The Surveillance Web

For Tina, Daisy, Billy and Joe-Bruce

The Surveillance Web
The rise of visual surveillance in an English city

Michael McCahill

Routledge
Taylor & Francis Group

LONDON AND NEW YORK

First published by Willan Publishing 2002
This edition published by Routledge 2012
2 Park Square, Milton Park, Abingdon, Oxon OX14 4RN
711 Third Avenue, New York, NY 10017 (8th Floor)

Routledge is an imprint of the Taylor & Francis Group, an informa business

ISBN 13: 978-1-903240-80-9 Hardback

British Library Cataloguing-in-Publication Data

A catalogue record for this book is available from the British Library

Contents

Contents

List of figures and tables

Figures

Tables

Acknowledgements

It gives me great pleasure to thank publicly some of the people who in various ways contributed to the completion of this book. I am indebted first of all to my family and friends. The precious memory of my dad, Bruce Arthur Stephenson, inspires me in everything I do and always will. I am also profoundly indebted to my mum Jessie Stephenson, and to Senga, Denis and Bruce who have all been a constant source of support. Thanks also to my dad (Denis McCahill: Glasgow's best tipster), Uncle Willie (Glasgow's worst tipster), my late-Uncle Michael and the rest of the McCahill clan in Glasgow. Up the Celts!

Cheers to Big Mike 'O' for introducing me to George Orwell and for teaching me to play the guitar. Thanks to Jon Joy and the 'King' (Mike Spurgeon) for jamming sessions and pizzas. To Si Hoyle (not ABBA) I would like to say 'Thank You For The Music'. A special thanks to my oldest friends Tina Scott and Chris Hassan ('Empty Tank') who encouraged me to leave the 'bookies' and head for night school. Chris has kept me in five-a-side games for the past fifteen years, and while most students were running up enormous debts I was able to rely on Tina to keep body and soul together in the Scott-McCahill household.

I would like to thank those friends and colleagues who contributed in a more direct way towards this book. Professor Keith Bottomley helped get the project started with his detailed and sound suggestions for improving the proposal I had written for ESRC (Economic and Social Research Council) funding. Other colleagues read and offered suggestions on selected chapters of the developing manuscript. Julie Seymour read and offered useful comments on the introduction and Chapter 1 while Clive Norris kindly read and offered comments on at least five different versions of the whole manuscript. Thanks to Chris Kirman for helping me to print off the thesis on which this book is based. A special thanks to Clive Coleman and Ian Taylor both of whom are sadly no longer with us. Their ideas and suggestions were gratefully received and are reflected in many places in the writing.

I would like to thank the ESRC for funding this project. Thanks to those who granted access to CCTV control rooms and to the CCTV operators who tolerated my presence and my inquisitiveness. My indebtedness and gratitude also to Brian Willan for his help and support throughout. Finally, thanks to Clive Norris. After marking an exam paper I had written in 1994, Clive decided that I might have a doctoral thesis in me. I owe him slightly more than the 'pint and pizza' he requested.

Michael McCahill
April 2002

Introduction

This book aims to make a significant and theoretically informed con-
tribution to the range of issues raised by the rapid growth in the use of
visual surveillance systems. It will locate and analyse the growth of
CCTV systems in relation to the central concerns of theorists of
modernity, and provide a micro-sociological account of the operation of
these systems in a range of different locales and institutional settings. In
this respect, the book intends to deal not only with the abstract categories
of 'grand theory'; it also attempts to explain how people living in
contemporary society experience these changes. However, before
outlining the contents of this book in more detail, this introduction will
briefly describe the book's approach to the study of surveillance and
society.

Surveillance and society

The starting point for this book is to view the relationship between
surveillance and society as a two-way process or as an interaction. In this
respect it looks at both the social impact of visual surveillance systems
and at how these technologies are shaped by existing social relations,
political practices and cultural traditions. Let me explain this two-way
relationship between surveillance and society by giving one or two
examples. The introduction of new surveillance technologies always has
a social impact, and this impact can be both positive and negative. This
process is best described by David Lyon when he says that surveillance
technology is always 'Janus-faced'; it 'both enables and constrains,

involves care and control' (Lyon, 2001: 3). In Scotland, for example, police officers decided to take 'DNA samples from all racial offenders ... in a covert attempt to stop attacks on ethnic minorities' (*Sunday Times,* 2 April 2000). Meanwhile, proponents of workplace drug testing have argued that this technology 'will reduce the number of deaths, accidents, and injuries caused by workers who have been using drugs' (Newton, 1999: 32). Also, in Lancaster the racist harassment of two local shopkeepers prompted Lancaster City Council to install three CCTV cameras which are monitored on a continuous basis in a Lancaster police station (*Guardian,* 3 April 1999).

The 'other face' of surveillance, however, arises from its capacity to reinforce existing social divisions along the lines of age, ethnicity, gender and class. For example, in the context of drugs testing, newspaper reports suggest some 'companies deliberately preyed on older workers with random drug tests in the hope that a positive result would release them from pension payments' (*Observer,* 12 December 1999). Another report suggests that managers of the London Underground are using drug tests 'as a disciplinary weapon, and picking on ethnic minorities' (*Independent on Sunday,* 22 November 1998). In his book, *Ur-ine Trouble,* Ken Holtorf (1998) shows that employers in the United States are using drug tests surreptitiously to screen female candidates for pregnancy. The Washington DC police department, for example, 'has admitted that it routinely subjected urine specimens taken for drug tests from female police officers ... to pregnancy testing without their knowledge or consent' (ibid.: 51). Meanwhile, in some parts of the United States welfare applicants who refuse to submit to drug testing will have their application for assistance denied (American Civil Liberties Union, 18 April 2000).

While surveillance always has a 'social impact', equally it is always shaped by existing social relations and cultural practices. In modern industrial societies, for example, surveillance processes were shaped by 'military competition between the nation states, the rationalization expressed in bureaucracy and the class imperatives of capitalism' (Lyon, 2001: 118). More recently, sociologists have argued that the emergence of a 'consumer society' is transforming surveillance processes. Zygmunt Bauman (1992, 1997), for example, argues that today consumerism con- tributes heavily towards the maintenance of social order. Bauman draws a distinction between the 'seduced' who become socially integrated by means of market dependency, and the 'repressed', who are controlled by the old disciplinary techniques of surveillance.

For some commentators the emergence of a 'consumer society' is also transforming the nature and meaning of surveillance. A documentary shown on Channel Four in 2001, for example, suggested that in a media-saturated consumer society surveillance is reinventing itself as a 'play-thing'. For instance, it was shown that in an attempt to attract the hip and the wealthy, architects of an upmarket restaurant in the United States appropriated CCTV as their design theme. As customers enter the restaurant their image is recorded by surveillance cameras and then displayed on TV monitors above the bar. As the architect who designed the scheme explained: 'Yesterday we were nervous that we were being watched and today we're nervous that we're not being watched' (Channel Four, 12 August 2001). Meanwhile, an advertisement by a US clothes manufacturer stated, 'you are on a video camera an average of ten times a day. Are you dressed for it?' (Channel Four, 12 August 2001). Where else but in a consumer society could surveillance be used to entice consumers and advertise products?

If the wider society and culture shapes surveillance processes, the way surveillance systems are applied in practice is shaped by the existing organisational and occupational concerns of those responsible for operating the systems. This two-way relationship between technology and society has been explored by a number of writers who have adopted the Social Construction of Technology (SCOT) approach (Bijker et al., 1987; Graham and Marvin, 1996). This approach rejects the notion that technological systems 'have some autonomous "logic" which "impacts" on cities as an external force' (Graham and Marvin, 1996: 104). Instead, it aims to show how 'individuals, social groups and institutions ... have some degree of choice in shaping the design, development and application of technologies in specific cases' (ibid.: 105).

In the context of police use of information and communications technology (ICT), for example, Peter Manning has stated: 'the vague notion that available, even conventionally acceptable technology will be used and employed without constraint of police practices and local political traditions is naïve and untenable' (Manning, 1992: 391). This is supported by the work of Ackroyd et al. (1992: 121–41) which showed 'how detectives incorporated ICT into existing police culture and work practices in ways that system designers and senior managers had not intended' (quoted in Gill, 2000: 19). Similarly, in their observational study of three CCTV control rooms, Norris and Armstrong (1998: 83) found that video-recorded images 'become another resource to be selectively utilised by the police in pursuit of their own organisational goals which are not coincidental with the full enforcement of law' (1998: 83).

In this book, the Social Construction of Technology (SCOT) framework will be used to tell a story about one city in the North of England (Northern City) and its relationship with CCTV. This 'thick description' of the construction of a surveillance network will explore the technical, social, economic and political aspects of the case under study. By using this framework the book hopes to avoid some the limitations in the existing literature on CCTV. This literature can be divided into three broad categories. First, there is an official, government/media line on CCTV which presents this new technology as a 'silver bullet' which can provide utopian solutions to complex social problems surrounding crime and disorder (Marx, 1992). Secondly, in the (administrative) criminological literature there is a concern with how effective CCTV systems are as a crime prevention measure (e.g. Skinns, 1998; Tilley, 1998). Thirdly, there is a growing sociological or critical literature that has drawn upon Foucault's metaphor of the panopticon to show how CCTV systems represent an extension of disciplinary power (Fyfe and Bannister, 1994; Reeve, 1998).

One thing that unites this diverse body of literature is its tendency to take as given the way CCTV systems are applied in practice. It is assumed that either visual surveillance systems have been introduced to detect and prevent crime or to extend the disciplinary potential of panoptic systems. What is often missing in this literature is a detailed micro-sociological account of the construction and operation of visual surveillance systems in different institutional settings. By adopting the SCOT approach this book aims to address a number of questions that have to date received little attention. For example, how does the introduction of surveillance systems fit in with existing political practices and cultural traditions? How is this technology applied in different institutional settings? How does the introduction of surveillance systems fit in with the existing organisational, occupational and individual concerns of those responsible for monitoring the systems? To get at these kinds of questions empirically required first-hand, lengthy involvement with those responsible for constructing and operating CCTV surveillance systems in a number of different locales and institutional settings.

What follows

In Part 1 of this book the growth of CCTV surveillance systems is located and analysed in relation to the central concerns of theorists of modernity. Chapter 1 draws on three theoretical strands (the 'electronic panopticon', 'post-Fordism' and the 'risk society') in an attempt to identify some of the technological, socio-economic, and political forces that are propelling the CCTV revolution. Drawing on the work of 'time-geographers' (e.g. Giddens, 1990) it is argued that one of the most significant impacts of the 'information revolution' has been the remarkable capacity of new surveillance technologies, such as CCTV, to transcend both spatial and temporal barriers. While Foucault has shown that 'discipline proceeds from the distribution of individuals in space' (1977: 141), the development of mass CCTV surveillance systems in public spaces means that surveillance is no longer confined to controlled and arranged spaces, such as the prison, and no longer requires the physical co-presence of the observer.

Having looked at some of the technological developments that are facilitating the introduction of CCTV technology, the chapter goes on to examine the broader socio-economic and political forces which are propelling the growth of this new technology. Drawing on the 'post-Fordist' literature (Harvey, 1989), it is argued that recent socio-economic restructuring has had major implications for changing strategies of crime control. As Stenson and Edwards (2001: 73) point out, increasing social polarisation and fragmentation has meant that 'multi-skilled professionals are increasingly segregated from peripheral, low- or no-income communities'. This polarisation, they go on to say, has seen strategies of crime control shift away from welfare and reintegration towards punitive goals of incapacitation, the militarisation of public space and exclusionary practices. Against this background of social fragmentation the increasing use of CCTV surveillance systems, it is argued, is bound up with attempts by local business and council elites to restore the 'feel good factor' in the 'entrepreneurial city', and with attempts to exclude undesirables from the new spaces of consumption.

Chapter 1 goes on to suggest that the rapid growth in the use of CCTV systems is also bound up with the emergence of the 'risk society' (Beck, 1992; Giddens, 1990). This section is divided into two parts. First, the growth and appeal of CCTV is located in the context of contemporary programmes of crime control which reject the 'meta-narrative' of 'progress' and the idea that people can be changed or societies transformed, and seek instead to regulate groups as part of a strategy of 'risk management'. Second, the emergence of a risk society is placed in the context of the emergence of 'neoliberal' or 'advanced liberal' strategies which seek to shift the responsibility for risk onto local state and non-state agencies (see Garland, 1997; Smandych, 1999; Stenson and Edwards, 2001). The growth of CCTV, it is argued, fits neatly with such strategies which enable the state 'to set up "chains of enrolment", "responsibilization" and "empowerment" to sectors and agencies distant from the centre, yet tied to it through a complex of alignments and translations' (Barry et al., 1996: 11–12).

The theoretical approaches outlined above are very useful for identifying some of the broad trends behind the emergence of a 'surveillance society'. However, as Stenson and Edwards have pointed out, they do tend to present very general, abstract narratives of change without examining how people in contemporary society experience these changes (2001: 74). In a similar vein, Ian Taylor has argued 'that most currently influential accounts of economic and cultural change operate at "far too generalized and indeed too global a level" (1996: 59) to be informatively applied to the detail of local cases and experiences' (quoted in Sparks, 2001: 202). Part 2 of the book, therefore, takes us from 'grand theory' to the 'real world' by examining the construction of a public-private surveillance network in Northern City. It begins in Chapter 2 by posing the following question: how did CCTV become the new 'common sense' in contemporary strategies of crime control? The chapter draws on 'various texts' – interviews, council documents and a local newspaper – to show how 'new modes of governance' (Garland, 1996) in crime control created a convergence of interests in Northern City which pushed CCTV to the top of the agenda. However, the chapter also poses a number of sociological questions that are ignored by writers working in the Foucaultian tradition. For example, which social groups are mobilised by the government's 'responsibilization' strategies? How do these strategies fit in with local cultural traditions and political practices?

Chapter 3 looks at how the 'surveillance web' constructed in Northern City works in practice. Here it is argued that despite the proliferation in the use of CCTV systems in both the public and private spheres very little is known about how private systems work in practice, and in particular how such systems may be linked with other private and/or public systems. Most of the existing literature on closed circuit television surveillance systems has taken as its object of analysis a separate and discrete CCTV system. For example, writers have looked at the construction of the Glasgow CCTV system (Fyfe and Bannister, 1994), or the effectiveness of the Doncaster CCTV system (Skinns, 1998), and so on. In contrast, Chapter 3 describes the operation of a 'surveillance web' by examining the electronic and human linkages between 30 CCTV systems in one city.

The three case studies in Part 3 of the book provide detailed observational studies of the operation of CCTV control rooms in two shopping malls, the workplace and high-rise housing schemes. Chapter 4 examines the exclusionary practices used in two contrasting shopping malls. It describes how exclusion works in practice and contemplates some of the likely consequences of these practices for the 'surveilled'. Chapters 5 and 6 show how CCTV surveillance systems, originally introduced to monitor the 'external threat' (i.e. shoplifters, burglars, intruders and other 'outsiders'), are increasingly used to monitor the 'internal threat' posed by workers and tenants. These chapters provide the book with a comparative element that directs attention to the 'context specificity' of new surveillance technologies.

Finally, Chapter 7 takes us back to theory and concludes by discussing the implications of the present study for theories of time-space, surveillance and social control.

Part I
Theory and Method

Chapter 1

Towards a contemporary theory of surveillance

This chapter aims to locate and analyse the growth of CCTV surveillance systems in relation to the central concerns of theorists of modernity. Over the last two decades the debate concerning the transition from 'modernity' to 'postmodernity' or 'late modernity' has pervaded much of the writing on contemporary society. This debate has drawn our attention to a variety of socio-economic, political and cultural changes that are taking place within many 'advanced' capitalist and industrial societies. Rapid technological changes, involving computer power and tele-communications infrastructures, which fundamentally adjust space and time barriers are implicated. So too is the process of global economic restructuring which has transformed the urban landscape giving rise to new patterns of social fragmentation, segregation and polarisation. For other writers the defining feature of the postmodern condition is the shift towards a new type of society structured around consumers and consumption rather than workers and production. This chapter is not so much concerned with the issue of whether or not these changes mark a significant break between the modern and postmodern eras. Instead the aim is to draw on these debates in an attempt to identify some of the recent technological, economic and political changes which are propelling the growth and use of CCTV surveillance systems.

Time-space distanciation and the panopticon

One of the central themes in recent sociological debates on surveillance and social control concerns the issue of whether the advent of modern video, computer and telecommunications systems have given rise to a *new surveillance*, qualitatively different from that which existed before (Marx, 1988; Lyon, 1994). David Lyon, for example, wonders if current surveillance trends should be considered as aspects of a deeper social transformation that requires the entire recalibration of sociological concepts (Lyon, 1994). In an attempt to come to grips with the New Surveillance many writers have seized upon Foucault's idea of the panopticon as a metaphor which captures neatly some of the features of contemporary society, linking changing technologies of surveillance with the debate over the emergence of the Information Age (see Lyon, 1993).

The panopticon was Jeremy Bentham's proposal, written in 1787, for an architectural system of social discipline, applicable to prisons, factories, workhouses and asylums. The design of the panopticon consisted of a tower in the centre surrounded by a ring-shaped building composed of cells, each housing an inmate. Control was maintained by the constant sense that prisoners were watched by unseen eyes. Not knowing whether or not they were under supervision, but obliged to assume that they were, conformity was the individual's only realistic option. Although Bentham's model prison was never built, it was nonetheless a crucial development for Foucault who believed that the principles of panopticism would 'seep out from their institutional location to infiltrate non-institutional spaces and populations' (Smart, 1985: 88).

The advent of time and space transcending technologies, such as CCTV, many writers believe, reflects this dynamic, extending the disciplinary potential of the panopticon to non-institutionalised public space. As Anthony Giddens points out, surveillance refers to two related sorts of phenomena. 'One is the accumulation of "coded information", which can be used to administer the activities of individuals about whom it is gathered ... the other sense of surveillance is that of direct supervision of the activities of some individuals by others in positions of authority over them' (1985: 14). In relation to the accumulation of 'coded information', the development of what Bruno Latour (1987: 227) calls 'immutable mobiles' (e.g. writing, paper, print, etc.) has long provided those in authority with a means of transcending temporal and spatial barriers and has extended the capacity of rulers to 'govern at-a-distance'. The 'direct supervision' of individuals, on the other hand, has been limited to relatively confined areas, such as small rural communities, or in the enclosed and controlled spaces of modern organisations (Giddens, 1985: 15). However, with the development of modern CCTV systems and telecommunications networks in public spaces, the 'direct supervision' of the subject population is no longer confined to specific institutional locales, nor does it require the physical co-presence of the observer. But there are limitations to the panopticon vision when applied to the use of CCTV systems as a mechanism of social control.

As Fyfe and Bannister (1994) point out, both Bentham and the proponents of CCTV argue that the power of the 'disciplinary gaze' lies both in its ability to induce conformity on the basis of a potential response, and to allow the possibility of a rapid intervention at any moment if something suspicious is detected. However, the extent to which CCTV surveillance systems mirror these panoptic principles in their operation and effects depends on a number of issues, including the context in which such systems operate. The recent growth in the use of open-street CCTV systems has been accompanied by a proliferation in the use of visual surveillance in a wide range of different institutional settings, including hospitals, schools, high-rise housing blocks and the workplace. In these relatively enclosed and controlled settings, individuals spend most of their day in the same building which means that they may be subject to more or less continuous monitoring from a centralised source. These individuals are also likely to be 'known' to those responsible for operating the CCTV system which allows for the attribution of any directly observed (or tape recorded) deviant behaviour to known and identified subjects. In this environment, CCTV surveillance, like the panoptic mechanism, 'makes it possible to see constantly and to recognise immediately' (Foucault, 1977: 200).

However, the activities of those monitored by open-street CCTV systems in public spaces are not restricted to an enclosed and controlled environment and this makes continuous monitoring virtually impossible. Moreover, as Norris and Armstrong (1999) point out, the street population monitored by open-street CCTV surveillance systems are unknown to the observer, which means that those watching the screens are unable to systematically identify and classify people in public space. As these authors point out, the response from those using such systems has been twofold. First, they are used to mobilise a response to crimes in progress and to provide the evidence for formal actions. Second, there is the potential to concentrate resources on the linking of images to named individuals to provide evidence for future actions. This is possible because the information (i.e. images) produced by CCTV is 'controllable, and not subject to the messiness or unruliness of time' (Simpson, 1995: 158). This allows deviant identities to be 'stored' in electronic spaces (on a computer file or videotape), ready to be 'lifted out' at some future, as yet unspecified, time and place.

CCTV and distanciated relations

One of the most important features of the 'electronic era' is that it has facilitated a new convergence between formally distinct surveillance systems. This means that today modern video technology can be combined with telecommunications systems such as fibre optics which enables the rapid transmission of data over long distances; powerful computers which allow for images to be stored, retrieved and analysed speedily and cheaply; and digital photography which (unlike silver-based photographic film) allows for images to be stored compactly, accessed by computer, manipulated freely and transmitted to remote locations through a variety of media (e.g. telephone lines and computer networks) within seconds of creation. As Mitchell (1992: 80) has written, 'in the electronic era an alliance of the computer, magnetic and optical storage media, and telecommunications networks is ... fundamentally altering patterns of image production ... image exchange has become far less constrained by space, time, and materiality than it ever was in the past'.

An example of how these systems are advancing is provided by a CCTV system developed by British Telecom, which can use ordinary telephone lines rather than expensive optic fibres, allowing cheap and rapid dissemination of images over vast distances (*Crime Prevention News*, 1993). As Graham and Marvin have pointed out, 'it will increasingly be possible to switch visual and video services across global distances as cheaply as data and voice'. They explain how 'the World Bank has already suggested the idea of using labour in Africa to monitor the CCTV camera systems in American shopping malls' and the 'CCTV monitoring for the computer group Tektronix is already carried out over 2,000 miles away from their Portland headquarters in Atlanta, Georgia' (1996: 155).

The development of optical networks and other telecommunications systems for the distribution of images, 'opens up the possibility of the unlimited transfer and re-routing of digitised video recordings' (Beck and Willis, 1995: 164). The police have not been slow to realise the potential of these developments and are beginning to concentrate resources on the linking of information (images) to named individuals to provide intelligence for future actions. For instance, in 1996 *The Guardian* newspaper reported that in the run-up to the 1996 European Football Championship, the National Criminal Intelligence Service (which holds details and pictures of around 6,000 suspected football hooligans) made its database available to all the other football grounds participating in the tournament, 'through the use of "photophones" enabling digitised photographs to be transmitted from one central location to a remote terminal in each stadium' (Norris et al., 1998: 267).

These developments are not merely bringing in their wake the potential to rapidly disseminate images over vast distances, they also provide the potential to store visual information in 'electronic spaces'. The ability to store visual information on computerised databases means that cameras can be linked with sophisticated computer software which can convert images into numerical data and automatically match facial features against a pictorial database of known offenders (Norris, 1996: 7). Facial recognition technology is developing fast, both for in-store security systems and wider city-centre networks (Graham and Marvin, 1996; Norris et al., 1998; Davies, 1996). However, as Norris et al. argue, although 'the prospect of being able to match a face from a city centre surveillance scene is advancing' it is 'still a long way off' (1998: 266). Police forensic technician, Leslie Bowie, gives some indication of how the police are likely to utilise this technology over the next few years. He says:

> The police may have a number of targets, a number of people that they're targeting or a number of suspects. It's really up to them to sort of harness this technology and to start taking good photographs of their suspects, put them on the database, code the faces, so when you get the crime scene images the computer can automatically search through the list of suspects and pull out a list of a few names that may have committed that crime.
>
> (*Crime Beat*, 1996)

Surveillance and sociation

In an essay entitled, 'New Urban Eras and Old Technological Fears: Reconfiguring the Goodwill of Electronic Things', Nigel Thrift provides a devastating critique of the literature on telecommunications technologies. This literature, Thrift argues, sinks 'very quickly into remarkably similar forms of "highway hype", "techno-babble" or "digital dreaming" ' (1996: 1466). For Thrift, much of the current literature on information technology gives the impression that the 'information space' created by the growth of telecommunications networks is 'an abstract and inhuman space strung out on the wire'. However, he goes on to point out that the rise of the information society does not necessarily signify a general erosion of the social and the move towards a more abstract, decontextualised, dehumanised and disenchanted world. In fact, the development of electronic communications systems often produces 'more, not less, sociation, much of it face-to-face' (ibid.: 1473).

The construction of CCTV surveillance networks has been facilitated by what Thrift might describe as 'patterns of sociation'. The CCTV Challenge Competition, for example, mobilised an army of partnerships and action groups who are pushing for CCTV. Once these systems are up and running they create a network of people who shape the application of visual surveillance systems. This raises the important issue of whether those who are pushing for CCTV may also be shaping its uses to suit their own interests. For instance, in many city centres the emergence of 'multi-agency partnerships' and 'city centre action groups', which were formed to coordinate the push for CCTV, has brought together the police, private security managers, department store managers, shopping centre managers and store detectives. These developments are increasing the integration of police and private security CCTV systems in city centres and facilitating information-sharing and liaison between those responsible for managing CCTV systems. For instance, in many city centres the newly formed action groups meet on a regular basis to exchange information and intelligence and discuss ways of encouraging a co-ordinated response to city centre security. The police, for instance, may have information on known shoplifters who are 'out and about' (Norris and Armstrong, 1999). The managers of private CCTV systems may have observed known troublemakers or shoplifters behaving in a particular pattern. These groups also discuss ways of improving communications between CCTV systems operators by, for example, introducing city-centre retail radio networks. As Coleman and Sim (2000) have shown in their study of the construction of Liverpool's city centre CCTV system, these developments have allowed the private sector to play 'a central role in constructing definitions of risk and danger in the city and who should be targeted to avoid these risks and dangers' (2000: 627).

It is in this sense that we may begin to talk about the construction of CCTV surveillance networks which can track individuals throughout the public and private spaces of contemporary cities. Today, in a typical town centre, for example, almost every small retailer, bank and building society has some form of CCTV coverage. Most of the major department stores and shopping centres have more sophisticated systems which are monitored from a control room by front-line operatives who are usually linked by radio to security guards on the ground. In most cities open-street CCTV surveillance systems monitor the behaviour of citizens as they wander through the public spaces in between the smaller private systems. Finally, in some cases a city-centre-wide 'radio link' connects all the actors (police, private security, store managers, etc.) involved in this surveillance network. In some cases those responsible for operating the CCTV systems in many of the large retail stores in city centres can take hard-copy 'printouts' and 'store' them in 'rogues galleries'. Anyone unfortunate enough to find themselves in a 'rogues gallery' may soon be monitored and/or excluded from retail outlets and shopping centres in a town centre.

The use of surveillance networks for exclusionary purposes reminds us that these systems are not only space and time transcending technologies, rather they are 'technological networks within which new forms of human interaction, control and organisation can actually be constructed' (Graham and Marvin, 1996: 54). This approach also draws our attention to the broader political and economic 'interests' that are promoting the use of CCTV systems. Thus while technological developments have been important in facilitating the introduction of electronic surveillance systems, the development of such systems must also be seen in the context of broader social and economic trends. The following section draws on the 'post-Fordist' literature to argue that the increasing use of CCTV surveillance systems is bound up with attempts by employers to manage the 'threat to profitability', and with attempts by local business and council elites to restore the 'feel-good factor' in the 'entrepreneurial city' (Harvey, 1989).

Post-Fordism and surveillance

In recent decades a number of writers have argued that the economies of many advanced industrial and capitalist nations have witnessed a shift from Fordism to post-Fordism (Harvey, 1989). In this literature Fordism is generally characterised in terms of a 'regime of accumulation' based on mass production and mass consumption, and a 'mode of regulation' summed up as the Keyensian Welfare State. Seen by many as the golden era of capitalism, this form of economic organisation provided relatively stable and state-regulated growth throughout the post-war period. By the 1970s, however, things began to change. A combination of falling demand for standardised, mass-produced goods, and the onset of globalisation (of markets, production, finance and communications) undermined the Fordist economic structures which hinged on the sovereignty of the nation state and 'on the relative immunity from foreign competition of indigenous companies' (Webster, 1995: 145).

While there is little agreement among theorists about the central features of the post-Fordist era (see Amin, 1994), most of the literature places great emphasis on the *flexibility* of the new 'regime of accumulation'. Thus, whereas Fordism was characterised as a regime of accumulation based on the mass production of standardised products by semi-skilled workers and geared towards mass markets, post-Fordism is said to have ushered in a system of 'flexible specialisation' which is based on skilled workers who produce a variety of customised products (Harvey, 1989; Piore and Sabel, 1984). One of the central themes in this debate concerns the role of information technology and telecommunications systems in providing new ways of organising more mobile modes of social life which can be more easily and flexibly controlled (Webster and Robins, 1993: 244; Harvey, 1989: 193).

In the workplace, for example, 'informationalism' improves the flexibility of production, enabling the introduction of total quality control (TQC) and just-in-time (JIT) systems that reduce costs and improve profit margins (Sewell and Wilkinson, 1992). Driven by a host of interrelated factors, notably intensification of competition through the globalisation of markets and widespread technological changes, enterprises are turning to these systems in attempts to remain viable. The popular prescriptions for achieving this involve flattening the organisational structure by shrinking middle management and pushing decision-making down the hierarchy. Employees are expected to take on wider task responsibilities with reduced direct supervision. In this context, strategic control over devolved work teams depends on the development of sophisticated electronic surveillance systems. Through the use of computer-based technology, for example, 'management can achieve the benefits that derive from the delegation of responsibility to teams while retaining authority and disciplinary control through the ownership of the superstructure of surveillance and the information it collects, retains and disseminates' (Sewell and Wilkinson, 1992: 282–3). As Winner (1992: 83–4) says:

> No longer are the Taylorite time-and-motion measurements limited by an awkward stopwatch carried from place to place by a wandering manager ... For telephone operators handling calls, insurance clerks processing claims, key punch operators doing data entry, rates of performance are recorded by a centralised computer and continuously compared to established norms.

While there is very little research on the extent and use of CCTV surveillance in the workplace, it would appear to be a thriving industry (Beck and Willis, 1995). As Sewell and Wilkinson (1992: 280) have reported, in many British supermarkets checkout operators have increasingly found themselves monitored by CCTV and electronic point of sale (EPOS) technology. A number of other studies have shown how CCTV systems introduced to target staff suspected of dishonesty have eventually proved more useful in checking whether staff were meeting company requirements, including compliance with till procedures or rules relating to refunds and exchanges (see Beck and Willis, 1995: 193). As we will see in Chapter 5, it is important to remember that the way surveillance systems work in practice depends upon how they fit in with existing social practices in the workplace. However, it is clear that such systems can be used as an instrument of disciplinary power exercised through the architecture of the panopticon, allowing management to see everything without ever being seen themselves.

The entrepreneurial city

As well as introducing *flexibility* into labour markets and production systems, the post-Fordist era is also said to have introduced *flexibility* into patterns of consumption (Webster, 1995: 151). Whereas the Fordist era was characterised by rigid mass-production systems that precluded flexibility in the design of consumer products, the new computerised production systems have enabled cost-effective small batch production runs, customisation of products and rapid changes in manufacturing procedures. This has created 'a leading role for consumption, reflected in such things as greater emphasis on choice and product differentiation, on marketing, packaging and design, on the "targeting" of consumers by lifestyle, taste and culture rather than by the Registrar General's categories of social class' (Hall, 1989: 118).

For some social theorists these developments are creating a new type of society structured around consumers and consumption rather than workers and production. Zygmunt Bauman, for example, draws a distinction between the 'seduced' and the 'repressed', and argues that in contemporary society consumerism contributes heavily to the maintenance of social order (1997: 14). The 'seduced', according to Bauman, become socially integrated by means of market dependency, while panopticon methods of social control are reserved for the 'repressed', those *flawed consumers* who are unable to respond to the enticements of the consumer market because they lack the required resources. This division between consumers and 'flawed consumers' is most clearly visible in the post-Fordist city where new strategies of social control are being devised in the new spaces of consumption (see Davis, 1990).

Any attempt to understand the forces that are shaping contemporary cities must look beyond a purely local perspective to the broader global political and economic changes that are restructuring city economies. As writers like David Harvey (1989) have shown, the end of the long postwar boom in western capitalist societies has triggered a massive restructuring which has radically altered cities. Globalisation and the intensification of global competition have torn away the traditional industrial fabric of many western cities through de-industrialisation (Graham and Marvin, 1996: 33). The effects of these developments have been most pronounced at the urban level where the construction of new urban spaces of consumption has been an almost universal response to de-industrialisation (Bianchini and Schweagel, 1991).

Another central feature of globalisation, according to Harvey (1989, 1993), is that it ascribes a greater salience to place, since firms, governments and the public come to identify the specificity of locations as an element for deriving competitive advantage. Place marketing, in this context, is said to constitute a critical element for success in the inter-regional competition for investment (Harvey, 1993). Thus over the last two decades 'managerialism', so characteristic of urban governance during the era of the Keynesian Welfare State, has been replaced by 'entrepreneurialism' as the main motif of urban action. This shift in urban politics is reflected in Britain which over the past 15 years has seen a crucial change in emphasis from an urban policy justified as a form of welfare initiative, to one based on functional economic terms aiming to introduce growth to areas of depression or industrial decline.

The emergence of this new economic realism can be seen in most cities. For example, as Seyd (1990) has shown in Sheffield, there has been a shift from 'socialism to entrepreneurialism'. In 1981 the city council established an Employment Department which was to develop a co-ordinated response to the economic crisis of the early 1980s, and which was to provide an alternative to Thatcherite economics. However, by the end of the 1980s the anti-capitalist ethos of the earlier period had disappeared. In its place came an increased emphasis on creating an image likely to induce capital to invest in the city, where 'consumerism' and 'leisure' are regarded as the two activities primarily capable of stimulating economic growth. In this sense, Seyd argues, 'Sheffield is no different from every other major city in Britain, all competing with each other to provide an attractive environment for private capital investment' (1990: 344). Increasingly therefore budgets are being set aside for image construction and advertising to extol the virtues of the city as a favourable business environment. This commodification of the city is now considered a requisite strategy in local economic development to lure external investment into the city.

It is against this background that town centre managers and 'image-makers' are promoting the use of city-centre CCTV surveillance systems as a means of providing a 'risk-free' environment designed to attract consumers and tourists. In one of the cities in Norris and Armstrong's

(1998) study, for example, a promotional video of the CCTV system 'emphasised not the detection of crime but the role CCTV was to play in revitalising the city centre's flagging fortunes by contributing to the "feel good factor" and encouraging the shopper back to the centre' (1998: 46). Similarly, in their campaign for city-centre CCTV, Glasgow District Council used 'the slogan CCTV doesn't just make sense – it makes business sense' (Fyfe and Bannister, 1994).

The exclusionary impulse

As town centres are increasingly portrayed as places of consumption for tourists and consumers the most recent phase of capitalist economic restructuring has generated levels of unemployment and homelessness not seen since the 1930s. The visibility of unemployed or homeless people on the streets or hanging around in shopping centres constitutes a crisis in the city's official representation and obstructs belief in the positive vision that the image-makers attempt to portray. In his book, *Crime Control as Industry*, Nils Christie (1993: 66) says in the 1990s:

> Poverty has again become visible. The homeless and the unemployed are out in the streets. They hang around everywhere dirty, abusive, provocative in their non-usefulness. We get a repetition of what happened in the 1930's, only more so since the inner cities have been rebuilt since then. Hiding places in slums and dark corners have been replaced by heated arcades leading into glittering shopping paradises. Of course homeless and/or unemployed persons also seek these public alternatives to the places of work and homes they are barred from. And as an equal matter of course they are met with agitated demands to get them out of sight and out of mind.

The problem of homelessness must, of course, be placed in the context of the broader spatial organisation of the city that is bound up with prevailing power relations. The dominant response to homelessness, however, is to treat it as an individual problem isolated from the realm of urban politics. According to the former Prime Minister John Major, for example, many of London's homeless choose to live that way – 'it is a strange way of life that some of them choose to live' (*The Guardian*, 25 April 1994). And more recently, Jack Straw (who was Shadow Home Secretary at the time) called for the streets to be reclaimed for law-abiding citizens from the 'aggressive begging of winos, addicts and squeegee merchants' (*The Guardian*, 6 September 1995). This theme has been taken up by local traders and 'action groups' throughout the country, like those in Bradford, who want to remove the homeless from town centres (*Five Live*, 28 April 1997) and those in Bridlington, who want to ban drinking in public places (*Hull Daily Mail*, 28 April 1997).

The desire to exclude undesirables from the new territories of consumption has led some to worry that CCTV may be used for the 'moral regulation' of city centres. Geoff Mulgan (1989), for example, argues that 'there is a danger that attempts to create a "convivial milieu" for economic and socio-cultural life in the city using CCTV may become attempts to purify space of those "troublesome others" – the underclass, the homeless, the unemployed – reducing exposure to what Sennet (1990) describes as "the presence of difference" ' (quoted in Fyfe and Bannister, 1994: 11). As Norris and Armstrong (1998: 45) have reported, 'targeting of the homeless, the vagrant and alcoholic ... was a regular feature' in two of the sites in their observational study of three CCTV control rooms. Moreover, these groups were targeted not because they caused any trouble or were engaged in criminal activities, but because of their 'capacity to convey a negative image of the city. In this sense targeting is more about the commercial image of the city than crime and reflects the values contained by the movement towards formal Town Centre Management programmes.'

A number of Home Office-sponsored studies on the 'threat to safe shopping' provide some support for the view that 'the boundaries between the consuming and non-consuming public are strengthening, with non-consumption being constructed as a form of deviance at the same time as spaces of consumption eliminate public spaces in city centres' (Sibley, 1995: xii). For instance, a study carried out in the Midlands found that nine out of ten of all recorded incidents related to nuisance rather than crime, and that tenants were particularly concerned about 'young people hanging around' (Phillips and Cochrane, 1988). Also, a Coventry study revealed that more than one-third of shoppers expressed concern about being 'insulted' on the street, particularly by unruly young persons and public drinkers (Ramsay, 1989). And a study carried out by Poole (1991) in Birmingham identified significant levels of public anxiety about people loitering on the street and teenage males displaying rowdy behaviour (see Beck and Willis, 1995).

While there is very little empirical work on the question of which subject populations are being targeted by the front-line operatives responsible for monitoring CCTV systems, the evidence so far suggests that such systems are being used mainly to target those groups that are 'out of place' in the new territories of consumption. For instance, Norris and Armstrong (1998: 85) found that 'Nine out of ten targeted surveillance's were on men, particularly if they are young or black.' Meanwhile, the Local Consultative Committee that was instrumental in pushing for the CCTV system in Wolverhampton argued that 'large groups, usually of young single people, simply assemble in places that happen to catch their fancy. Their mere presence is a nuisance to people who want to use the streets and shopping centres in a more conventional way... ' (quoted in Graham and Marvin, 1996: 20). Finally, Bulos (1995: 9) have reported that the use of CCTV to revive a town centre in their study resulted in 'young people being displaced by town centre improvement schemes to ... environments which are unsafe for them such as alleyways and subways'.

As Sibley points out, these studies suggest that 'it is not adolescent males as a social category, or even "unruly" groups of young people per se, who are seen as threatening; rather, it is their presence in spaces which comprise part of "normal family space" which renders them discrepant and threatening' (1995: xii). According to Zygmunt Bauman (1997: 14), these *flawed consumers* are:

> the dirt of post-modern purity ... people unable to respond to the enticements of the consumer market because they lack the required resources ... They are the new 'impure', who do not fit into the new scheme of purity. Looked at from the now dominant perspective of the consumer market, they are redundant – truly 'objects out of place'.
>
> (1997: 14)

For some writers this exclusionary impulse is leading to the erosion of democratic public space in town centres throughout the UK. In a recent study on the growth of town centre management (TCM), for example, Reeve (1996) has argued that public spaces may increasingly be replaced by pseudo-public spaces like those in shopping malls, where commercial imperatives dominate and what goes on, and who participates, is intensely regulated and tightly controlled so that profitable consumption is maximised. Reeve argues that in many respects town centre managers 'regard the town centre as if it were primarily a space for personal and individuated consumption, and that one consequence of this has been the development of design, management, policing and promotional strategies similar to those employed in the privatised public space of the shopping mall' (1996: 2). In this respect, town centre management initiatives are intended to 'attract a spending public in preference to those perceived as anti-social and "unaesthetic"' (1996: 18). Reeve goes on to point out that there is no evidence as yet of TCM schemes aiming to actively discriminate against undesirables in order to massage the social space of the town centre into something more socially acceptable to consumers. However, he also suggests that:

> The institutional apparatus – the formalised involvement of the private sector in TCM; the technology, such as CCTV; and hiving off of the responsibility for town centre security and policing to the private sector – are in place or beginning to be in place to allow the effective implementation of the values of the private interest in town centres above those of the more disinterested state'.
>
> (1996: 33)

As Beck and Willis (1995) point out, 'the identification and exclusion of known or suspected persons', which is currently practised in many shopping centres, is not really 'an option which is open to the Town Centre Manager' (1995: 89). However, the increasing use of bye-laws to restrict various activities in public space (Reeve, 1996), and the increasing use of open-street city-centre CCTV systems mean that the police may soon have a means of excluding 'undesirables' from the public spaces of city centres. This growing army of unemployed and homeless, described by some as a new 'underclass', is increasingly seen, not as a social group to be integrated, but as 'a *risk* to be policed' (Nelken, 1994: 4, emphasis added). In this respect, current trends in crime control can be seen as part of a broader shift in the public agenda away from issues of economic inequality towards a focus on the distribution and control of risks (Beck, 1992; Giddens, 1990), where 'the values of the unsafe society displace those of the unequal society' (Ericson and Carriere, 1994: 102).

The risk society

Whether one focuses on the sociological preconditions of the emergence of a 'risk society' (Beck, 1992; Giddens, 1990) or on the genealogical account of risk as a form of 'governance' (Barry et al. 1996), it is clear that risk is a central feature of contemporary society. But why has risk become such a major concern in contemporary society and how is this development related to the emergence of a 'surveillance society'? As Reiner et al. (2001: 177) point out, while the idea of a 'risk society' has had a major influence on criminological discourse, there is a certain ambiguity about what is involved. Reiner et al. suggest that on the one hand the idea of a 'risk society' refers to changes in the extent and nature of risk. One of the central themes in the work of Beck and Giddens, for example, is that the risks we face today are quite different from the risks inflicted by nature on technologically more primitive societies. For instance, today risks such as pollution, global warming and rising crime are 'manifestations of the humanly "manufactured uncertainty" of late modernity' (Stenson, 2001: 24).

However, Reiner et al. go on to suggest that the idea of a risk society also implies a shift in cultural sensibilities and in strategies for dealing with risk. In this respect, the emergence of a risk society concerns the broad move against Enlightenment faith in reason and progress which has taken place during the twentieth century. The loss of faith in humanly engineered progress has seen the project of modernity shift from programmes of 'problem-solving', based on scientific rationality, towards 'risk-anticipating', based on 'reflexivity' (Bauman, 1992: 25). Current trends in crime control can be seen as illustrations of this wider move against the idea of humanly engineered progress. Feeley and Simon (1994: 173), for example, suggest that the last decade has witnessed a paradigm shift in the criminal process from the 'old penology' to the 'new penology'. The old penology, these writers point out, worked at the level of the individual criminal and involved diagnosis of the problem, intervention and treatment. The 'new penology', on the other hand, is 'actuarial' and seeks to regulate whole populations and groups as part of a strategy of managing danger.

Stan Cohen (1985) suggests that these developments are bound up with a 'master shift' in the discourse of social control from a concern with the mind (and issues of motivation, thought and intention) to a concern with the body (and issues of observable behaviour). This 'master shift' has given rise to strategies of control which instead of trying to change the individual offender, aim to alter the physical and social structure in which individuals behave (seen in the move towards the cashless society and the building of locks into the steering columns of cars). There is also a shift away from strategies of social control which are reactive (only activated when rules are violated) towards proactive strategies which try to predict the dangers one wishes to prevent (see Cohen, 1994; Marx, 1988). In this respect the 'master shift' is part of a broader reorientation of social control policy which encompasses such things as testing employees for the use of drugs (see Gilliom, 1994) and mass DNA testing (see Nelkin and Andrews, 1999).

The last decade or so has witnessed an exponential increase in the use of new surveillance technologies which are designed to regulate groups as part of a strategy of managing danger. The introduction of these new technologies is often justified in terms of their ability to monitor 'risk' groups who pose a serious threat to society. However, once these systems are introduced, the concept of dangerousness is broadened to include a much wider range of offenders and suspects (see Pratt, 1999). On 10 April 1995, for example, a National DNA Database was set up in the UK by the Forensic Science Service (FSS) on behalf of the Association of Chief Police Officers (ACPO). The database was originally established as a forensic source for helping identify those involved in serious crimes (i.e. murder and rape). However, an amendment to the Criminal Justice and Public Order Act 1994 allows samples to be taken without consent from any person convicted or suspected of a recordable offence (Home Office, 1999). The trend towards more 'inclusive' databanking is also evident in those cases involving the retention of samples submitted on a voluntary basis. The police have already conducted 118 'mass screens', resulting in 48 hits and seven convictions (Werrett, 1999).

Latest figures show that over one million DNA profiles from suspects have been put onto the database, plus around 73,000 profiles from evidence found at scenes of crime (*The Guardian*, 1 September, 2000; Forensic Science Service 2000). Meanwhile, the government recently announced a £109 m cash boost for the Database which is expected to see an extra 3 m samples added to the DNA database by 2004 (*The Guardian*, 1 September 2000). In light of these developments we may be tempted to agree with Stan Cohen (1985) when he argued that, 'For many visionary ideologues and observers the day is ending for all forms of individual intervention. The real master shift about to take place is towards the control of whole groups, populations and environments – not community control, but the control of communities' (1985:127).

Risk and individualisation

One of the key motors of social change in the emergence of a risk society is the process of 'individualisation' (Beck, 1992; Lash, 1994). In 'late modernity', Scott Lash argues, agency is increasingly freed from structure (Lash, 1994: 111). This process is, of course, nothing new. The break-up of traditional communities, the decline of organised religion and geographical mobility are all important elements in the development of modern industrial society. However, in the past, the erosion of collective institutions 'took place in conditions where new forms of solidarities were created' (Furedi, 1997: 67). In this respect, the transition from 'traditional society' to 'modern society' broke down the old traditional structures of extended family, church and village community. However, as Scott Lash (1994) points out, these traditional structures were replaced by a new set of structures, including the nuclear family, trade unions, the welfare state, government bureaucracy and an unconditional belief in the validity of science. What's happening today is that a further process of individualisation has set agency free from 'these (simply) modern social structures' (Lash, 1994: 114).

The process of individualisation is related to the emergence of a surveillance society in a number of ways. As Norris and Armstrong (1999: 21) have pointed out, individualisation was one of the central factors behind the emergence of a 'stranger society', a process which has been intensified in recent years. Social and geographic mobility aided by the development of mass transportation systems 'has meant that people no longer spend their lives in the communities into which they were born and brought up' (1999: 21). The decline of traditional communities and the demise of stable employment patterns 'results in a significant drop in information, about neighbours, acquaintances, or chance encounters in the street' (Young, 1999: 70). As Young argues, 'less direct knowledge of fellow citizens ... leads to much less *predictability* of behaviour' and a greater wariness in our 'stance towards others' (ibid.: 70). In this respect, individualisation contributes to an intensification of social isolation, insecurity and the 'fear of difference' (Bannister et al., 1998).

In contemporary cities, the possibility for chance encounters with strangers is reduced further by the development of segregated residential, retail and business areas, and the privatisation of public space (Norris and Armstrong, 1999: 23). As Richard Sennett (1990: 201) points out, today the shopping mall is situated far from tracts of housing, the school is on its own 'campus', and factories are hidden in the industrial park. These techniques, Sennet argues, are 'increasingly used in the city centre to remove the threat of classes or races touching, to create a city of secure inner walls' (ibid.: 201). These developments are most clearly pronounced at the urban level where the need to manage space – and particularly to separate different kinds of people in space – 'is a pre-eminent consideration of contemporary urban design' (Christopherson, 1994: 409; Davis, 1990, 1992; Bannister et al., 1998). In the United States, for example, Mike Davis has shown how the development of secured 'skyway' systems and 'gated communities' are eliminating 'the democratic admixture on the pavements' (1990: 231). In some cities 'overstreet malls' have 'created a virtual spatial apartheid in the city, with middle-class whites above, and blacks and poor people below' (Boddy, 1992: 141). Urban geographers have identified similar trends in the UK where the development of gated residential communities, the private policing of semi-public space and the deployment of CCTV systems 'should also be seen as part of the fortress impulse' (Bannister et al., 1998: 27).

Kevin Robins (1995: 61) believes that 'we must consider the implications of these developments – the scale of the metropolis, its fragmentation, the fortification of space, the surveillance cameras, and so on – for the collective emotional life of the city'. He asks, 'when we no longer live the complexities of the city directly and physically, how much more difficult does it become to cope with the reality of those complexities [and] to what extent does such insulation … encourage paranoid and defensive mechanisms?' According to Spitzer (1987: 50) 'The more we enter into relationships to obtain the security commodity, the more insecure we feel; the more we depend upon the commodity rather than each other to keep us safe and confident, the less safe and confident we feel … ' (quoted in Ericson, 1994: 171).

Thus while the introduction of CCTV systems is cited by many politicians and practitioners as an effective way of reducing crime and the widespread 'fear of crime', it may be that such strategies are adding to the fear and insecurity already brought about by wider processes of 'deregulation' and 'privatisation'. Bauman (1997: 204), for example, suggests that as expenditures on collective welfare are cut, 'the costs of police, prisons, security services, armed guards and house/office/car protection grows unstoppably'. The only winner in this shift of resources from welfare to law and order, according to Bauman, is 'the universally shared and overwhelming sensation of insecurity' (ibid.: 204).

Risk and governance

As a number of writers have pointed out, many of the programmes of practical action which flow from strategies of 'risk management' increasingly are addressed not to central-state agencies such as the police, 'but *beyond* the state apparatus, to the organisations, institutions and individuals in civil society' (Garland, 1996: 451; O'Malley, 1992; Fyfe, 1995). In this respect the move towards a 'risk society' must also be understood in terms of its relation to more specific political struggles over the nature of the welfare state and the emergence over the last two decades of neoliberal political programmes. As Stenson and Edwards point out, the introduction of new surveillance systems, and

> the new statutory requirement for local community safety partnerships to undertake crime audits, are among the host of ways in which new powers have … created a new 'governmentality'. This refers to the new means to render populations thinkable and measurable, through categorisation, differentiation, and sorting into hierarchies, for the purposes of government.
>
> (2001: 22–3)

Following the demise of the Keynesian welfare state in many of the advanced capitalist nations, an emphasis on individual responsibility for managing risk 'finds converts from all parts of the political spectrum' (Barry et al., 1996: 1). Pat O'Malley (1992) has written of the emergence of a new form of *prudentialism* where insurance against future risks becomes a private obligation of the active citizen. In the context of crime control there has been no shortage of public pronouncements from politicians in the UK designed to encourage the 'active citizen' to take responsibility for the prevention of crime. In 1988, for example, the Conservative minister John Patten stated that: 'preventing crime is a matter for all of us. At the very centre of our ideas on how to control crime should be the energy and initiative of the active citizen' (Patten, 1988: v–vi; quoted in Fyfe, 1995: 180). The findings of the 1996 International Crime Victimisation Survey (ICVS) would suggest that the public are beginning to accept the consumerist responsibility of the individual for the management of risk. This study has shown that 'England and Wales are the most security conscious countries in the industrialised world'. The research shows that England and Wales 'tops the international league for home security devices with more than three-quarters of homes boasting an alarm, or special door locks, or grilles on windows or doors' (*The Guardian*, 27 May 1997).

Responsibilisation strategies are also designed to offload the responsibility for risk management from central government on to local state and non-state agencies and organisations, hence the increasing emphasis on public/private partnerships, inter-agency cooperation, inter-governmental forums and the rapid growth of non-elected government agencies. The former Conservative government established a series of organisations and projects, such as 'The Safer Cities' programme, whose remit is to act as a focus for the multi-agency crime prevention partnership and to facilitate contact and cooperation between local agencies and interests. In this sense the state takes on the role of providing *empowering* knowledge and education in order to pass on the necessary skills to responsible citizens. Nowhere was this more evident than in the case of the introduction of CCTV systems. Thus in 1994 the Home Office published a CCTV instruction manual which offered advice to councillors, business people and the police on the need for CCTV, the situations in which it might be useful and how CCTV systems should be installed. In October of the same year the government launched its 'CCTV Challenge Competition' which received 480 bids. From these bids 'more than one hundred schemes received a share of the £5 million funding, with a further £13.8 million levered in from other partnerships' (Davies, 1996: 178).

The CCTV Challenge Competition mobilised an army of action groups and task forces who were all competing with one another in a frantic race for CCTV. These powerful coalitions drew 'elements from the press, the media, the police, local authorities, retailers, insurance companies, surveillance industries and property interests' (Graham et al., 1996). The systems constructed by these 'partnerships' produce a mass of information (i.e. images) which also encourages greater communication and liaison between the different actors involved, providing the police with new structures of information exchange and cooperation. In this sense, the growth of CCTV fits neatly with neoliberal strategies of rule that enable the state 'to set up "chains of enrolment", "responsibilization" and "empowerment" to sectors and agencies distant from the centre, yet tied to it through a complex of alignments and translations' (Barry et al., 11–12). The composition of such networks allows the state to 'govern at-a-distance', while leaving 'the centralised state machine more powerful than before, with an extended capacity for action and influence' (Garland, 1996: 454).

From theory to method

Up to this point, the central aim of this chapter has been to identify some of the broad social, political and cultural changes in late modernity which are propelling the growth and use of CCTV surveillance systems. Drawing on the work of 'time-geographers' (e.g. Giddens, 1990) we have seen how one of the most significant impacts of the 'information revolution' has been the remarkable capacity of new surveillance technologies, such as CCTV, to transcend both spatial and temporal barriers. The chapter has also focused on the broader social and economic forces that are propelling the growth of CCTV. Here we saw that the increasing use of CCTV surveillance systems is bound up with attempts by employers to manage the 'threat to profitability', and with attempts by local business and council elites to restore the 'feel good factor' in the 'entrepreneurial city' (Harvey, 1989). Finally, the chapter went on to consider the view that the rapid growth in the use of visual surveillance systems is part of the shift towards programmes of crime control which seek to regulate groups as part of a strategy of 'risk management'. It is now time to leave the 'grand theory' of late modernity behind as we turn our attention to the 'real world' in an attempt to see what effect these developments have had in one city in the north of England.

The setting and the sample

The setting chosen for this study was Northern City, a recession-hit city in the north of England with a population consisting of a quarter of a million people. In principle, the thesis could have provided a case study of any city in the country, but Northern City did provide an interesting case study for the rise of visual surveillance systems. For instance, despite being a large city with one of the highest crime rates in Britain, Northern City was one of the very few major urban conurbations in the country that did not have an extensive open-street CCTV surveillance system in operation. When I began the research for this book I had anticipated that the introduction of a publicly funded city-centre CCTV system was imminent. However, when, three years down the line, the council still had not installed a city-centre scheme my proposed study of 'a city under visual surveillance' looked to be in danger of becoming a study of the only city in the country that was not under visual surveillance!

However, as the research progressed it became clear that the absence of a city-centre CCTV system in Northern City was interesting for two reasons in particular. First, as the local newspaper (the *Daily Echo*) had reported, the Labour-dominated city council were 'split' over the issue of introducing a city centre CCTV scheme. The public row over CCTV, which had been documented by the *Daily Echo*, reached a high-point in 1992 when the newspaper reported how the Director of the Technical Services Department had banned several councillors from making un-announced visits to an existing council-operated CCTV control room which monitored various council properties. So it was clear that there might be a story to tell about how 'responsibilization strategies' had generated conflict among the local elites of Northern City. The second interesting aspect to this story was that despite the well documented council opposition to the introduction of city-centre CCTV, Northern City was in fact one of the first major cities in the UK to introduce surveillance cameras to monitor public space (in the city-centre bus station and car park). From reading the local newspaper it was also clear that Northern City did in fact already have an extensive public-private CCTV network, which included cameras operating in the city centre, hospitals, high-rise housing schemes, etc.

Having chosen the setting for the case study, the next issue was to decide how to sample within the case along the dimensions of *people* and *context* (Hammersley and Atkinson, 1983: 46). The decision about which informants should be selected was loosely based on what Glaser and Strauss (1967) call 'theoretical sampling'. As Hammersley and Atkinson (1983: 117) explain, 'theoretical sampling' means that 'who is

23

interviewed, when, and how will be decided as the research progresses, according to one's assessment of one's current state of knowledge and one's judgement as to how it might best be developed further'. In the preliminary stages of the fieldwork the idea was simply to speak to anyone who had been involved in the construction and operation of Northern City's CCTV network. The eventual sample comprised 60 people. This included tape recorded interviews (where permission was granted) with the following people: 27 security managers, 10 managers of city-centre department stores and high-street retailers, 8 elected members of the city council, 6 paid council officials, 6 managers of local industrial concerns, and 3 security officers. One-third (34 per cent) of these interviews resulted in at least one site visit to the CCTV control room where further informal interviews were carried out with whoever was present at the time. These site visits (and the in-depth observational studies which were carried out later in the study) were very important in terms of providing an adequate representation of the people involved in the operation of the CCTV systems. Many of the security managers who were interviewed, for example, tended to provide an 'organisational gloss' in their account of how the CCTV systems worked in practice. Informal discussions with the front-line operatives in the CCTV control room, on the other hand, often provided a different version of events from those provided by the management.

One of the aims of the study was to tell the story about the debate that had taken place within Northern City over the introduction of a public open-street CCTV system. A useful starting place for tapping into this story was the local newspaper that had reported extensively on how the council was split over the issue of installing a city-centre CCTV system. After reviewing this debate in the local newspaper I was able to draw up a list of people who seemed to be 'key players' in the debate over city-centre CCTV. This list included one or two 'maverick' councillors who were opposed to CCTV and several members of the Chamber of Trade who were leading the campaign for a city-centre CCTV system. In the early stages of the research these interviews allowed me to document the debate over the introduction of a publicly funded city-centre CCTV system. However, they also began to focus my attention on the linkages between the ideological network of entrepreneurs who were campaigning for a publicly funded city-centre CCTV system, and the existing operational network of people involved in Northern City's existing public-private CCTV network. For example, leading members of the Chamber of Trade who were pushing for city-centre CCTV were also involved in powerful coalitions consisting of business leaders, councillors and the police. At this stage my interest began to switch from documenting the debate over the introduction of a publicly-funded city-centre CCTV system towards mapping the public-private network which was leading to new forms of 'hybrid policing' in Northern City. Thus, while it was originally anticipated that any description of a city's visual surveillance network would require access to the police, it soon became apparent that Northern City's CCTV network was operated entirely by council officers and private security personnel. These developments appeared to fit neatly with government-initiated 'responsibilization' strategies which are leading to fragmentation in risk management across myriad public and private sector institutions (Garland, 1996).

The connections between the network of entrepreneurs and the operational network of those responsible for constructing the existing public-private surveillance network became clearer during interviews. For instance, one interview with a shopping mall manager was conducted in his private suite which contained a control pad and a 24-inch TV monitor displaying the images from all of the shopping mall's CCTV cameras. During this interview the manager was constantly interrupted on a mobile radio link. On two occasions he stopped the interview to talk to CCTV operators on the shopping mall radio link. During the first conversation a CCTV operator informed the manager that a 'banned person' had just entered the mall. In the second conversation the shopping mall manager was told that one of the lifts in the centre had broken down. During this conversation the shopping mall manager glanced at his TV monitor to observe the lift in question. In this respect, the interviews could also be regarded as mini-observational studies. During this interview I observed the shopping mall manager communicating with CCTV operators and using the surveillance system in his office. These observations drew my attention to two things. First, that the shopping mall manager was not only involved in the campaign for city-centre CCTV, but was also involved in the operation of a public-private CCTV network. And second that shopping mall surveillance systems are used not only to monitor shoppers, they are also used as a general managerial tool (i.e. to deal with lift breakdowns).

Taking account of variations in context was a major concern of the study. Interviews and site visits were arranged with those responsible for operating CCTV systems in a wide range of settings. These included hospitals, high-rise housing schemes, universities, factories, a newspaper publishing plant, a chain of medium-sized convenience stores, a public network (bus station, car park, cleansing depot and shopping arcade), high-street retailers, department stores and shopping malls. By providing a detailed empirical account of the operation of these systems the study addresses a number of important issues. Firstly, it provides an original account of the operation of CCTV systems in the 'private' sector (e.g. workplace, high street retailers, department stores, etc.). Secondly, by focusing on the linkages between the public police and private security it provides a detailed descriptive account of how 'hybrid policing' works in practice. Thirdly, it shows how the interests of the 'private' sector are beginning to influence the nature and practice of policing in contemporary society.

Insider accounts

In general the interviews were 'reflexive' in the sense that I entered the interview situation with a broad list of issues to be covered and used a combination of non-directive and directive questions (Hammersley and Atkinson, 1983). The interview guide, which contained the list of issues to be covered, was constantly modified for subsequent interviews to pick up on themes that were emerging from the analysis of earlier interview transcripts. The interview usually began with a series of 'non-directive' questions that were designed to encourage the interviewee to talk in detail about a particular issue. For example, during site visits to CCTV control rooms I would refrain from asking direct questions, such as: 'are your cameras used to monitor the workforce?' Or (in the case of high-rise housing schemes) 'are your cameras used to monitor tenants?' Instead, I would ask a series of open-ended questions that would be followed by a number of probes. The following question, which I asked during site visits to the industrial workplace, is fairly typical:

Question: What kinds of problems do you get on a site like this and how does CCTV help you tackle these problems?

Probe for:

- external problems (burglaries, break-ins);
- internal problems (worker malpractice);
- any other uses (general managerial tool);
- worker resistance.

This kind of questioning encouraged the interviewees to talk freely about the uses of CCTV and focused my attention on issues that would not have been revealed with more directive questions. However, non-directive questions do not always encourage interviewees to talk freely, especially when some of the issues involved are sensitive. During site visits to the workplace, for example, many security managers were reluctant to talk about the use of CCTV to monitor the workforce. One way to get around this problem was to confront the interviewee with what one already knew from previous interviews. This kind of questioning went something like this: 'The security managers at other sites have told me how their CCTV system is particularly useful as a general managerial tool. Have you found this to be the case on this site?' This kind of question was often successful in encouraging the interviewees to talk more freely about sensitive issues. It is also important to remember to follow up a directive question with something like: 'That's interesting. Can you give me some of examples of how this works in practice?' Another way of encouraging informants to talk about sensitive issues is to conduct group interviews. In the present study, site visits to CCTV control rooms were very important in this respect. During these visits several security officers would be present and they would often prompt one another into telling various 'CCTV stories'. On one occasion a CCTV operator working at an industrial site explained how he had spotted a night-shift worker 'nipping for a pint' during working hours. Meanwhile, on another site a CCTV operator described how the police had used the CCTV control room to monitor the movements of a shop owner who was suspected of receiving stolen goods.

Data collection and analysis

As part of the fieldwork for the present study observational research was conducted during site visits to 20 CCTV control rooms. More detailed observational work was carried out in the control rooms of two shopping malls (144 hours) and a concierge system in a high-rise housing scheme (24 hours). As Hammersley and Atkinson (1983: 146) have pointed out, the central issues faced by the researcher carrying out observational research concern *what* to write down, *how* to write it down and *when* to write it down. The decision of when to take fieldnotes depends to some extent on the context of the setting under scrutiny. In the present study, this decision was influenced by the way electronic communications technology shaped social interactions in the CCTV control rooms. For instance, during 'live' CCTV incidents fairly extensive notes could be taken without undue disruption. The CCTV operators were usually too busy monitoring the TV screens or communicating with those outside the system on mobile radio links to be worried about me scribbling notes in the corner of the control room. Taking notes while CCTV operators communicated with those outside of the control room also seemed less intrusive than recording face-to-face conversations conducted in my presence, perhaps because of the impersonal nature of these electronically mediated interactions. In contrast, to take notes when people visited the control room (shopworkers, police officers, security officers, etc.) to have an informal conversation with the security officers would have been highly inappropriate. In this situation I would usually sit and listen or join in the conversations which could be written up later, perhaps during a targeted surveillance when note-taking was less conspicuous.

In terms of *what* to write down it is important that in the early stages of observation the researcher adopts a wide focus until more specific issues are identified which can then be followed up. Having said this the researcher can identify some of the key issues to be explored by reading the relevant literature and by carrying out interviews which can act as mini-pilot studies conducted before the main period of observational research begins. In the present study, for example, the researcher adapted a quantitative observation schedule used by Norris and Armstrong (1998) to record four types of data in their observational study of open-street public CCTV surveillance systems: *shift data* (including the number of operatives on each shift, who visited the system, etc.), *targeted suspicion data* (including the reason for suspicion, type of suspicion, how the surveillance was initiated, etc.), *person data* (e.g. age, race, sex and appearance of suspect) and *deployment data* (recording all deployments initiated by the system operatives) (Norris and Armstrong, 1998: 108).

The observation schedule was adapted to account for some of the differences between public and private CCTV systems and for the different theoretical emphases of the two studies. As we have already seen, two central themes of the present study are a concern with the 'context specificity' of visual surveillance systems and the exclusionary potential of CCTV. Thus, in the *targeted suspicion data* the categories of 'property management' and 'personnel management' have been included in the *reason for suspicion* in attempt to record the uses of CCTV as a general managerial tool while in the deployment data and person data a number of questions have been included to record the social characteristics of those ejected from shopping malls. The requirement to complete the observation schedule (which was filled in the day after a period of observation) provided a checklist of things to write down in shorthand as each targeted surveillance occurred (i.e. incident number, time began, reason for suspicion, who it was initiated by, how it was initiated, was a suspect identified, etc.). As well as jotting down fieldnotes that would allow me to complete the observation schedule and describe each targeted surveillance in detail, close attention was also paid to the 'situated vocabularies' employed by the security personnel (Hammersley and Atkinson, 1983). These provided valuable information about how the security officers organise their perception of the world and in particular focused my attention on the tension between the formal, organisational goals of the institution and the informal, occupational concerns of those responsible for operating the systems.

An attempt was also made to write down any analytic ideas that arose during the process of data collection. For instance, on my first day in the control room of City Centre Mall, one of the things I wanted to do was count the number of interactions between security personnel on a City Centre Radio Link (CCRL). This radio link provides a means of communication between the security personnel (CCTV operatives, security managers and security guards) in all the major department stores, high-street retailers and shopping centres in the city centre. However, counting the number of transmissions on the radio link proved to be impossible because the CCTV operator who was on duty during my first shift in the control room liked to listen to the latest tunes on Radio One. Moreover, when his favourite songs came on air he turned up the volume and would often forget to turn it back down again when the song had finished. This, of course, was infuriating for me because it meant that I couldn't listen to the conversations between the security officers and the police on the City Centre Radio Link. However, when I typed up the fieldnotes the next day and reflected on this problem I realised that if I couldn't hear the messages then neither could anyone else in the control room. This was a perfect example of how the human mediation of technology placed limits on the integration of CCTV systems, and needless to say from that point onwards I paid much closer attention to this issue and looked for more examples during the following periods of observation.

As this example shows, data collection and data analysis are not distinct stages of the research process. Indeed, the process of analysis begins in the early stages of the fieldwork well before all the relevant material has been collected. In the present study, the analysis of interview transcripts, observational fieldnotes and documents began in the first few months of research. The material was analysed as it was collected and this mini-analysis was used to guide the collection of further data for further mini-analyses in a cyclical development. In this way the researcher moves up and down, and forwards and backwards, through the data as it is collected and analysed in order to identify and explore the main dimensions of the research topic.

In terms of the actual mechanics of analysis, the researcher usually draws 'up an outline comprising his or her current idea of the principal themes to emerge from the data, along with any analytic ideas he or she has accumulated during the fieldwork' (Fielding, 1993: 168). The separation of the data into analytic themes requires the 'cut and paste' procedure, a process that has been speeded up by the use of the word processor. On the completion of my fieldwork I was left with over 300,000 words of fieldnotes. These were made up of notes from 60 interview transcripts, observational studies of three CCTV control rooms and notes from site visits to a further 20 CCTV control rooms. Finally, selected extracts from a wide range of documentary sources were typed up. This included every news article on CCTV that appeared in *The Northern City Daily Echo* between 1 January 1990 and 1 August 1998.

This material was cut and pasted into a series of files, including an *analytic file* that placed analytic categories and related items together into 'mini-analytic files'. These mini-files eventually became sections of material organised around the themes of 'time-space distanciation', the 'panopticon', 'human mediation', 'hierarchy of response', 'conflict', 'resistance', 'context specificity', 'intimacy' and so on. This material was in turn re-analysed and re-coded over and over again. The results of this analysis are presented in the remainder of this book which aims to bridge the gap between the 'macro' and the 'micro', between 'grand theory' and the 'real world', by telling a story about one city and its relationship with visual surveillance systems.

Part 2
The Rise of Visual Surveillance in
Northern City

Chapter 2

The story of Northern City

In 1984, the year of George Orwell's Big Brother, Northern City had very few, if any, visual surveillance systems operating in public space. Today the city has an extensive public-private CCTV network comprising of over 800 cameras (see Table 2.1). The construction of this network began in 1988 when the government announced its Safer Cities programme. This programme aimed to set up crime prevention projects and establish local non-state or semi-state structures which would help govern crime problems by means of inter-agency cooperation and the activation of local initiatives. As the following extract from a Home Office document illustrates, the Safer Cities programme fits neatly with new modes of governance based on 'responsibilization' and the formation of a 'partnership' approach to crime control. The author spells out some guidelines on how to provide:

> direct assistance in creating *networks* between those developing strategies in different areas ... make money available to pump prime *multi-agency work* ... maintain contacts with key policy making personnel ... foster *network developments* between agencies you wish to see working in *partnership* ... develop *multi-agency schemes* ... develop a feel for *multi-agency* crime prevention work ...facilitate communication between *partners* whose co-operation is potentially mutually beneficial ... create *multi-task, multi-agency patch teams* ... and make sure *local structures* are robust enough to take the strategy forward.
>
> (Home Office, 1992: 30–32, emphasis added)

Table 2.1 Active and proposed CCTV systems in Northern City

	Active Systems							
Title	'Shopnet'	Housing estate mall	Civic One	Medi-size store-net	Hospital network	Workplace	The housing network	University
Area watched	City centre dept stores and shopping centres	Shopping centre, car parks and loading bays	Car park, bus station station depot and arcade	Supmkt isles and entrances	Entrances, exits, car parks, and hospital wards	Perimeter fencing, car parks and factory floor	High rise flats, car parks and estate offices	Campus buildings, computers and car parks
Number of cameras	Total: 235 External: 39 Internal: 196 Covert: 1	Total: 16 External: 8 Internal: 8 Covert: 0	Total: 23 External: 17 Internal: 6 Covert: 0	Total: 198 External: 22 Internal: 176 Covert: 0	Total: 28 External: 4 Invernal: 24 Covert: 0	Total: 72 External: 48 Internal: 24 Covert: 9	Total: 222 External: 48 Internal: 174 Covert: 0	Total: 14 External: 4 Internal: 10 Covert: 0
Stated objectives	Prevent shop theft	Deter and detect shop theft	Reduce crime/fear of crime	Deter and detect shop theft	Deter and detect car crime, staff safety etc.	External threat and internal threat	To reduce crime/fear of crime vandalism and unauthorised access	To deter/detect crime
Year	1994	1993	1991	1992	1994	1987–1997	1987–1997	1992
Monitoring agency	Private security and the police	In-house staff	Council employees and the police	In-house staff	Hospital staff	Private security	Council employees	In-house staff
Initiator of system	City centre traders	Shopping centre owners	Council and police	Supmkt mangt	Hospital security manager	Mangt and security managers	Council – housing dept and police	University security manager
Capital costs: who pays?	City centre traders	Shopping centre owners	Council and safer cities	Supmkt owners	Hospital	Business owners	Council and estates action programme	University
Revenue costs: who pays?	City centre	Shopping centre owners	Council	Supmkt owners	Hospital	Business owners	Council	University

Table 2 continued

		Proposed Systems		
Title	City Centre CCTV	Park and ride	Industrial estate	Sheltered housing
Area watched	City-centre streets	Car park	Industrial estate, business premises and entry roads	Houses and car park
Number of cameras	Total: 20 External: 20 Internal: 0 Covert: 0	Total: 3 External: 3 Internal: 0 Covert: 0	Total: 24 External: 24 Internal: 0 Covert: 0	Total: 8 External: 8 Internal: 0 Covert: 0
Stated objectives	To reduce crime/fear of crime and attract more visitors to the city centre	To reduce crime/fear of crime and encourage use of car park	To reduce car crime, burglaries, vandalism etc.	To reduce crime/ fear of crime
Year	?	?	May never start	?
Monitoring agency	Council employees and police	Council employees	Private security	Council employees
Initiator of system	City centre traders and the police	Council	Council, police and industrialist	Council – Housing Dept
Capital costs: who pays?	Council and city centre traders	Council	Industrialist, council and Home Office grant	Council
Revenue costs: who pays?	?	Council	Industrialist	Council

The former commander of the city-centre police subdivision, Super-intendent Harry Paten, first proposed plans for a city-centre CCTV system in Northern City in January 1990. Superintendent Paten represented Northern City police force on the Safer Cities Steering Committee and had set up a Working Party on City Centre Disorder comprising city-centre traders, councillors and the police. This group had intended to introduce a camera system covering the whole of the city centre. However, in the face of council opposition the scheme was eventually scaled down to provide coverage of the council-owned bus station and city-centre car park. As the *Daily Echo* reported in October 1990, Northern City was one of the first cities in the country to introduce CCTV surveillance cameras in public space as part of its Safer Cities programme:

CCTV BID TARGETS CITY'S BUS STATION:
Northern City's bus station and major car parks are likely to become the first city centre areas to be monitored by CCTV cameras. The council's Policy Committee has recommended consideration of TV cameras at both the bus station and certain car parks to crack down on crime. The proposal needs rubber-stamping by the powerful Labour Group at the Guildhall and the full council before it becomes reality. Although councillors are split over the issue, it is expected yesterday's recommendations moved by the council leader will eventually become accepted.

(24 October 1990)

As the newspaper reported, the council were split over the issue of introducing the system. The Council Leader explained to me how there were:

... two groups on the council, one lobbying for cameras and one opposed on civil liberties grounds. There was a lot of concern about 1984 and all that. So we had a concern on civil liberties grounds about gay people for example. Should we be able to watch people entering gay bars? Should we be able to watch people going into cinemas to see certain films? Should we be able to watch people going into church? I mean I'm a believer, so I've already got God watching me. The last thing I need is cameras monitoring my behaviour as well.

Despite the reservations of some councillors the CCTV system went ahead and has been up and running since February 1991. There are eight cameras located around the bus station, three fully functional (i.e. pan/tilt/zoom) and five fixed. In the car park there are three fully functional cameras mounted at a high level on a support tower which is situated in the middle of the car park. All video signals from the cameras on both sites are routed into Uniplex Series 2 multiplexers located nearby for encoding into a single video signal. The camera pictures are then relayed to the council's Guildhall central monitoring station via a relay station on the top of a nearby building by microwave radio links. The pictures are also relayed from the council's central monitoring station to the nearby police station (which is 185 metres away) by microwave video/telemetry link, which enables the control of the cameras to be handed over to the police when required.

The city council provided £75,000 of the funding, with another £75,000 coming from the Home Office-backed Safer Cities Project. Thus, although many councillors were opposed to the introduction of a city-centre CCTV system, most of them fully supported the introduction of cameras to monitor a bus station, a city-centre car park and other council properties throughout the city. As several councillors explained:

> I supported the car park and bus station systems because that car park is our property and we are protecting people's cars who go in to the theatre. We put them in the bus station at the time because we were protecting our buses and the people who use those buses. Now I'm not very certain whether I would support them in the bus station at present because we don't own any buses and it maybe that the private operator should have put the cameras in and looked after his own buses.
>
> (City councillor)

> We were going to introduce cameras at the industrial estate, but that's to protect property owned by us. The people there pay the council to let our buildings so it's our responsibility to protect that property. It's the same with the bus station, we own the bus station; we don't own the buses anymore but we own the bus station.
>
> (City councillor)

> We've also got cameras in the Art Gallery and on the Marina. We had a couple of arson attacks on there. The people who own the boats pay the council to have their boats there so security is our responsibility.
>
> (City councillor)

As part of the Safer Cities programme two further CCTV surveillance systems were installed by the city council in October 1993. Following a number of break-ins at a council-owned public cleansing depot situated three miles from the city centre, six cameras were mounted externally to monitor the main office building, car parks, storage areas and the depot perimeter. One fixed camera is used specifically to monitor the main gate, which has been made remotely operable from the city council's central monitoring station. Also in 1993, following an armed robbery at a council-owned shopping arcade six miles from the city centre, six cameras were installed to monitor the public area of the arcade and a council housing estate office. All cameras on both sites are wired back to an on-site control room. They are also connected into a video compression system which transmits the pictures back to the council's central monitoring station via the integrated services digital network (ISDN) line system. Images from both systems are monitored remotely on a periodical basis at the council's central monitoring station in the city centre.

The council's CCTV systems were soon hailed as a great success in the *Daily Echo* by senior police officers and members of the Chamber of Trade. In 1993 representatives of the Chamber of Trade, impressed with the council's CCTV systems, joined forces with the police and asked the city council's Technical Services Department to determine the cost of providing CCTV coverage of the city centre with a view to the project being financed jointly by local trading organisations and the city council. The final report stated that an enquiry had been made on the council's behalf by the Northern City Safer Cities Project to the Home Office with regard to obtaining grant aid for the proposed town centre CCTV system. However, the Safer Cities Steering Committee reported that the Home Office had confirmed that there would be no grant aid available for this project and that there would be no council money available for the project either.

The council's position on the funding of city-centre CCTV was summed up by a local councillor who led a public campaign against the introduction of CCTV:

Well, to be perfectly honest, I think the businesses themselves should fund the system because it's the businesses that's really come to us and asked for it. Now they're saying that their insurance's are horrendously high in the city centre and they want it. Now if they want it to protect their property and their businesses they should pay for it. I wouldn't actually expect them to pay for it in the car parks or in the bus station, but if it's down the streets on their property I would expect them to pay for it because we should not be spending public money to protect the insurance policies of businesses.

(City councillor)

The CCTV Challenge Competition

When the city council installed CCTV cameras in the city-centre bus station and car park, they had made provisional plans to extend the system to other areas of the city. The council had modelled their CCTV programme on the CCTV systems at King's Lynn and Northampton which were both drawn up with a view to expanding the CCTV systems very much in mind. In a feasibility study for a city-centre CCTV system the council stated that typical areas for expansion in Northern City included:

> important buildings like the Guildhall, museums, art galleries etc.; depots, car parks, leisure centres, housing department properties, problem areas on housing estates, bus stations, traffic control systems, and also non-council properties such as industrial estates, British Rail facilities, out of town retail outlets, hospitals and schools.
>
> (CCTV Feasibility Report, Northern City Council)

When it became clear that there was to be no more funding from the Home Office-backed Safer Cities Programme, plans to expand the CCTV network were put on hold. However, the announcement in 1995 of the government's CCTV Challenge Competition encouraged the city council to apply for Home Office funding towards the capital costs of three new CCTV systems. These were to be installed in the city's high-rise flats, a major industrial estate and the city centre. But once again these proposals created conflict among the local elites of Northern City.

While many councillors stated that they were opposed to the introduction of (city centre) CCTV on the grounds of civil liberties, a number of schemes had been approved over the years by various council committees, including the Housing Committee which had agreed to install surveillance cameras in the city's high-rise blocks. These CCTV systems were installed as part of the Estate Action Scheme in the mid-1980s. Since this period a total of 222 fixed cameras (48 external cameras and 174 internal cameras) have been installed in the city's 16 tower blocks and 26 estate offices. Following the recommendations of a local neighbourhood management committee (NMC), a 24-hour concierge service began at three blocks of flats in 1992. Installed at a capital cost of £180,000, the service is self-financing in revenue terms with a direct charge of £3.00 per week per tenant. In 1997 the council made a bid to the Home Office for a new concierge system at another site, and upgraded internal and external colour CCTV cameras for the existing concierge system. This bid failed, however, partly due to the fact that the council failed to secure any private funds towards the system. The housing officer responsible for submitting the bid told me:

> One of the things that I suppose would have gone against us, what they're keen on in all these bids, is to try and get partnerships and get some private funding. It's not so much that they're bothered about the fact that we can put up half a million pounds ... they'd be a lot happier if it was a quarter of a million from us and a quarter of a million from the private, or some contribution from the private sector. But when you're talking about a place like Oakwell Estate there's one or two shops and a few empty units that've been vandalised and things, you're not really gonna attract any private funds. There's nobody really got any incentive to put some money into protecting those estates.

The council had more success in the second round of the government's Challenge Competition when in 1995 they made a successful bid for funding towards a 26-camera system to be installed at the Northern City industrial estate. The estate comprises of approximately 250 acres. It has 212,600 square metres of business floor space already developed and this accommodation is occupied by 128 companies. The employment generated by the occupiers of the estate is at present in the region of 4,250 people. The estate is occupied by a vast array of industrial and commercial concerns with ancillary service-type operations also present. Types of industrial uses range from manufacturing, engineering and haulage, through to food processing and hi-tech computer companies. There is also an area on the estate which had been designated as a retailing/leisure area and this had attracted major national retailers, two public houses, a bowling alley, bingo hall, other small retailers and a bank.

As a council feasibility report stated, the estate was subject to a high level of crime that was increasing faster than anywhere in the police sector area and normal police and private security measures were not stemming this increase. Apart from the obvious financial cost of crime – in 1992 alone the tenants of the estate had spent in excess of £200,000 on security and a further £175,000 to rectify the costs of crime – occupiers were facing other problems. For instance, businesses were experiencing great difficulty in obtaining insurance cover, and when insurance was obtained the premiums were relatively high. Also, existing companies were not willing to expand operations on the estate and new companies were not prepared to relocate in this area. The report states that the council would benefit, as owners and managers of the estate, as the area would become more attractive to both existing occupiers and prospective new developers. This improved attractiveness should then lead to an increased demand for premises which could then be reflected by higher industrial land values. With an effective CCTV scheme in place the council, and other private landlords on the estate, should be able to market the vacant units on the estate with greater success.

The police were also keen to install a CCTV system on the industrial estate which they had long identified as a 'problem area'. As some of the industrialists explained, the police had on previous occasions attempted to persuade the industrialists to support the introduction of cameras on the site:

> The police came to us and said: 'We're failing you fellas, you know we are, we know we are, but there's not a lot we can do about it. So how about having a go yourself?'
>
> (Factory manager)

> It was a reincarnation of a scheme they tried to get off the ground about six years ago and for various reasons it didn't get very far, although a lot of effort was put into it. The local police did a lot of work a couple of years ago, came round to sound out people's feelings, put a lot of leg work in, quite literally leg work, walking around the estate, chaps from Banton (the local housing estate) – it was a sergeant with the backing of an inspector, to try and get people re-interested in it.
>
> (Factory manager)

However, the main catalyst for the most recent attempt to set up a CCTV system was provided by the government's announcement of the CCTV Challenge Competition. As the estate manager from the Council's Technical Services Department told me:

> I became the estate manager approximately two years ago. From about 1987 onwards the police have identified the problem of crime on the estate. Since 1987 they've been trying to get this CCTV system going on the estate. So over the years they've had a few good

attempts and got quite close. But I think the main catalyst for this recent attempt was the government's CCTV Challenge Competition. We got the details through, unfortunately it came onto my desk 'cause I was then deemed to be the manager and they said: 'There you go, write us a proposed report basically on what you intended to do'. And that was basically the catalyst ... There was meant to be an organisation called ... I wrote the report and it refers to the Northern City Industrial Association, at the time there wasn't one really. There was one in essence, it had been used in the past, but at the time it was dormant basically. What we did, we made the application for the grants, it was successful, then we had to go back to these people and say: 'Look we've got the grant, let's reactivate the proposals, get yourselves organised into this working party'. So it was ourselves and the police to start with then we drew in the industrialists as we went along.

The council's bid for a £50,000 grant towards the capital costs of the system was successful. All the police and the council had to do now was persuade the industrialists to contribute towards the other half of the capital costs and the ongoing revenue costs. Thus in 1995 the council, along with the police and several of the industrialists, set up a partnership called the Northern City Industrial Association (NCIA) which was to manage the operation of the CCTV system. Various different types of schemes and methods of purchase were looked into and after due consideration it was decided that the most beneficial approach would be for the Northern City Industrial Association to develop its own fibre optic cable link then rent the necessary equipment from a security company. The £50,000 grant represented approximately 50 per cent of the capital costs of developing the fibre optic cable link and it was proposed that the remaining funding would be provided by members of the Industrial Association with contributions based upon each occupier's 1995 rateable value. Funding of the yearly rental charges for the equipment, monitoring and management were to be collected from the occupiers of the estate based upon banded rateable values. As 'expert advisors' in risk management it fell to the police sell the idea to the industrialists:

... it was arranging meetings, talking at the various meetings briefly, trying to get support. The police put on some excellent lectures, even organised one of the earlier public meetings at the Police Training College with people from the CCTV industry explaining the different types of cameras, what we could have, what we couldn't have, where the costs penalties came in, how to look at the whole business of getting it up and running.

(Chairman of the Northern City Industrial Association)

There was a meeting organised by the police at Northern City College where they showed us films. There has always been, certainly at the public meetings, a good display of graphics, probably slides, and very well-informed people, some of them ex-coppers who are now in the CCTV business, good speakers all of them to a man, who were perfectly able to answer the most searching questions be they technical or philosophical. There was no reason for anyone who was remotely interested not to have been fully informed.

(Factory manager)

However, some of the industrialists were sceptical of the attempt by the police to 'offload' the area:

In my opinion the police wanted to offload this area to a private company. And yes, sure they would respond to that private company if they were called to but they didn't wanna police the area. That's my opinion.

(Factory security manager)

They were there in an advisory capacity. A couple of times we met up at the police station. They were under pressure from the traders and the business people in the area to do something about the level of crime. So it was half a 'cop out' on their side to say well, you know, 'we'll sponsor the scheme to a degree and give you a quicker response', and so and so forth, but it was only a way of taking a bit of heat off them.

(Factory manager)

The main sticking point, however, came on the question of funding. Some of the industrialists believed the council should pay for the system:

We kept banging our heads against a brick wall. We had to really grab these people by the throat and say: 'JOIN THE SCHEME'. And because of that you lose your impetus ... and every time I went to these places they just weren't interested. Basically I got abuse: 'Why aren't you paying for it? Why aren't the council paying for it? We pay enough in rent. We get nothing from the council'.

(Estate manager)

Other industrialists thought that some of their neighbours might gain free coverage without contributing towards the system:

> There were plenty of people who were dropping out. Because you've got the old 'why should I pay for it when I've only got a £500,000 turnover and the factory next door with their £8 million turnover, they're gonna pay for it so I'll get free coverage'.
>
> (Factory security manager)

> We've tried two or three times to get some sort of conglomerate for the estate and a lot of the companies to pull together but they don't, the big ones tend to have to drive it. The ones that suffer the most tend to have to drive it, the rest just think, 'well I'll get the spin off of them. If he wants to pay for a camera and it looks across my buildings as well, brilliant'. And there is a lot of that.
>
> (Factory manager)

> Oh yes, they sent us some plans on where the cameras were going to be sited which in all honesty gave the little units around that corner there some terrific coverage for their twenty pounds a week or whatever, and it gave us very, very little at the back of our site for our £140 a week. So I'm afraid there was too many people getting away with it if you like.
>
> (Factory security manager)

Another group of industrialists who had to pull out of the scheme included local managers of national concerns who wanted the system but had to go along with the decisions made by the head office:

> There were other support problems and I would have thought they wouldn't have been insuperable, but in some cases they appeared to be. There are plenty of companies on the estate that are not actually owned and controlled from this area, they are simply outlets of multinationals and there are a number of them. And in each case the local management team was not able to make the financial decision as to whether or not they would be able to join or not. They have no on-site directors and they weren't able to make that financial decision.
>
> (Factory security manager)

> Local managers agreed. But if you look at the names of these companies most of them are offshoots of a national company and

when it came to signing the agreement form they didn't have the authority to sign it, it went to head office. Obviously when they look at the total of all their outgoings it's just more money out. They don't understand the day-to-day problems of having a bike nicked, or somebody's car being vandalised.

(Factory manager)

Those councillors and industrialists who had set up the private security company which was to be responsible for managing the CCTV system had also intended to charge businesses in other areas of Northern City to have their premises monitored remotely from the new CCTV control room which was to be based in the centre of the industrial estate. However, some of the security managers on the industrial estate were sceptical of these plans. As one of them told me:

All of a sudden this cleverly formed – shall I choose my words carefully? – new company, which was being managed and directed by local directors around here, was gonna be one serious profit-making organisation as far as I could see. I'm saying no more than that. You know, for me it should have been non-profit making. Not exactly belt and braces but something like that system that would envisage one guy monitoring the TVs in a central area, you know, and probably a response unit. Whereas ... I smelt a rat at the end of it to be honest.

As each industrialist withdrew their support the cost of setting up the system increased and eventually became too great for the few remaining industrialists who were still committed. Some of the industrialists wanted to go ahead with a smaller system but, as the estate manager explained, in the end the whole project ground to a halt:

We sent round the agreement forms, draft agreements to join the company, a direct debit mandate, and an information pack to around one hundred large companies and we gave them three weeks to reply. After three weeks we hadn't got one back. So we extended the time period by a couple of weeks and after ringing round and badgering we ended up with something like fifteen ... So that's where we are at the moment. I've sent all the agreements back and the direct debits that people did bother sending. We've wrote back to the interested people who were going to join and said: 'look we're putting it on hold at the moment'. We haven't disbanded the company, we've suspended its operations. The cash is being held by the council and we're just waiting to see if we can get other areas of funding.

The £50,000 grant that the council received from the first round of the government's Challenge Competition was eventually returned to the Home Office. The Northern City Industrial Association has been disbanded and there are no plans at present to install a CCTV system on the industrial estate. Once again it was not civil liberties concerns that scuppered the proposed system on the industrial estate, but disputes about who should be 'responsible' for funding.

The Challenge Competition and the entrepreneurial city

Back in the city centre the government's CCTV Challenge Competition gave a new impetus to those 'entrepreneurs' who were pushing for a publicly funded city-centre CCTV system. The 'key player' in Northern City's network of entrepreneurs is Neil Lawson, a man with a dynamic personality and a reputation for working very well with the city council. Lawson, a former department store manager, arrived in Northern City in 1994 when he became the manager of City Centre Mall, a £65 million retail leisure complex situated in the middle of the city centre. A few months later he was appointed chairman of the Chamber of Trade, and more recently became the deputy chair of the City Centre Task Force and a member of Northern City Vision Ltd. The Council Leader set up the City Centre Task Force (with a little encouragement from the Chamber of Trade) with the aim of revitalising the city centre. Lawson heads a 'management group' on the Task Force which is responsible for dealing with security issues in the city centre. The vice-chairman of the management group is the city centre police commander, Superintendent Jack Sampson, who is also a member of Northern City Vision Ltd and the City Centre Action Group (CCAG). Northern City Vision is a public-private partnership which provides a strategic framework for making bids to the government's Challenge Fund which provides Single Regeneration Budget (SRB) grants. As a member of Northern City Vision Lawson, along with the editor of the *Daily Echo*, chairs an 'image group' which has recently raised £50,000 to commission a major consultant to revamp the image of Northern City.

In January 1996 Lawson and other members of the Chamber of Trade set up a City Centre Action Group (CCAG) which holds bi-monthly meetings in Lawson's office in the basement of City Centre Mall. The chairman of the CCAG is Chris Danton. Danton is the manager of a major high-street retailer, vice-chairman of the Chamber of Trade and a member of both Northern City Vision Ltd and the City Centre Task Force. The

CCAG was set up with the aim of addressing a number of issues related to the management of the city centre. As Danton explained:

> It was again going back three and a half or four years … there has long been a Chamber of Trade and a Chamber of Commerce in the area … erm … I felt, along with quite a few other … erm … mainstream retailers, that the city centre deserved a bit of focused attention. And we encouraged the Chamber of Trade to, if you like, allow a sub-group – which is what the City Centre Action Group (CCAG) is – which could encompass non-members of the Chamber of Trade so that we could actually bring in the various other things that go on in city centres to allow a sort of across the board representation. So while the CCAG does have many retailers in it, it also includes the banks, the building societies, the licence trade, the police, the buses, you know, the civic society, you name it. We've got people in most areas who can give a view about certain things. CCTV became one of the planks of our strategy.

The City Centre Action Group's main aims are to coordinate the push for CCTV, and encourage the council to create a role for a town centre manager. The formation of the CCAG has allowed members of the Chamber of Trade to gain access to key members of the city council. Council representatives attending the CCAG meetings include the council's Chief Executive, the head of the council's Policy Unit, and the Director of the Technical Services Department. The Technical Services Department is responsible for carrying out the feasibility studies for all CCTV systems, and for drawing up proposals and CCTV bids to the Home Office. As several members of the Chamber of Trade explained, getting these 'key players' on board was an important breakthrough in terms of changing the council's position from one of total opposition to city-centre CCTV to supporting CCTV in principle:

> Oh yes, it was 'NO!' It wasn't even on the agenda. Now it's on the agenda. The issue they're concerned about now … is the cost. It's gonna cost about £30,000 for maintenance …so we spend £300,000, we get the system in up and running and it's gonna cost about £30,000 per year to run it, maintain it and that's what they're concerned about, the running costs. Who's going to pay for that? Year one, year two, year three, etc. Of course we want the council to pay for it and they want us to pay for it. It's a debate.
>
> (The manager, City Centre Mall)

Liaison with the council has improved dramatically over the past two years or so since we formed the CCAG. They started coming to the meetings, we always have representatives from the council, it's usually the paid officers from the Technical Services Department that we have but there's always at least two people from the council at the meetings.

(The manager, city centre department store)

The council's position has changed a heck of a lot. I mean when the City Centre Action Group first started it was 'we won't even talk about that', whereas now it's changed from 'we won't talk about it' to 'we really want it, but' ... Like now the thing that's really good is that the councillors who come to the meetings, they really want it so they keep battling back and putting cases.

(The manager, high-street retailer)

It was just lobbying. We met with the council, we've had constant meetings with the members of the Technical Services and then really we got the biggest, the council's Chief Executive and the head of Technical Services and his team in the Planning Department. We had a meeting with the Chief Executive during the late summer and he virtually said: 'Yes, I think we can come up with the money. Leave it to us'.

(The manager, high-street retailer)

The government's CCTV Challenge Competition was not completely responsible for mobilising the network of entrepreneurs in Northern City behind the push for CCTV. The emergence of a 'partnership culture' also has to be understood against the background of political and economic changes at the local level. In the mid-1990s, Northern City, like most cities in the UK, began to experience substantial changes in the complexion of its local political institutions, including the rapid growth of non-elected local government agencies, local authority implementation agencies, public/private partnership organisations and inter-governmental forums. The background to these developments can be traced to the policies of post-1979 conservative governments. These political administrations routinely rejected what they saw as the in-adequacies of the interventionist, social democratic state and im-plemented policies designed to ensure that representatives of the private sector were involved to a greater degree in defining the 'urban problem', in developing solutions and in operationalising them. These changes were founded on the shared assumption that the attraction of external (and increasingly global) investment is the key to securing the future prosperity of the city in the face of heightened inter-urban competition (Hubbard, 1996: 1441–2). This transformation of the political landscape has shifted attitudes on the part of local authorities that have seen their independent room for manoeuvre reduced and the incentives to achieve their objectives through cooperation with the private sector increased.

This shift in local urban governance was reflected in Northern City by the establishment of various public-private partnerships set up by the council with the aim of regenerating various parts of the city, including the city centre. For example, in 1995 a loose association of organisations interested in the future of regeneration in Northern City came together to discuss the changes which were taking place in UK government and European policy on urban regeneration. The partnership became Northern City Vision Ltd in 1995. One of the group's first tasks was to develop a City Regeneration Strategy to provide a strategic framework for using existing resources more effectively and for bids for additional finance including bids to the government's Challenge Fund which provides Single Regeneration Budget (SRB) grants. In its first annual report the regeneration manager stated that:

> Sustainable urban regeneration cannot be achieved by organisations working in isolation. We need to work together to understand the issues we are dealing with and to develop effective policies and projects for dealing with them … Northern City Vision is committed to building an effective partnership and improved understanding of the Challenge Fund culture.
>
> (Northern City Vision, 1996: 9)

During the same period city councillors also began to recognise that rapid social and economic changes – including the introduction of the supermarket, the creation of shopping centres in towns and cities, and the emergence of out-of-town shopping centres – were having a devastating impact on the city centre. In July 1995 the city council commissioned a consultant firm to review shopping in Northern City. A detailed assessment of the city centre's health was carried out and comparisons with main competing towns were made. The report recommended:

(1) The development of a new City Centre Partnership between the public and private sectors.

(2) The preparation of a City Centre Strategy and Action Plan.
(3) The establishment of a City Centre Management Team, with members of the public and private sector, to act as an advisory body to the city council.

In the light of these recommendations the council set up a City Centre Task Force comprising city-centre traders, the police, voluntary organisations and councillors who sat on various committees which had an interest in city-centre regeneration. In the opening statement of the Task Force's Action Plan it was reported that:

> Rapid economic and social change, the growth of increasing competition from rival town and city centres and strong pressures to develop more out-of-centre facilities present new challenges ...to reassess and redefine the functions of the city centre and to enhance its qualities and future role.
>
> (Northern City Strategy and Action Plan)

As several writers have argued, these developments in local urban governance mean that it is increasingly 'competition between places ... which provides the driving force for new regeneration strategies' (Cochrane, 1993: 95). Many of the city-centre traders in Northern City believed that the acquisition of a city-centre CCTV surveillance system was an essential part of the Task Force's broader strategy of attracting consumers back from the out-of-town shopping centres and from other cities in the region. As the manager of one high-street retailer and member of the Task Force put it:

> All towns have gone down this road. It's the 'feel good factor' – okay, you're never going to compete with Meadow Hall and Northern City feels the competition from Meadow Hall ... we can't compete. We can't provide parking space for so many thousand visitors and a totally covered environment. What we can offer though is a wide range of stores, a history and theatres. But you want people to feel secure and CCTV goes a long way to creating feelings of security ... You know, I don't think I'm competing with Allders and Hammonds. I think Northern City is competing with York or Leeds or Meadowhall. That's the real prize.
>
> (The manager, high-street retailer)

Against this background of spatial competition between localities and cities the City Centre Task Force's vision is that of a city which will be 'a safe, vibrant and attractive place to live, work and visit – the heart of a dynamic European City' (City Council Strategy and Action Plan: 6). The local-level recognition of the importance of 'place marketing' as a critical element for success in the inter-regional competition for investment has been described by some writers as a shift towards 'entre-preneurialism' which involves cities striving 'to forge a distinctive image and to create an atmosphere of place and tradition that will act as a lure to both capital and people "of the right sort" ' (Harvey, 1989: 295). Through their involvement in these public-private partnerships city-centre traders expressed their concern that the absence of CCTV in Northern City meant that the city centre was perceived as unsafe and that this was having a detrimental effect on their attempt to sell the city centre to tourists and consumers. According to many city-centre traders the issues of safety, inter-urban competition and the development of a consumer-orientated environment all crystallised around the issue of city-centre CCTV:

> CCTV comes into everything. The 'feel-good factor', the security of people, vehicle security and so on. CCTV is an umbrella which takes in a number of these issues. If you look at what's happened in places like Bradford and Wolverhampton, what's happening in these cities since CCTV came in is the emergence of a 'cafe culture' and so on. I mean Leeds is talking about all night shopping and things like that.
>
> (The manager, high-street retailer)

> Well CCTV fits into the vision because we've got to make the city safer. It is perceived that the city isn't safe for people to come in during the day and especially at night. What we're trying to do is get a twenty-four hour city. A city that is really active 24 hours a day. The city if you like comes alive between nine o'clock and five o'clock and is very 'no-go' out of those hours which is silly. And we want to get into the European mode of having street cafes, entertainment, wine bars, bistros, this sort of thing. So we've got to move towards a 24-hour city.
>
> (The manager, City Centre Mall)

This model is, of course, dependent on their being a large middle-class and an affluent working population who enjoy good transport links to these new places of consumption, all of which is wishful thinking in the case of Northern City.

The local media and CCTV

The importance of getting the media on board in local campaigns for CCTV is made explicit in the Home Office document, *CCTV: Looking Out For You* (1994). In this instruction manual those wanting to set up a city-centre CCTV system are advised to 'form a multi-agency working party comprising all interested parties'. This includes the police, relevant local authorities, crime prevention panels, representatives of retailers, car parking operators, town centre managers, the Chamber of Commerce and 'a representative of the media, for example the editor of a local newspaper' (1994: 12). In Northern City the growth of public-private partnerships and local multi-agency networks made the Chamber of Trade's task of 'getting the media on board' a lot easier. In 1995, for instance, Neil Lawson (the chairman of the Chamber of Trade) was appointed as chairman of an 'image group' which he chairs with the editor of the *Daily Echo*. Also, in January 1996 Lawson and other members of the Chamber of Trade created the City Centre Action Group (CCAG) whose meetings are attended by a representative of the *Daily Echo*.

Having a representative of the local newspaper attend CCAG meetings was particularly useful for members of the Chamber of Trade. As one city-centre trader explained: 'what happens is the newspaper's representative comes down to the [CCAG] meetings and if there's anything of interest then we'll give them a script to see if they're interested in publicising it'. From 1996 onwards the *Daily Echo* joined forces with the Chamber of Trade in a campaign to have a city-centre CCTV system installed in Northern City. As the manager of one high-street retailer put it, what the newspaper did was:

> lend their 'journalistic muscle' to the campaign ... And from there it gets into people's hands and they understand. It's a communication exercise in trying to educate the public if you like on to what the real reasons for wanting CCTV are.

In this way the 'entrepreneurs' in Northern City became the 'primary definers' of news stories in the *Daily Echo*. As Hall et al. (1981) have shown, the concept of 'primary definition' explains how powerful groups in society enjoy privileged access to the media as news sources, providing the interpretative frameworks within which journalists then construct their story. This does not mean that journalists are necessarily biased towards the powerful or that they have no independence. Rather, it draws attention to 'the more routine structures of news production to see how the media come in fact, in the "last instance", to reproduce the definitions of the powerful, without being, in a simple sense, in their pay' (1981: 57). The bureaucratic nature of news organisation is such that it creates an easy interface with the bureaucratic organisation of powerful social institutions and elite groups. As van Dijk (1996) points out, because the *discourse access profile* of elite groups is much greater than that of ordinary citizens, it opens up the means for the powerful to define situations through the media without having to issue direct instructions. In the context of the present study, this means that an organisation like the Chamber of Trade, for example, has the resources to provide news organisations with a steady flow of information, while the latter have the resources to receive and process this information quickly and efficiently. As Fairclough (1992: 22) points out, institutions which enjoy access to the media:

> are established by official authority, by social status or by commercial success; they are organised, with a bureaucratic structure which embodies spokespersons, and a regular scheduling of statements; and they have the resources to pay for publicity and public relations. Thus, the most convenient sources for journalists to monitor are also, necessarily, institutions and persons with official authority and/or financial power.

While recognising that journalists employed by the *Daily Echo* may themselves have taken the initiative in the definitional process (Schlesinger and Tumber, 1994: 19), the influence of the City Centre Action Group (CCAG) on the newspaper's coverage of CCTV stories is quite clear. For example, between 1 January 1990 and 30 June 1998 a total of 186 CCTV stories were printed in the *Daily Echo*. Closed-circuit television first broke as a news story in the *Daily Echo* on 24 October 1990. Only six articles appeared in the newspaper during this year followed by a total of eight articles in 1991. The Chamber of Trade began its public campaign for city-centre CCTV in the newspaper on 13 April 1992. Ten CCTV stories were printed during this year, followed by 21 in 1993, 17 in 1994 and only 10 in 1995. However, following the formation of the CCAG in January 1996, a total of 51 CCTV stories appeared in the *Daily Echo* during the same year, and 49 articles followed in 1997. Thus, over half (54 per cent) of the CCTV stories that appeared in the newspaper between January 1990 and June 1998 appeared in the two-year period immediately following the formation of the CCAG at the beginning of 1996.

In the 186 CCTV stories that were printed by the newspaper a total of 272 'voices' appeared (i.e. 272 people were quoted directly or indirectly in the 186 CCTV stories). One-fifth (21 per cent) of these voices belonged to members of the Chamber of Trade, one-quarter (24 per cent) to the police, and one-quarter (26 per cent) to Northern City councillors. Most of the other voices comprised supporters of CCTV. These included British Rail and brewery spokespersons, members of the Safer Cities Committee, safety groups and residents groups, MPs and Home Office ministers, private security personnel and private security industry representatives, members of the legal profession, and various entrepreneurs who were responsible for setting up CCTV systems in local hospitals, schools and universities. Those (councillors) who were opposed to the introduction of CCTV, on the other hand, appeared in only two articles.

In the *Daily Echo's* coverage of CCTV, therefore, the news actors who appeared most frequently were city councillors, the police, city-centre traders and other people in positions of authority. As Fowler (1991: 22) points out, the effects of this division between the 'accessed' and 'unaccessed' are clear:

> an imbalance between the representation of the already privileged, on the one hand, and the already unprivileged, on the other, with the views of the official, the powerful and the rich being constantly invoked to legitimate the status quo.

In this respect the news media do not provide a neutral reflection of the 'world out there', rather they provide an ideological construction of reality which naturalises 'a preferred range of truth claims (to the detriment of alternative ones) as being the most *obvious, reasonable* or *rational* ones available' (Allan, 1998: 108–9). This social construction of reality encourages us 'to accept as *natural, obvious* or *commonsensical* certain preferred definitions of reality, and ... these definitions have profound implications for the cultural reproduction of power relations across society' (ibid.: 105). Having looked at how production schedules and conventions for access to stories affect the content and presentation of the CCTV stories that appeared in the *Daily Echo*, we will now look a little closer at the stories themselves.

CCTV in the *Daily Echo*

Many of the issues surrounding the debate over the introduction of a city centre CCTV system fit very neatly with the professional and cultural assumptions that underlie a journalist's judgement about what is news and what is not. As a number of writers have argued, a 'good story' should include events which have 'negative' consequences; events which are 'dramatic'; events which concern 'elite' persons; events which have the potential for 'conflict'; events which prioritise the 'present over the past' and the 'simplistic over the complex'; events which are part of an ongoing 'newsworthy theme'; and events which take place in close 'proximity' to the reader (Hall et al., 1981; Bell, 1991; Chibnall, 1981; Norris and Armstrong, 1999; van Dijk, 1998). The very first CCTV news item published by the *Daily Echo* shows how CCTV scores high on a number of these news values:

CCTV BID TARGETS CITY'S BUS STATION
Northern City's bus station [*proximity*] and major car parks are likely to become the first city centre areas to be monitored by closed-circuit security cameras. The city council's Policy Committee has recommended consideration of TV cameras at both the station and certain car parks to crack down on crime [*unambiguity*]. The proposal needs rubber stamping by the powerful Labour Group [*elite group*] at the Guildhall and the full council before it becomes a reality. Although councillors are split over the issue [*conflict*] it is expected yesterday's recommendations [*recency*] moved by council leader, Coun Paul Dowy, will eventually become accepted [*newsworthy theme*].

(24 October 1990)

Over the next two years this ongoing 'local story' with potential for 'conflict' among local 'elite groups' provided good copy for the newspaper:

'SPY' CAMERAS RULE BREACHED – CLAIM (27 January 1992)

TV SPY ROOM BAN (15 February 1992)

WOULD-BE EURO MP SPARKS WAR OF WORDS (23 December 1993)

COUNCIL ROW OVER CCTV (7 January 1994)

Other news values were also drawn upon to sustain the 'news life' of CCTV, including an emphasis on 'violent' and 'dramatic' crimes which were usually followed by a call for city-centre CCTV:

VIOLENT CRIME SHOCK (in-set 'Local town's CCTV rolls today') (26 March 1996)

NEW CCTV CALL AFTER SHOOTING (9 April 1996)

POLICE PLEA IN HUNT FOR GUN THUGS (13 June 1996)

PCs PELTED WITH BOTTLES IN BRAWL (15 May 1997)

The three main discursive strategies, however, that dominated the newspaper's coverage of CCTV stories included: (a) *the silver bullet*; (b) *in-group versus out-group*; and (c) *winners and losers*. The silver bullet news frame claims that 'CCTV CRACKS CRIME'. The in-group versus out-group frame suggests that 'good' people like 'us' support CCTV and 'bad' people like 'them' do not. Finally, the winners and losers news frame attempts to mobilise support for CCTV by arguing that 'we must have CCTV because everyone else has got it'.

The silver bullet

As Gary Marx (1992) has argued, many contemporary strategies of crime control are presented as 'silver bullets' which can provide utopian solutions to complex social problems surrounding crime and disorder. The dominant discourse surrounding CCTV fits neatly with this idea of a 'technical fix' and is a common feature of the language of politicians who claim that CCTV is a 'friendly eye in the sky' which will 'put criminals on the run'. The silver bullet news frame dominated the *Daily Echo's* coverage of CCTV stories and is summed up by the following headlines:

SPY CAMERAS CRACK CRIME (18 January 1992)

HOW TV CAN CUT CRIME (20 January 1996)

CAMERAS WINNING CRIME WAR (14 March 1996)

CCTV CRACKS SHOP CRIME (4 March 1998)

One of the main themes of the silver bullet frame was the use of facts and figures which showed how CCTV was winning 'the war against crime'. In the *Daily Echo*, senior police officers were the main providers of statistics which confirmed the effectiveness of the silver bullet:

CAMERAS CLICK WITH CHIEF
Chief Constable X has backed Northern City's controversial closed circuit TV security system, saying it is reducing crime and disorder ... between November 1 and February 11, only four vehicles were damaged at the city centre car park compared to seven in the same

period last year. Thefts from vehicles were down by 65 per cent and theft of cars was down 80 per cent.

(12 March 92)

SPY CAMERAS CRACK CRIME

Spy cameras installed at city centre trouble spots have drastically cut crime, police figures show. And councillors are now calling for CCTV to be extended to other parts of the city centre to crack down on rowdy revellers and thieves. The cameras have been monitoring Northern City's bus station and city centre car park – hotspots for public order offences and car crime – since the end of November. Figures just released indicate they have been remarkably successful. The bus station has seen a 60% drop in public order offences, while the car park is 80% down on reports of damage to cars compared to 1990.

(18 January 92)

Despite the *Daily Echo's* claim in the second extract above, that reductions in crime had led councillors to call for CCTV to be extended, there was no direct quote from any councillor in the article, nor did any councillor appear in the article as a 'news actor'. The newspaper also translates the imaginary call for cameras by councillors into the newspaper's own language which depicts the 'out-group' as 'rowdy revellers' and 'thieves'.

The use of police statistics on crime rates became a key strategy in the Chamber of Trade's public campaign for CCTV. This campaign began on 13 April 1992 when a representative of the Chamber used police figures to argue that the success of the council's existing CCTV cameras justified the extension of cameras throughout the city centre:

CALL FOR MORE CITY SECURITY CAMERAS

Latest crime figures are the strongest argument yet for more security cameras in the city centre, it was claimed today ... The sharpest drop in recent months has been in areas now covered by a closed-circuit television security system. Northern City Chamber of Trade secretary Mr Roy Lane said today: 'the security cameras in the city centre car park and the bus station have reduced a great deal of the trouble and car crime. People are aware the cameras are there and are not going to do anything. It is absolutely wonderful. These crime figures are a strong argument for more cameras. It is a fact and you cannot get away from it'.

(13 April 1992)

If the public were not convinced about the effectiveness of CCTV by the newspaper's publication of crime figures, then surely, the newspaper argued, no one could oppose CCTV when it has been shown to capture child abductors and terrorists. This was the theme of many articles which used some of the sensational and highly publicised CCTV 'success stories' that appeared in the national media to argue that CCTV would prevent the same thing happening in Northern City:

BID TO BOOST SECURITY
Chamber of Trade Secretary Mr Roy Lane said the Chamber had been pushing hard for CCTV and had assured the council it would try to raise money to offset the cost. 'Surely no-one can object to CCTV anymore on the grounds of loss of civil liberty, when they are going to gain a great deal more', said Mr Lang. 'Televisions in Oxford Street and other areas have shown people putting things in litter bins. It helps catch *terrorists*'.

(14 June 1993, emphasis added)

CAMERA BID TO TACKLE CRIME
Mr Roy Lane, secretary of the Northern City Chamber of Trade, said … 'Recent events such as *terrorists* and *child abductors* being caught on video I think have convinced many of the public concerned about civil liberties that there is more good than bad in having the cameras'.

(7 June 1993, emphasis added)

CAMERA CASH WORRIES
'… I don't have a problem with people paying an extra £3.80 a year on their council tax bill for CCTV', said councillor Ian Mail. 'Anything that will stop another *James Bulger* abduction is worthwhile'.

(30 August 1997, emphasis added)

On other occasions the newspaper used these exceptional cases to justify the introduction of smaller CCTV systems in local schools and hospitals:

SCHOOL IN DRIVE TO BOOST SECURITY
Headteacher Barry Darley has spearheaded moves to bolster security since 16 children and their teacher were slaughtered by Thomas Hamilton at *Dunblane* Primary School, Scotland.

(4 May 1996, emphasis added)

SCHOOLS TO STEP UP SECURITY MEASURES
INITIATIVES to make schools safer following incidents like the *Dunblane massacre* will be thrashed out in Bradley today.
(23 March 1998, emphasis added)

ETERNAL VIGILANCE ON THE HOSPITAL WATCH
Bidding is in the pipeline for a CCTV system at the Northern City Royal Hospital while eight cameras watch all entrances of the Maternity Hospital following previous baby snatches, including that of *Abbie Humphries* from a Nottingham hospital in July 1994.
(12 April 1996, emphasis added)

In-group versus out-group

The in-group versus out-group news frame involves the rhetorical construction of a binary opposition between 'us', law abiding citizens of Northern City, and 'them' (the surveilled), 'mindless thugs', 'vice girls', 'rowdies' and so on. The following headlines are typical of the negative lexicalisation of the out-group:

TV WILL 'SPY' ON BUS THUGS (21 December 1990)

STORES DEMAND ACTION ON YOBS (7 January 1993)

THUGS FORCE TRADERS OUT (13 December 1996)

Here the newspaper is not merely reporting the statements of the 'primary definers', it is also framing them in a popular rhetorical style that makes such statements seem to respond to the popular demand for CCTV. As Fairclough (1992: 11) argues, when the statements of 'primary definers'

are translated into a newspaper's version of popular language ... there is a degree of mystification about whose voices and positions are being represented. If the voices of powerful people and groups ... are represented in a version of everyday speech ... then social identities, relationships and distances are collapsed. Powerful groups are represented as speaking in a language which readers themselves might have used, which makes it so much easier to go along with their meanings. The news media can be regarded as effecting the ideological work of transmitting the voices of power in a disguised and covert form.

In many cases the out-group occupy a passive position or a 'patient position', as people who are affected by the actions of others. In the following headlines the out-group are passive individuals who are about to be captured by the silver bullet:

THUG: WE'VE GOT YOU IN THE PICTURE (13 December 1991)

CCTV TO NET PLAYGROUND DRUGDEALERS (3 October 1996)

ROWDY FOOTBALL FANS CAUGHT ON VIDEO (17 August 1996)

CAUGHT ON CAMERA: PROSTITUTES AND CLIENTS TO BE FILMED BY POLICE (27 November 1997)

On other occasions the text had the effect of ascribing a high degree of responsibility or agency to the negative actions of the 'out-group'. Consider the labelling of news actors and the lexical style in the following extract:

VANDALS CAPTURED ON FILM
Five *teenage louts* are in the frame for *wrecking* a 30ft stretch of seating at a local railway station in a *'frenzied attack'* of *mindless violence.* Security cameras caught the *hooligans* in action as they *tore the seats apart with their bare hands* ... Sgt Harris said '... They did not stop until they reduced them to matchwood. I still don't know how they did it and I shudder to think what sort of mentality they have – perhaps they were on *drugs* ... *rail passengers* are having to stand out in the cold waiting for trains because of the behaviour of a few *mindless vandals'*, he said.

(7 January 1994, emphasis added)

As the last extract illustrates, the portrayal of the out-group as 'mindless thugs' who 'are not like us' was often done by associating them with the use of drugs. In several cases the 'druggies' were pitted against those who were installing CCTV systems to fight the 'war against drugs':

COUNCIL WINS LANDMARK EVICTION CASE
A SECRET spyhole camera has helped convict a suspected city *drug dealer* in a landmark legal case.

(5 September 1997, emphasis added)

ETERNAL VIGILANCE ON THE HOSPITAL WATCH
From drug addicts 'shooting up' in toilets to people slashing their wrists in

hospital corridors, there's nothing Northern City Royal Hospitals NHS Trust support services manager Gavin Mason does not know about.

(original emphasis)

CCTV TO NET PLAYGROUND DRUG DEALERS

Teenage *drug dealers* and *yobs* are being targeted in a new battle to clean up the city's schools. A mobile spy camera designed to catch the *young thugs* off guard will be set up overnight to catch *dealers* at work in school playgrounds. It will be able to video the *young criminals* at work during the daytime and provide invaluable evidence if they are arrested by the police … The idea behind the new strategy comes from the *Northern City West Crime Prevention Panel Chairwoman, Mrs Lynda Holmes.* She said she hoped the covert nature of the spy cameras would be a major deterrent to young *drug dealers*.

(3 October 1996, emphasis added)

In these articles members of the in-group receive their full names and titles (e.g. Northern City West Crime Prevention Panel Chairwoman, Mrs Lynda Holmes) which gives added weight and authority to their pronouncements. In contrast the out-group are described simply as 'thugs' or 'dealers'. However, there is an alternative representation of the out-group to that of the 'mindless thug'; this is the 'rational actor' who thinks in cost-benefit terms – weighing up the risks, potential gains and potential costs, and then committing an offence only when the benefits are perceived to outweigh the losses. This is the rational actor who only carries out his or her shoplifting activities in towns not covered by CCTV. In the following articles, for example, police officers and traders argue that the absence of CCTV surveillance in their town will make them vulnerable to relocation crime from those areas that are already protected by such systems:

FRESH BID FOR CCTV

A fresh bid to secure funding for a city centre CCTV system is expected to be launched this week. As the Echo revealed, Northern City is the only major city in the region not to have extensive CCTV cover. Even small towns like Grimthorpe and Collingwood have better street camera systems. Police chiefs and traders fear criminals from outside the city regard the central shopping area as an easy touch because of the absence of cameras.

(25 September 1996)

RADIO LINK-UPS TO FIGHT CRIME
CRIME-fighting traders are to *launch* a radio link-up scheme to bolster their moves to *combat* crime ... Woolworth branch manager Mike Marshall ... has already been involved in a scheme at Bishopthorpe and he warned that shoplifters are now turning their attention away from Bishopthorpe to towns like Bradley.

(23 March 1998, emphasis added)

The newspaper is expressing a contradictory view of the 'out-group' here. This contradictory view of the offender reflects official criminological discourse which, as David Garland (1996: 461) has argued, is increasingly dualistic and polarised:

There is a *criminology of the self*, that characterises offenders as rational consumers, just like us; and there is a *criminology of the other*, of the threatening outcast, the fearsome stranger, the excluded and the embittered.

(original emphasis)

The *Daily Echo* uses both of these images to generate support for the introduction of CCTV surveillance systems. Surveillance cameras are needed, according to the newspaper, to monitor the behaviour of the 'mindless thugs' and 'druggies' who threaten our schools and hospitals. However, cameras are also needed to monitor the behaviour of the 'rational actors' who, on discovering that a town centre is monitored by CCTV, are likely to catch a train to the nearest town without CCTV coverage where they can carry out their shoplifting activities with less chance of being caught.

The active citizen
In contrast to the out-group, who were portrayed either as passive (about to be captured by the silver bullet), or with a high degree of responsibility for their negative actions, the in-group were portrayed as agents and received a high degree of responsibility for their positive actions. This representation of the in-group reflects neoliberal discourse which over the last decade has encouraged 'active citizens' to take responsibility in a number of policy areas, including law and order (see Fyfe, 1995: 179). The extracts below illustrate some of the typical rhetorical features of this strategy:

MPs PLEA ON CCTV FOR TOWN
A *CAMPAIGNING MP* is *urging* government ministers to make a local town's bid for *crime busting* security cameras a priority.
(2 December 1996, emphasis added)

CCTV DECISION
Campaigners fighting for *crime-busting* CCTV cameras will be making bids in the future for help from the government to set up a system in the city. CCAG chairman Colin Danton of X store ... promised they would continue *beavering away* to get CCTV installed as it was a sure way of *fighting* the fear of crime.
(21 June 1996, emphasis added)

SCHOOLS SEEK SECURITY HELP
A *CRIME-FIGHTING* team hope to step up security at city schools after a successful summer *crackdown*. West Northern City Crime Prevention Panel lent a state of the art closed circuit television to concerned schools in their area over the summer holidays. Now the *determined group* have *launched* a fund-raising *mission* to have more equipment on offer.
(17 October 1997, emphasis added)

In some articles and leader comments the *Daily Echo* praised the work of the 'active citizen':

TOWN'S CCTV EXAMPLE
WELL done to those Hillburn police officers who have come up with an inspired way to help fund a new CCTV system in Hillburn. Savings made in overtime payments and economising in the office are now being directed towards the camera scheme for the town launched last month. This imaginative move shows the local police force is committed to driving crime off the streets.
(Leader comment, 3 April 1998)

BIG PUSH FOR CITY CAMERA WATCH BID
Scores of people from hard-up grannies to wealthy businessmen have put their hands in their pockets in an effort to stop the spiral of city centre crime ... store manager John Hockey said even pensioners had come into his store and asked if they could also donate a few pounds towards CCTV.
(23 February 1996)

As well as campaigning for city-centre CCTV systems to be installed in Northern City and the surrounding towns and villages, the *Daily Echo* also praised the work of local 'entrepreneurs' who were installing smaller systems in places such as schools and hospitals:

COST-EFFECTIVE CRIME FIGHTER
There are some good ideas so simple, that you are left wondering why they took so long to emerge. One such idea has emerged from the Northern City Crime Prevention Panel. The value of surveillance cameras in reducing crime is well understood. The high cost of comprehensive systems is the main reason they are not used more widely. The crime panel came up with the answer: a mobile unit to be set up on an irregular basis to cover known troublespots. The unit is to be used in schools to weed out drug pushers and vandals. Given the relatively modest outlay involved, *the scheme should provide food for thought for parents, school governors and councillors everywhere. Those who cannot afford costly schemes would do well to consider a more subtle approach.* The use of a combination of dummy cameras and/or a 'live' mobile video unit could prove a very useful and cost-effective deterrent.

(4 October 1996, emphasis added)

Finally, from around 1996 onwards, the *Daily Echo* teamed up with *Crimestoppers* and began to publish mugshots taken from CCTV footage in the newspaper. In these articles 'active citizens' were encouraged to phone in with the names of people captured on film by various CCTV systems in Northern City:

DO YOU KNOW THEM? (20 June 1996)

PLEA TO READERS TO IDENTIFY 12 MEN (11 July 1996)

DO YOU KNOW MAN ON B&Q CAMERA? (19 August 1996)

WANTED: DO YOU KNOW THESE PEOPLE? (17 January 1997)

POLICE WANT TO TRACE THIS WOMAN (4 August 1997)

In one article, the *Daily Echo* printed pictures taken from CCTV footage of a young mother and her two children with the headline: 'MOTHER FAGIN'S YOUNG HELPERS'. The newspaper reported that a mother and her two young children had been captured by a local supermarket's

CCTV system 'carrying out a Fagin-style raid' in a local market town on the outskirts of Northern City. The article encouraged people to phone in with the names of the suspects who were clearly seen as members of the out-group. The newspaper pleaded with local residents to provide information on the suspects who, as the newspaper put it, 'spoke in a rough Northern City accent', and were clearly not 'one of us'. The description of the woman as Mother Fagin also depicted her as 'other' and conjured up Dickensian images of the 'dangerous classes'. In this sense, the article combined all three discursive strategies: 'active citizens' were encouraged to phone in with information on Mother Fagin (in-group versus out-group) who had been captured on film (silver bullet) while shoplifting in a town without extensive CCTV coverage (winners and losers).

Winners and losers

The government's CCTV Challenge Competition played an important part in the *Daily Echo*'s coverage of CCTV stories. The Challenge Competition gave a temporal coherence to the newspaper's reporting and generated a sense of urgency among those who were trying to raise their half of the capital costs to set up a CCTV system. The following headlines appeared in 1996 in the run-up to the deadline for the second round of the government's Challenge Competition:

23 August: NEW CALL FOR CAMERAS IN CITY CENTRE

10 September: LAST-DITCH BID TO WIN CCTV CASH

25 September: FRESH BID FOR CCTV

18 October: DECISION ON CITY CENTRE SECURITY CAMERAS IS DELAYED

11 November: CCTV BID SET TO GO IN

14 November: LATE BID FOR CCTV CASH IN BRADLEY FAILS

20 November: CASH CRISIS PULLS PLUG ON CCTV

For many local activists the competition for CCTV became a competition among neighbouring towns and cities. As the *Daily Echo* reported:

RESORT STEPS UP DRIVE FOR ANTI-CRIME CAMERAS
Seaside shopkeepers are renewing their crime fighting campaign to

have town centre surveillance cameras installed following a *rival* resort's plan to set up a similar scheme.

(26 June 1995, emphasis added)

CRIME SPREE LEADS TO CALLS FOR CCTV
A SPATE of serious crimes including an armed robbery and three ram-raids has sparked new calls for closed circuit television in a local town ... Local businessman Jim Lane said ... *'There is a public outcry that we have not got CCTV and places like Collingwood have backing from the council'*.

(22 December 1997, emphasis added)

Others left behind in the dash for CCTV began to express a concern that they could become victims of 'relocation' crime from those areas now covered by CCTV. During this period of the *Daily Echo's* news coverage of CCTV stories many of the news actors began to use the issue of 'displacement' to call for the installation of city-centre CCTV systems:

NEW CALL FOR CCTV
CALLS for closed-circuit TV cameras for the town centre were repeated today after new figures showed the success of other schemes. The calls from traders and police chiefs follow the success-ful introduction of cameras in two local towns where crime figures plummeted by as much as 76 per cent. But the success of these schemes may be at the expense of Northern City, with some traders claiming that criminals could turn to areas without cameras, sending crime figures through the roof.

(27 September 1997)

In one article the *Daily Echo* gave its official backing to one town's bid for CCTV in its 'Eye on Crime' campaign. This article illustrates how the Challenge Competition created a sense of urgency among the entre-preneurs who were campaigning for CCTV and a sense of fear that those left behind in the race for CCTV cameras would become an easy target for criminals:

ECHO BACKS CCTV SCHEME
The Echo today pledges its support for closed circuit television in Bradley as time runs out this week for a last chance bid for the scheme. It all hinges on businesses pledging enough cash towards

the system, and our 'Bradley's Eye on Crime' campaign is backing the call all the way. Traders are being warned Bradley could become a soft target for crime if it ends up as the only town in the area without CCTV cover. The last ditch attempt is important because there will be no more Home Office funds to help after its current CCTV Challenge pays out. Trader Paul Garland ... warned: 'If Bradley ends up the only town in the country that doesn't have CCTV – or certainly one of the few – then we will be very vulnerable to what they call re-location crime'.

(16 February 1998)

The fear among traders and police that their towns could become a 'soft touch' led many to look for alternative strategies to deal with local problems:

SHOPS ON SHOPLIFTING ALERT
CRIME-fighting traders are launching a new instant alert system to combat shoplifting. Shopkeepers are determined Bradley will not be a soft target for criminals after the town's latest quest for closed-circuit television funding failed. A new telephone alert system to warn traders about criminal activity is now on trial in the town centre revealed Bradley crime prevention officer PC Jack Stone: 'As Bradley has not yet been successful in obtaining a CCTV system, the traders need to look at alternative means of identifying criminal activity in the town', said PC Stone. He warned criminals may be turning their attention away from shopping centres covered by CCTV to unprotected towns such as Bradley.

(21 November 1996)

UNDERCOVER POLICE TARGET TOWN GANGS
Covert cameras and plain clothes police are to be used to crack a dramatic rise in crime on Bradley's car parks and streets ... Sector Commander at Bradley Chief Inspector Alan Hall is determined that town car parks and sleepy villages will not be easy targets for the raiders.

(19 September 1997)

Telephone alert systems and covert camera operations were just some of the many strategies devised by those who missed out on Home Office funds in the Challenge Competition. Other towns in the region began to use private-sector CCTV networks linked by mobile radio networks to tackle relocation crime. Others compiled 'rogues galleries' of known 'shoplifters' and 'troublemakers' and distributed the photographs to other retailers in the area:

RADIO LINK-UP'S TO FIGHT CRIME (23 March 1998)

POLICE TARGET DIRTY DOZEN: THIEVES HIGHLIGHTED IN ALBUM OF SHAME (30 August 1997)

SHOPS TARGET DIRTY DOZEN (16 January 1998)

Summary

In this chapter we have seen how 'new modes of governance' in local crime control strategies have brought together powerful coalitions including the press, the police, local authorities, city centre retailers, private security managers, insurance companies and surveillance industries. These developments created a convergence of interests in Northern City that pushed CCTV to the top of the agenda. However, we have also seen how the success of 'responsibilization' strategies depends upon how they fit in with local cultural traditions and political practices. As Stenson and Edwards (2001: 76) point out, the development of public-private partnerships 'provide an opportunity for exchange relationships based on trust', but they also 'create opportunities for short-term, self-interested, competitive behaviour'.

In the face of opposition from the city council, local activists in Northern City have yet to succeed in their campaign for a publicly funded city-centre CCTV system. However, 'new modes of governance', which brought together the police, councillors and the business community, has already led to the creation of extensive public-private CCTV networks throughout the city. These developments are leading to the creation of new forms of 'hybrid policing' in city centres that blur the public-private divide. For example, in Northern City the chairman of the Chamber of Trade, Neil Lawson, has developed an extensive local network which is increasing the private sector's involvement in the policing of the city centre. Through his involvement in various action groups, Lawson has worked closely with senior members of Northern City police force. This has enabled him to set up a City Centre Security Group (CCSG) which is a loose coalition of private security personnel and the police working in the city centre. So while those campaigning for cameras have yet to win the 'battle' for publicly funded city-centre CCTV, it could be argued that they have already won the 'ideological war' for an expansion of visual surveillance systems throughout the public and private spaces of Northern City. The question of how this surveillance network works in practice will be addressed in the following chapters.

Chapter 3

The surveillance web

The 'surveillance web' described in this chapter is made up of the electronic linkages between 30 CCTV control rooms. As Figure 3.1 shows, some systems are more integrated than others (i.e. linked to more CCTV control rooms). The system with the highest level of integration is the 'shopnet' system which is on the left-hand side of the map. This is a public-private city centre CCTV radio network which is made up of two shopping centres (City Centre Mall and Pullmans Shopping Centre), four major department stores, seven high-street retailers and the city-centre police station. The city centre radio link (CCRL) is used by the security personnel as an 'early warning system' and is designed to let other members of the 'shopnet' system know if any 'shoplifters' or 'troublemakers' are heading towards their premises.

The operation of the 'shopnet' system is coordinated by the City Centre Security Group (CCSG), a loose coalition of private security personnel and the police. This group holds bi-monthly meetings in a vacant unit in City Centre Mall which is currently used as a conference room. The chairman of the CCSG is the operations manager of City Centre Mall. The security manager of High-Street Retailer 1 is the group's treasurer. The chairman of the group describes how the radio link was set up:

> Well we have a City Centre Security Group in the city centre which at the moment has about twenty members and the twenty members are made up of the two shopping centres and the major stores in the city centre, as well as the city centre police station. And basically it was born through the retailers in the city centre trying to have an

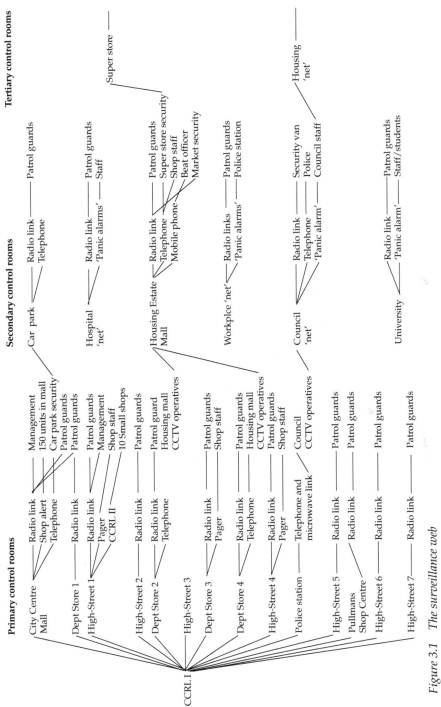

Primary control rooms

Secondary control rooms

Tertiary control rooms

City Centre Mall — Radio link → Management / 150 units in mall / Car park security / Patrol guards
Shop alert → Patrol guards
Telephone

Car park — Radio link — Patrol guards
Telephone

Super store

Dept Store 1 — Radio link — Radio link

High-Street 1 — Radio link → Patrol guards / Management / Shop staff / 10 Small shops
Pager
CCRL II

Hospital 'net' — Radio link → Patrol guards / Staff
'Panic alarms'

High-Street 2 — Radio link — Patrol guards

Dept Store 2 — Radio link → Patrol guard / Housing mall / CCTV operatives
Telephone

Housing Estate Mall — Radio link → Patrol guards / Super store security / Shop staff / Beat officer / Market security
Telephone
Mobile phone

High-Street 3

Dept Store 3 — Radio link → Patrol guards / Shop staff
Pager

Workplce 'net' — Radio links — Patrol guards / Police station
'Panic alarms'

Dept Store 4 — Radio link → Patrol guards / Housing mall / CCTV operatives
Telephone

High-Street 4 — Radio link → Patrol guards / Shop staff
Pager

Council 'net' — Radio link → Security van / Police / Council staff
Telephone
'Panic alarm'

Housing 'net'

Police station — Telephone and microwave link → Council / CCTV operatives

High-Street 5 — Radio link — Patrol guards

Pullmans Shop Centre — Radio link — Patrol guards

University — Radio link → Patrol guards / Staff/students
'Panic alarm'

High-Street 6 — Radio link — Patrol guards

High-Street 7 — Radio link — Patrol guards

CCRL I

Figure 3.1   The surveillance web

71

effective deterrent towards the criminal element that try to penetrate their businesses. And basically each member purchases their own radio. We have a 'base station' which is situated on top of one of the department stores. And through that we can communicate to each other, giving each other information of known criminals heading towards their businesses. And with that information they can then take the necessary action to stop these people coming into their businesses and trying to get away with the goods basically.

The two shopping centres in the 'shopnet' system both have dedicated CCTV control rooms on site where front-line operatives monitor the images displayed on the screens on a continuous basis, as do nine of the other eleven retail stores. The other two high-street retailers have less sophisticated CCTV systems which are tape recorded but not monitored on site in a control room. Between them the CCTV systems in this private sector network include a total of around 235 cameras, 39 external cameras and 196 internal cameras. As Figure 3.1 shows, all the CCTV operatives involved in the operation of the 'Shopnet' system can talk to each other directly and to the police on the city centre radio link (CCRL).

The CCTV operatives can also communicate directly with the patrol guards, shop staff and management in their own stores through the use of in-store radio links, telephones, panic alarms and pager systems. The CCTV operatives based in the control room of City Centre Mall, for example, have a shopping centre radio link (SCRL) which allows them to communicate with ten patrol guards, four cleaning staff, five members of the management team and two store detectives who are based in the CCTV control room of a clothes store within the shopping centre. There is also a computerised 'Shop Alert' system which allows instantaneous communication between the CCTV operatives and the staff in the centre's 150 units (i.e. shops, restaurants, offices). The operations manager of City Centre Mall described how the system operates:

... basically it's a small keypad that is put into a shop and on that keypad is a window display where I can send a message to you and you can read it. And you can send a message to me but on our system it's limited 'cause we only want you to send two messages: one, somebody's attacked you, a 'personal attack' we call it; and two, 'shop theft': somebody is stealing from your shop. And to send those two messages ... to send one you press two numbers simultaneously and to send the other is a code 79. And this piece of equipment is electronically connected to a VDU in the control room.

And when you press that button it sets off an audible alarm in the control room and it comes up on the VDU floor plan of the centre and the security officer in the control room would then dispatch a security guard to that problem to go and assess the situation and try and (a) if it's somebody being attacked stop them, and (b) if it's somebody that's having something stolen to assist them in apprehending the thief to bring them to justice.

The Shop Alert system can also be used by the CCTV operatives to send a wide range of messages to the stores within the shopping centre. For instance, the 'message library' can be used to send the following messages: *Stolen Credit Card In Use, Look Out For Forged Ten Pound Notes*, and so on. When the operatives send a message to the stores they can see all the units within the shopping centre light up on a floor plan which is displayed on the computer screen. As the operative sends the message all the units on the screen turn from grey to green. Then gradually each unit on the computer screen turns from green to blue which indicates that the shop staff have acknowledged the message. The following extract from the fieldnotes describes how this system works:

At 13.59 a patrol guard (who has been informed by a shop worker that someone has used a forged £10 note in their shop) calls the control room on the shopping centre radio link [SCRL] and tells Alan [the CCTV operative] that he has been told by a shopworker to be on the lookout for forged ten pound notes. Alan logs in to the Shop Alert computer and in the 'message library' finds a message warning shop staff that forged notes are in use. When Alan sends the message all the units in the mall immediately light up green on the computer screen which means they have received the message. Gradually, each unit on the computer screen turns from green to blue which indicates that a member of staff in the shop has acknowledged the message.

Although the Shop Alert system provides a means of instant communication with a number of actors who are widely separated in time and space it does not allow the CCTV operatives to provide detailed descriptions concerning, say, the appearance or location of 'known' persons. To do this the computerised Shop Alert system has to be used in conjunction with 'old' technology, i.e. the telephone. For instance, if a CCTV operative sees or is told that a 'known' person has entered a shop within the shopping centre they may choose to send a message to the shop on the Shop Alert system (e.g. *Shoplifter In Your Store Please Ring*

Security). The shopworker then rings the control room and is given a description of the suspect by the CCTV operative. This happened in the incident described below when one of the patrol guards contacted the control room on the shopping centre radio link to tell the operatives that a suspected 'shoplifter' had just entered Clothes Are Us:

> Trevor puts a camera on the entrance to Clothes Are Us and walks across to the Shop Alert computer system. He logs in and using the mouse goes into the menu and selects the 'message library'. This displays a list of messages on the right-hand side of the screen. Trevor highlights a message – *suspect persons in your premises please contact control* – and then using the mouse highlights the shop in question on a map of the centre displayed on the screen and presses the enter button to send the message which will be received in the shop on a message pad fixed to a wall usually close to the till. A few seconds later an employee of Clothes Are Us calls the control room by telephone. Karen takes the call and says, 'Hello, do you know you've got three known shoplifters in your store'. Karen puts the phone down and tells Trevor that the staff in the shop have got the suspects under their sights.

A combination of CCTV surveillance cameras linked with panic alarms, radio links and mobile and fixed telephone networks allows for a high degree of integration between the police and private security systems in the city centre. However, the 'surveillance web' is not confined to the city centre. The 'shopnet' system, for example, is also integrated with CCTV systems on the outskirts of Northern City. We can illustrate this by briefly examining the operation of a CCTV system set up in 1994 at Housing Estate Mall which is six miles away from the city centre.

Housing Estate Mall is situated in the middle of a large council estate called Banton which is one of the most deprived areas in Northern City. The shopping centre provides a focal point for many of the estates residents. It is built on the same grounds as a local public house, post office, night club, health clinic and social services office. There is a police station across the road from the shopping centre and just beyond the police station is the city's largest comprehensive school. The CCTV system at Housing Estate Mall was introduced, according to Kevin Smith, the security manager, to help tackle the local 'drugs problem'. Housing Estate Mall has 13 CCTV cameras: five colour cameras covering the entrances and main shopping areas within the centre, and eight black-and-white external CCTV cameras covering the loading bays and two large car parks. All the CCTV cameras are fully functional (pan/tilt/

zoom). The reasoning behind installing all fully functional cameras, according to Kevin Smith, was 'so there's nowhere for the "druggies" to hide. "Druggies" always congregate in little corners or out of sight places.'

The integration between the shopnet system and Housing Estate Mall is made possible by a number of 'interpersonal' links between the security personnel employed by Housing Estate Mall and other members of the 'surveillance web'. For example, two security managers, currently working in Department Store 2 and Department Store 4, are former employees of Kevin Smith's. Also, the security manager employed by Department Store 2 is the brother of Danny, a security guard and CCTV operative who works at Housing Estate Mall. This informal network allows the security officers to share information about 'known' persons with other members of the surveillance web. For example, the security personnel employed by Housing Estate Mall often ring Danny's brother at city centre Department Store 2 with information about 'known' persons that may be heading for the city centre. Housing Estate Mall has several external cameras including one in the middle of a car park which overlooks a bus stop outside of the shopping centre. If the CCTV operatives at Housing Estate Mall see any 'known' persons waiting for a bus to take them to the city centre they can telephone Danny's brother to let him know that 'one of the "regulars" is on his way on the number 36 bus'. The security manager of city centre Department Store 2 can then share this information with his patrol guards on the in-store radio link and with all the other city centre stores, shopping centres and police on the CCRL (see Figure 3.1).

The security personnel at Housing Estate Mall also have direct electronic linkages to other members of the surveillance web. The CCTV operative, for example, has a direct radio link with four full-time patrol guards, the shopping centre cleaners and the shopping centre secretary. Also on the shopping centre radio link (SCRL) is a security officer employed by the indoor market which is inside the shopping centre but under different ownership. The market security officer monitors the images displayed by a very limited CCTV system comprising three ancient-looking black-and-white fixed CCTV cameras which cover the back entrances to the market. If the security officer in the market sees any 'known' or 'banned' persons trying to sneak into the centre through the entrance at the back of the market he contacts the shopping centre's CCTV control room on the SCRL and gives the CCTV operative a description of the suspect. The CCTV operative in Housing Estate Mall's control room also has a direct link with Shaun, the local beat officer. Shaun has given the security manager his mobile telephone number and asked the security officers to give him a ring if any 'wanted' persons enter the shopping centre. Hardly a day goes by without Shaun visiting the control room to speak to the security personnel who, Kevin says, 'are used as an information service by the police'.

The council network

The absence of a city-centre CCTV system in Northern City has meant that at present it is not possible to integrate a public open-street CCTV system with other CCTV systems such as the 'shopnet' system. However, as Figure 3.1 shows, the 'council net' does have a number of direct electronic linkages with other CCTV systems. The 'council net' comprises four separate CCTV systems which are all monitored at the council's central monitoring station in the city centre by two council officials and one private security officer. As part of its Safer Cities programme the city council installed CCTV surveillance systems at both the city centre bus station and one of the council-owned city-centre car parks. There are eight cameras located around the bus station, three fully functional (i.e. pan/tilt/zoom) and five fixed. In the car park there are three fully functional P/T/Z cameras mounted at a high level on a support tower which is situated in the middle of the car park. All video signals from the cameras on both sites are routed into Uniplex Series 2 multiplexers located nearby for encoding into a single video signal. The camera pictures are then relayed to the council's Guildhall central monitoring station via a relay station on the top of a nearby building by microwave radio links. The cameras are monitored and recorded on a continuous basis, i.e. 24 hours a day, 365 days a year.

The pictures from the council's CCTV systems located in the bus station and car park are also relayed from the council's central monitoring station to the city centre police station (which is 185 metres away) by microwave video/telemetry link, which enables the control of the cameras to be handed over to the police when required. In theory this would allow the public 'council net' system to be integrated with the private 'shopnet' system. As we have seen, the security personnel involved in the operation of the 'shopnet' system also have a direct radio link to the city centre police station through the city centre radio link. This allows the security officers to communicate directly with the police Interview Team. In theory this would mean that the police could monitor the cameras overlooking the bus station and watch for the arrival of 'known' persons who could then be passed on to the security personnel involved in the operation of the 'shopnet' system via the CCRL. However, the Police Communications Headquarters has recently moved from the city-centre police station to a new station eight miles away. This means that the police in the city centre station no longer use the facility to take control of the council's cameras. Meanwhile the council officials who monitor the cameras on the bus station and car park do not have access to the city centre radio link (CCRL). This means that at present there is no integration between the public-private 'shopnet' system and the public 'council net' system.

Two further CCTV surveillance systems were installed by the city council in October 1993, one at a public cleansing depot, approximately three miles from the city centre, and one at the Radcliffe Shopping Centre. At the cleansing depot six cameras are mounted externally on the main office building and four of the cameras monitor car parks, storage areas and the depot perimeter. At the Radcliffe Shopping Centre six cameras are mounted internally to a housing estate office and the public areas of the Centre. All cameras on both sites are wired back to an on-site control room and connected into a Frowds Digiscan Video compression system which transmits the pictures back to the council's central monitoring station via the integrated services digital network (ISDN) line system. Both systems are monitored remotely at the council's central monitoring station in the city centre and recorded on a continuous basis at the two sites.

The council's security manager says that very little ever happens on these two sites and that basically these systems are just a part of the council's alarm monitoring services. He says:

> When the alarm goes off … an alarm signal comes down the ISDN line which switches on the camera. But the alarm's never activated for that to go off. So it's just an added security measure.

If anything does happen at the Shopping Centre the security personnel 'pass it straight to the police'. If anything happens at the cleansing depot, on the other hand, the security officers go down there with the police because they're contracted to patrol the depot and they have the keys to let the police onto the site. The council official's main priority, though, is to monitor all the alarm systems on council property throughout the city. The security officers can be contacted by all the different council departments on a pager system, two internal and four external telephone lines, and a fax machine. The officers also have two patrol vehicles which have a digital radio and handset so that the patrolling security officer can be contacted from the control room.

The council's computerised alarm system provides a direct 'panic alarm' link between the CCTV operatives in the council's central monitoring station and the 'housing net' CCTV systems. The 'housing net' comprises of a total of 222 fixed cameras – 48 external cameras and

174 internal cameras. There are three colour cameras in each of the city's 26 estate offices and nine in each of the 16 high-rise blocks of flats which are spread across the city mainly on the large council estates. The most recent system was installed in 1996 and has nine colour cameras. The other eight blocks of flats have black-and-white cameras. Some of these systems are over ten years old and have several cameras that are out of action. The cameras in the estate offices were installed two years ago. The person responsible for installing the cameras in the estate offices was a paid council official employed by the Technical Services Department. According to him there are cameras in

> ... all the estate offices of which there's about twenty. We went round and depending on the size we put two or three colour cameras into each one of the offices when we upgraded the counters and things making them with bullet proof glass. This was when we had a problem with a few armed robberies. So we should be able to get a decent image of somebody now if anybody does it again.

The CCTV systems in the high-rise blocks have been installed gradually since the late 1980s. Most of the CCTV systems consist of CCTV cameras in vandal-resistant housings sited in each lift, in the ground floor lobbies and at both the front and back entrances. These are connected to a 'Krammer' controller which enables all cameras to be recorded simultaneously on a single time-lapse video tape recorder. This unit incorporates a sequential switcher which feeds a monitor within the custodian's office, and also connects to the tenants' communal television aerial system on a dedicated channel. This latter feature enables the tenants themselves to monitor the system. Furthermore, when used in conjunction with the digital call audio system it enables visual identification of callers before admitting them into the flats. The council official told me that one of the unintended consequences of allowing the residents themselves to view the images displayed by the cameras was that some tenants would sit and monitor the system on their television and when a they saw a neighbour leaving the flats they would go straight to the person's flat, break in and steal their goods.

In 13 of the 16 high-rise blocks the images displayed by the cameras are not monitored on site on a continuous basis. However, at Hampton (which comprises three blocks of flats) there is a full-time concierge system in operation. Concierge staff employed by the Housing Department monitor the images displayed from the cameras in three high-rise blocks on a continuous basis, i.e. 24 hours a day, 365 days a year. The 26 estate offices, eight caretakers' offices in the high-rise flats and the concierge CCTV control room all have a button for the 'panic alarm' system which sounds in the council's central monitoring station. When the alarm sounds in the council's control room, the operatives can either ring the police immediately or come down to deal with the problem themselves. The concierge staff also have a desk number for the local police station. Trev, one of the concierge staff, tells me that he does not ring the police very often but that they often visit the control room after an incident has occurred:

> Yes they come and they ask us to review tapes. We had one the other day where we were looking for a stolen car off the car park. But you have to stop all the cameras on the monitor to review the tapes. But yes, we have good liaison with Haldon Police Station, Transport Police, Bradley Police, the Child Protection Unit, the Divisional Intelligence Unit. We don't have much to do with the town centre police. Sometimes if there's a ram raid the police will ask us to look out for the car coming back onto the estate so I'll get on the roof and look out for it.

Liaison between the concierge staff and the police has recently been formalised by the signing of an Information Sharing Agreement between members of the Housing Department and Northern City Police Force. Under the agreement, senior housing staff and senior operational police staff have already started to meet regularly to discuss appropriate cases and to share information to be better able to take civic tenancy enforcement or criminal action respectively. Some of the requests made by the police include that the Housing Department will give information (including photographic information) to individual police officers on request; will make available free of charge empty houses and flats for the use of police officers as vantage points to mount covert observations; and an agreement that Northern City Divisional Commanders will always be informed of the council's intention to use private detectives to gather evidence in specific cases, and that this evidence will be available to the police on request. In return, the council are to receive details and confirmation of convictions/cautions which are relevant and relate to the grounds of possession covered by the terms of Section 84 and Schedule 2, Housing Act 1985 of named council tenants or members of their family, excluding juveniles. The council can then use this information in order to progress legal action through the civil courts for enforcement of the council's tenancy agreement, or commence injunctive proceedings through the civil courts to enforce the tenant's compliance with the terms of their tenancy agreement with the council.

Other systems

The CCTV systems with the lowest level of system integration, in terms of direct electronic linkages with other systems (see Figure 3.1), are the four hospitals, the university, and the 11 industrial workplaces. However, these systems do have electronic links with patrol guards on other sites and like all the CCTV systems in the figure are also used as an information pool by Northern City police force. The hospital's central control room is based at the Royal Hospital half a mile away from the city centre. From this site the CCTV operators (who are employed by the hospital) monitor the images displayed by a total of 28 cameras on a continuous basis (i.e. 24 hours a day, 365 days a year). There are 12 cameras located at the Royal Hospital, eight cameras at the Maternity Hospital, and eight at Northern City General Hospital. The pictures from the cameras at both the General and Maternity come back to the central control room on an ISDN. The cameras at the three hospitals are made up of internal and external cameras which monitor the entrances, 'tea bars', car parks and a drugs rehabilitation unit.

The CCTV operative employed by the hospital has a radio link with guards contracted from a private security company who patrol the Royal Hospital, the Maternity Hospital (which is about twelve miles away) and the General Hospital (which is around eight miles away). The security manager responsible for the operation of the hospital's CCTV network is a man in his mid-forties called Gavin Macleod. He says:

> The CCTV operatives direct the guards because within the system we've got an emergency number which anyone can ring direct to the control room. So anybody with an emergency can ring the control room and the controller dispatches a guard. So, for instance, if somebody rings from the General Hospital and says, 'we've got a stranger prowling around the corridor', the controller will dispatch a guard to that location. They'll also monitor the situation and if need be they'll call in back-up from the company because the security company also have one of our radios, so they're tuned into all the transmissions that take place.

Mcleod is about to install a 'panic alarm' system which will enable the hospital staff to contact the control room in emergencies. As he explains:

> We're installing a ... Euro-Panel, it's one of the 'intelligent panels', you can interface all sorts of things into it. For instance, you can have panic attack alarms. It works by means of a transmitter, so that

there's a transmitter on the ward, er if anybody's under attack they just press that, that sends a signal straight to the control room to let them know there's a panic attack activation on Ward X and the controller will then dispatch a guard to that location. The other benefit of a panel as well is that I can dial in from home through the modem and see what's happening. So you don't physically have to come out.

Macleod says that he also works closely with the police, particularly when dealing with the problems posed by the local 'druggies' who, according to the security manager, use the hospital toilets to 'shoot up'. McLeod has recently installed a hard-copy printout machine which has enabled him to create a dossier of the 'druggies':

We've got a separate video if we wanna record a particular incident, we can record that separately. We've also got the facility to produce photographs from the system and we've built up a 'Rogue's Gallery' of the troublemakers er, we say to the police, 'can you give us the name of this person?' So there's interchange between us and the police because of the facilities we've got up there are obviously of use to other people other than ourselves in the area we're working in, so there's that working relationship between us and the police, both with equipment and information.

At Northern City University the CCTV system has recently been upgraded by the new security manager who is a former head of the CID where he served for over thirty years. He also runs a private investigation company and took on the job at the university as a back-up to his company. The CCTV system comprises 20 cameras, 11 internal and 9 external. The images are monitored in a control room in the Administration Building on a full-time basis, i.e. 24 hours a day, 365 days a year. Sixteen of the 20 cameras are on the university campus. These include five external cameras, one (P/T/Z) monitoring the main thoroughfare in the campus, three (P/T/Z) cameras monitoring the car parks, and one fixed camera focused on a postgraduate building. The other 11 cameras are situated in various buildings, including some recently installed colour cameras in the Student's Union building. These cameras monitor the entrance to the building and the Student's Union Shop. The other four external cameras monitor the buildings and car parks of another campus some eight miles away which the university has recently taken over.

The CCTV operative in the university control room can communicate directly with the patrol guards based at the other University campus, and the Security Manager plans to extend this link when he introduces a patrol unit at the new campus. He says:

> The cameras up there … come down the telephone line to the control room here. We were going to monitor up there as well but I think that's ridiculous actually, I think in the end it will all be monitored in one control room here … We haven't got security up there at the moment but I've had a meeting with the Audit Group and we've budgeted for four more security guards so we can go into roving patrol with a vehicle and they'll be able to respond to any problems we have at the new campus.

The 11 CCTV systems in the industrial sector are also relatively isolated in terms of direct links to other systems or to the police with the exception of one pharmaceuticals manufacturer that has a panic alarm which sounds in the local police station about half a mile down the road. The security arrangements on the 11 sites are all very similar. On nine of the 11 sites the CCTV control room is situated at the entrance to the site which is usually just beyond an access control barrier that is operated by the security officers in the control room. At every site visitors must report to the control room and sign a visitors book. The control rooms on nine of the sites are monitored on a continuous basis by private security officials, i.e. 24 hours a day, 365 days a year. In the other two sites one has a CCTV monitor placed in the management office which is monitored by the management periodically, and on the other site a private security guard monitors the images at night time when the factory is closed. A typical factory has around ten cameras including a combination of fully functional and fixed cameras. These cameras are usually positioned to monitor the entrances, exits, perimeter fencing, car parks, contractor loading bays and factory floor.

Although the majority of the CCTV systems in the industrial workplace are used to monitor the 'internal threat' of worker malpractice, they are also used to monitor the 'external threat' of intruders coming onto the site and are very useful for the police. Police use of CCTV systems in the industrial workplace can be both 'reactive' and 'proactive'. For example, the security personnel report that in the course of their work they sometimes observe incidents taking place beyond the perimeter fencing of the site. These are reported to the police who then come along to the control room to collect the tape:

> … we've caught kids breaking into the tools factory across the road [the CCTV operative zooms in on the factory]. I saw two kids

messing about with that barrier, followed them, watched them fill plaggy bags [plastic bags] with the stuff they'd nicked, then I phoned the police who caught them filling their car boot. The police then came to the control room to collect the tape.

(CCTV operative, caravan manufacturer)

Other security officers described how the police have used their CCTV systems in a more 'proactive' way by bringing blank tapes to the control room and asking the CCTV operatives to monitor activities which were beyond the perimeter fencing of the site but in range of the CCTV cameras. The security manager of a newspaper publishing plant, for example, said that the police had brought a tape to the control room and asked him if he would record people visiting a second-hand electrical shop. The plant has three external P/T/Z cameras and one of them is about fifty yards away from the electrical shop which is suspected of receiving stolen goods. Meanwhile, a CCTV operative employed by a frozen foods factory said that the police had used one of the cameras on the site to monitor a person who was suspected of drug dealing. I asked the CCTV operative if the police came to the control room to watch the monitors and he replied:

No, they gave us a tape and we were taping it 24 hours a day on one channel. They were watching this house here (the security officer zooms in on a house across the road). The guy used to go out on Friday night and come back on Monday morning and apparently what it was, he was drug dealing so we caught him on camera. We were recording what time of the day and night people came in, the registration numbers of cars, what people looked like, and as I say it was all on tape.

The 'surveillance web' described above transcends both spatial and temporal barriers. It allows communication with others widely separated in space and facilitates instantaneous communication with a wide range of people, many of whom are involved in the operation of completely separate CCTV systems. In short, this 'electronic network' of CCTV systems, panic alarm systems, faxes, radio links and telephones allows the individual 'strands' of the CCTV network to become a 'surveillance web'. However, when we turn our attention to the question of how this 'web' works in practice, we will find that the reality is a little more complex. Put simply there are no 'electronic linkages' in the surveillance web without 'human linkages' (although see Norris et al. (1998) for an account of the rise of automated visual surveillance systems). And when we turn our attention to the human mediation of technology we will find, for example, that some people turn their pager systems off, some people do not listen to radio messages, some people will listen to radio messages and ignore them, and others will only answer radio messages if they *know* the person at the other end of the line. So what I want to do now is look at the surveillance web once more. Only this time we shall look a little closer at how the human mediation of technology places limits on the possibility of system integration. However, we shall go on to see that it is in fact the 'human' linkages within the 'electronic web' which makes system integration possible.

The human mediation of technology: limits to system integration

One of the things that makes system integration possible is the use of electronic media, such as mobile radio links and 'panic alarms', which allow instantaneous communication between the security personnel who are involved in the operation of completely separate CCTV systems. However, as Thrift (1996: 1471) points out, while electronic communications media may provide a means of rapid communication across a wide geographical area, it does not automatically follow that such space-transcending technologies are 'able to communicate their essential properties of instanteneity and speed to their users'.

Many of the security managers who were interviewed stressed the importance of having a rapid means of communication between those involved in the operation of the surveillance web. Take the Shop Alert system, for example. The operations manager of City Centre Mall described what he saw as the main strength of the system:

> Yes, we had a problem when we first opened where to get a message to every shop took minutes. Now it takes about three seconds because of a piece of equipment ... called a 'Shop Alert' ... It's a very effective system. It can also be used to inform our tenants that somebody is trying to buy goods with forged ten and twenty pound notes. And again by inserting a message in and pressing a button within three seconds it's round the centre: 'Be aware of forged twenty pound notes, fifty pound notes'. A very useful tool because it's saving time, people's time. Within seconds you can send them.

The Shop Alert system is indeed a very effective piece of technology. Unlike the individual stores within the public space of the city centre which are not 'wired up', every single person working in City Centre Mall (the Shop Alert alarm sounds on the message pad in all the shops, restaurants, offices, etc.) can be instantly informed of any incident that has come to the attention of the CCTV operatives in the control room. However, this is assuming that everyone in the centre hears the alarm, and not only hears the alarm but reads the message displayed on the message pad. As the incident described below demonstrates, this is not always the case:

> Alan [CCTV operative] sends a message to all the units within the centre – *Look out for forged ten pound notes* – but one or two of the staff working in the shops do not acknowledge the message. After a couple of minutes Alan notices that one or two of the units displayed on the computer screen are still green which indicates that they have not acknowledged the alarm. He picks up the SCRL microphone and asks one of the patrol guards to go into those shops to ask the shop staff if they have received the message. Alan turns to me and says, 'some of them just turn the alarm off on the keypad and don't even bother to read the message'.

Other 'panic alarm' systems in the surveillance web were hardly used at all. In the housing department's CCTV network, for example, all of the estate offices and high-rise flats have a panic alarm button which sends a message directly to the computerised alarm system in the council's central monitoring station in the city centre. When the CCTV operatives in the central monitoring station receive a message on the alarm system, they can either ring the police immediately or attend to the scene themselves. However, according to the neighbourhood housing manager (NHM) responsible for managing the concierge system at Hampton, the 'panic alarm' system is hardly used at all. During a visit to his office the NHM said:

> … do you see that button there? [the NHM points to a button on the wall in the estate office]. That's a panic button and if I were to press that now it would go through to the council's CCTV control room in the Guildhall and automatically they would ring the police. They've also got one in the concierge CCTV control room and if the housing staff in there press the button they [the CCTV operatives at the central monitoring station] would ring the police immediately … But I think through experience that doesn't happen very often. There's been examples where the concierge have actually had to summons the police when they've been on their own, you know

when someone's been getting really difficult. A couple of occasions in the last year or so where they've actually activated the panic button, but it doesn't happen very often.

The NHM goes on to say that when the button is pressed the response from the police is not very quick. He says:

It's hit and miss really. From our experience when we pressed it in here [the estate office] it's taken fifteen minutes plus, you know, which is certainly outside the police's targets for 999 calls.

The operation of the city centre radio link (CCRL) in the 'shopnet' system provides a perfect example of how the human mediation of technology places limits on the integration of the individual CCTV systems which make up the surveillance web. The CCRL, we can recall, provides a means of instantaneous communication between the CCTV operatives and security officers in two shopping centres, four department stores, seven high-street retailers and two police officers based at the city-centre police station. The security personnel employed by the city-centre department stores had previously used a pager system but this did not provide a quick enough response. As the security manager of a department store explained:

We used to have a small pager which had text on it. You'd sit and read it and there'd be spelling mistakes and all sorts of problems with that, erm, and it was thought that it would be better if we had a common link. You know, the voice is a lot quicker than these visual read-outs that had to be run through and transcribed and sent out.

When a CCTV operative receives an 'early warning' message on the CCRL, there are a number of things he or she can do. The CCTV operative may simply repeat the description to the patrol guards on the in-store radio link and take no further action. The operative may look for the suspect on camera and monitor their behaviour. If the operative sees the suspect leave the store, or is told by a patrol guard that the suspect has left the store, he or she may use the CCRL to pass the suspect on to a neighbouring store. The operative can also choose to deploy a guard to the store entrance either to deny access or to 'observe' the suspect. And, finally, the operative may use the CCRL to contact the police at the city centre police station. However, on many occasions none of these actions are taken. This is because some CCTV operatives can't hear the messages, some can hear the messages but choose to ignore them, and some can hear the messages but lack sufficient knowledge of the technology to respond quickly to the incident that has been brought to their attention.

To respond quickly to messages received on the CCRL the CCTV operative must first be able to hear the messages that are sent. But this is not always possible. In the CCTV control room at City Centre Mall, for example, the CCRL is sometimes turned down so low that it is impossible to hear the descriptions coming from the other stores in the city centre. This depends on which of the CCTV operatives is on duty. Alan, for example, likes to listen to the latest pop tunes on Radio One so he turns the radio up loud and has the CCRL turned down low. When Jim is on duty, on the other hand, he turns Radio One off which means that he can hear the messages that are sent by other stores on the CCRL. If there happens to be a lot of noise in the control room when a message comes across on the CCRL Jim picks up the mobile radio and puts it close to his ear so he can hear the messages.

There are other reasons why the city-centre security personnel cannot hear the messages that come across on the CCRL. For instance, the security manager employed by one high-street retailer spends his working day between the CCTV control room and the shopfloor and does not like to carry the mobile radio for the CCRL. This is because he is a plain-clothes detective who likes to remain discrete when patrolling the shop floor. But when the security manager receives messages on the CCRL while patrolling the shopfloor the mobile radio makes a loud bleeping sound which draws attention to him and blows his cover. To avoid this problem the security manager has given the mobile radio for the CCRL to a uniformed patrol guard and asked him to pass any messages received on the CCRL to the security manager by contacting him on the in-store radio link which doesn't make a loud bleeping sound.

Some CCTV operatives may hear radio messages but decide not to do anything about them. For example, during a typical eight-hour shift (09.00 to 17.00) at City Centre Mall there are likely to be at least thirty to forty descriptions of known 'lifters' or 'troublemakers' sent on the CCRL, but only two or three of these are likely to be 'acted upon' by the operatives. The two following examples are fairly typical:

At 15.09 Kevin receives an 'early warning' message with a description of a 'known' shoplifter sent to the control room from High Fashion on the CCRL. Carl says 'thank you' but does not inform anyone else about the message and makes no attempt to find the suspect on camera.

At 14.47 a store detective who works for one of the stores within the shopping centre contacts Darren on the CCRL and tells him that there are three males on the ground floor who have been trying to get stuff into their bag. Darren says, 'yes we'll try and get them on camera', and then continues with some paperwork.

The decision or ability to act upon messages received on the CCRL is also influenced by whether or not the CCTV operative has sufficient knowledge of the CCTV system which will allow him or her to respond quickly to any incident. In the following incident, Karen, who has been employed by the shopping centre for only three weeks, is in the control room to relieve the full-time CCTV operative who is on a tea break:

At 09.40 a store detective from one of the stores within the shopping centre which has its own CCTV system contacts the control room on the SCRL and informs the CCTV operatives that two known 'troublemakers' have just entered Sportsworld. Karen, who has only worked at the centre for a few weeks and who is only in the control room to cover for one of the *stand-in supervisors*, has to look at the map of the centre and the list of camera positions on the main desk in front of the monitors before she can attempt to track down the two suspects. Karen eventually realises that she needs a fully functional camera on level two close to the escalator in order to monitor the entrance to Sportsworld. By the time she gets this camera on the 'spot monitor' we can hear in the control room that the patrol guards are passing the two suspects onto one another, and one guard calls the control room on the shopping centre radio link to let Karen know that the suspects have now left the building by the West Arcade.

A lack of technological know-how also affected the operation of the council's CCTV network. The city council has cameras monitoring the city-centre bus station and a city-centre car park. The images displayed by these cameras can be relayed to the city-centre police station which allows the police to take control of the cameras as and when required. When the council's CCTV system was first installed in 1992 this facility was used on a regular basis by the police, mainly to monitor a city-centre pub which is located inside the bus station. However, according to the council's Security Controller the police no longer use the link:

... they [the police] haven't used the link since we first moved in ... cos they don't know what they're doing with the keyboards.

Sometimes we have to talk them through it. But the last time they used it was the middle of last year. It was this car park thing and they wanted to have a look and we did it for them in the end, because we were trying to explain to him on the phone how to use the panel and he was all over the place. So I said, 'I'll tell you what, you tell me and I'll do it'.

Intimacy and system integration

As well as providing a means of instantaneous communication between the security personnel involved in the operation of the surveillance web, electronic media also uncouple the need for the communicator and receiver to be present while interacting. As Meyrowitz (1985) has argued, electronic media are 'placeless'. Electronic communication systems, he says, have led 'to a near total dissociation of physical place and social place' to the extent that 'when we communicate through telephone, radio, T.V., or computer where we are physically no longer determines *where* and *who* we are socially' (emphasis added). However, those involved in the operation of the surveillance web do not lose their 'sense of place'. Whether or not the security personnel communicate with others widely separated in time and space depends to some extent on *where* the other security personnel are located and, more importantly, *who* is at the other end of the electronic link.

For example, the geographical location of some of the stores which have access to the city centre radio link (CCRL) places limits on the possibility of system integration. The main function of this link is to allow the security personnel to send each other 'early warning' messages about known 'troublemakers' and 'shoplifters' who may be approaching their store. The passing of information on the CCRL can come directly from CCTV operative to CCTV operative, or it can come via a patrol guard. The security manager of City Centre Mall described how this works:

… what they'll do is, for example, say he's coming from Pullmans Shopping Centre, they will inform Bargain Basement, which is also in Pullmans Shopping Centre, the guard will then stand at the door, monitor the movements and if he sees him crossing the road going to Department Store 1 he'll then contact Department Store 1 and say, 'Right, in his last known location he was heading up towards you going past Burger Bar'. If he doesn't go into Department Store 1 and goes up the street and is heading towards City Centre Mall or High Fashion, they'll get onto High Fashion and the guard in High Fashion will come out and monitor his movements. If he then comes into City Centre Mall or approaches City Centre Mall they get on to us and say, 'He's coming in via the West entrance'. So we can then get guards down there to monitor their movements and again if they don't come in here and they go down Black Street we'll inform CD World or whatever. It's just a chain-reaction basically.

However, because the security personnel tend only to send messages to their neighbouring stores this leads to breaks in the chain of communication and means that some stores do not always get descriptions of 'known' people passed on to their security officers. These breaks are caused by the geographical location of the different stores in the city centre and by the human mediation of technology. One major high-street retailer, for example, is at the far side of the city centre and is isolated from the main activity on the CCRL which takes place between the main group of stores which are situated near the bus station. The close proximity to the bus station is very useful for the security personnel working in this cluster of stores because it allows them to see 'known' persons arriving by bus in the city centre. Anyone arriving in the city centre by bus who wants to reach the main shopping area must walk across one of two pedestrian crossings which lead into the city centre. The two pedestrian crossings are directly opposite the main cluster of stores and this allows the security personnel (who usually have a patrol guard standing by the shop entrance) to get a good look at people arriving. Those department stores and high-street retailers that are situated in a more central position in the city centre do not have this advantage, as Simon, the security manager employed by the major high-street retailer, explains:

At the other side of the city centre they can see them coming in off the buses. There's Department Store 2, which is just by the bus station, he often comes across [on the CCRL] and says, 'somebody's just come off the bus'. That will give us an 'early warning' who to look out for.

However, Simon goes on to say that the location of his store creates some problems in terms of receiving early warning messages on the CCRL. Firstly, the nearest member of the 'shopnet' system to his store is City Centre Mall. As we have already seen the CCTV operatives in this control room very rarely listen to the messages that they are sent on the CCRL. This means that Simon cannot rely on the security personnel at City Centre Mall to pass 'early warning' messages on to the CCTV operative in the CCTV control room. Secondly, the store where Simon works, along with around thirty smaller shops, is situated in a busy pedestrianised area. Very few of these smaller shops have full-time security personnel which means that they do not qualify to go on the CCRL.

These problems have led Simon to set up an additional city centre radio link (CCRL II). The reason for setting up CCRL II was, according to Simon, because he felt that his store was 'a little isolated from the majority of stores that are clustered around Pullmans Shopping Centre near the bus station'. Simon no longer listens to the CCRL directly. What he does instead is leave the mobile radio for the CCRL in the CCTV control room where the CCTV operative listens to the transmissions from the two radio links, CCRL and CCRL II. Simon, who spends most of his time on the shopfloor, now has an ear piece which allows him to listen to CCRL II where a combination of private security guards and shop staff in around twelve of the smaller stores in the pedestrianised area share information on known 'shoplifters' and 'troublemakers'.

Thus, although the city centre radio link (CCRL) provides a common link between all the 'key players' involved in the operation of the 'shopnet' system, the security personnel are still more likely to liaise with those in close proximity to themselves than with those stores at the other side of the city centre. This would suggest that distance still provides a barrier to communication between those involved in the operation of the surveillance web. There is another explanation for this, however. Rather than *distance* creating a barrier between the security personnel, a more important obstacle to communication may be the issue of whether or not the person at the other end of the electronic link is *known* by the person sending the message. This of course may be related to physical distance since the chances of meeting other members of the surveillance web and thus knowing them is related to spatial proximity.

The importance of knowing the person at the other end of the electronic link was evident in the operation of many of the CCTV systems within the surveillance web. The security personnel employed by Housing Estate Mall (which is on a large housing estate six miles from the city centre), for example, said that they preferred to deal with the local police station rather than the new Police Communications Headquarters which is about ten miles away from the shopping centre. In the following incident the security manager of Housing Estate Mall contacts Dave in the control room and asks him to let the police know that he is detaining a shoplifter in a chemist:

> Dave rings the police and tells them that they are detaining a person for shoptheft. When he comes off the phone he says to me, 'Haldon [the new Police Communications Centre] are such a pain in the arse. Some of them don't even know *who* we are or *where* Housing Estate

Mall is. We have got a number direct to Banton Police Station and the CID have given us a list of names and people they want. So we can ring them direct and they'll come straight out'.

On another occasion Steve is in the control room when he rings the police to let them know that there is a 'wanted' person outside the shopping centre and that if they come to the control room he will point the person out to the police:

Steve rings the police and is asked to hold. He turns to me and says: 'This is what happens. You get arsed about. They don't even know *who* we are or *where* Housing Estate Mall is. We just lose interest in the end. It was much better before when we got put through to Banton cause we got a lot more done'. Steve gets fed up and hangs up. A few minutes later the phone rings and Kevin answers. Kevin talks to the police and then puts the phone down and says, 'they want to know where he is now, twenty minutes later'.

The importance of intimacy in facilitating liaison between those responsible for operating separate CCTV systems was illustrated by the network of friends, interpersonal links and even relatives that provided a number of linkages between the members of the surveillance web. In the 'shopnet' system, for example, the security manager employed by High-Street Retailer 2 said that he mostly uses the CCRL to pass information on to the security officers in Department Store 1. Department Store 1 is very close to High-Street Retailer 2 and forms a part of the main cluster of stores by the bus station. However, two other stores on the CCRL are even closer to High-Street Retailer 2 but the security manager does not liaise with the security personnel in these stores as much as he does with the security officers in Department Store 1. The high level of information flow between High-Street Retailer 2 and Department Store 1 is due to the fact that the security managers 'know' each other quite well'. As one of the security managers explained:

The store detectives from across the road at Department Store 1 sometimes visit. Sometimes they'll come across on their dinner hour to talk about, you know, who's out and about, so and so's out of prison, are you busy, that type of thing. We're not supposed to show tapes to each other but we do it.

Similarly, the most frequent sender of messages on the CCRL to the control room of City Centre Mall is High Fashion. The Security Manager employed by High Fashion was previously employed as a security officer at Bargain Basement in the city centre. Two of his colleagues at Bargain Basement were Jim and Trevor who now work as CCTV operatives at City Centre Mall. Trevor and Jim do not use the CCRL very often but when they do it is usually to send an early warning message to High Fashion where they address the security manager by his first name.

Interpersonal links were also very important at Housing Estate Mall. Most of the security personnel (patrol guards and CCTV operatives) have worked previously as security officers in other retail stores. Steve, for example, was previously employed as a security guard by Supermart (a supermarket located in Housing Estate Mall) and High-Street Retailer 1 in the city centre. He has also worked in the sentry alarm monitoring control room in the city centre. Andy also used to work as a security guard in Supermart which, he tells me, has four CCTV cameras and two patrol guards. Although the patrol guards employed by Supermart are not on the shopping centre's radio link, Andy says: 'if we see someone enter their store then we'll tell the guards'. This was supported by Dave, another former employee of Supermart, who stated:

> On Sundays nothing happens much, although Supermart stays open when we close so we put a camera on the door and give them a bell and say, 'you've got so and so in', cause they get a lot of 'rubbish' in when we're closed.

Kevin Smith, the security manager of Housing Estate Mall, has also worked with many of the security personnel who are currently involved in the operation of the surveillance web, including some of the security managers employed by the major stores in the city centre. According to him:

> Most of them's worked for me in the past. Yes, we liaise with them quite a lot. If we have any of our banned shoplifters, they'll try and get in here and when they realise they can't they'll get on a bus and go into town. And if we know they're just out for shoplifting we'll inform town and tell them that he's coming. Then you usually get a call back in the afternoon saying: 'We got him Kevin'. So we all help each other.

Smith has also maintained contact with two of his former employees who recently left Housing Estate Mall to work at the local Superstore:

Two of my best guards have gone to work as Assistant Security Managers at Superstore. They're still using our assistance with putting names to faces or whatever, 'cause obviously a lot of them's gone from here to Superstore, it's new pickings, it's unknown. So the locals are real upset. They thought they were going to an unknown store where they had free pickings and they saw two guards who worked here for four years saying, 'you're not coming in here'.

Interpersonal links also allow the security team at Housing Estate Mall to liaise closely with the local police. Dawn, the main CCTV operative, is a former special constable who has previously worked in the operations room of the police station which is just a few yards across the road from the shopping centre. Dawn knows most of the officers who visit the control room including the former beat officer with whom she spent some time on patrol. Hardly a days goes by at the shopping centre without at least one visit to the control room by the police. Sometimes Shaun, the beat officer, spends almost the whole day in the centre either on the mall or sitting in the control room chatting to the CCTV operative and watching the monitors. This informal liaison leads to a high level of integration between the control room and police deployment practice. For instance, Shaun has given the security personnel a list of 'wanted' persons and asked them to give him a ring (either at the local station or on his mobile phone) if they see any 'wanted' suspects inside the shopping centre or hanging around outside the centre but in view of the external cameras. As Smith explained:

We don't get involved in it, we monitor it and we inform the police and we'll track them on camera so that they can come here and say, 'Where is she Kevin?' And I can say, 'she's there'. We can follow them around the whole centre. They'll be coming to meet somebody, whether it's to get their giro from the Post Office, or to go in Careers or the Probation Service or whatever. So it's using all sorts of methods. We was asked to keep an eye out for one lad, they said: 'If he comes in would you let us know?' He'd escaped from one of these Secure Units and we could tell the police 'yes he's in here'. I mean normally we would have gone and thrown him out cos he's a banned person from here, but we left him and just monitored him on camera and we could point them straight to him.

The surveillance web and classification

As Nigel Thrift (1996: 1473) argues, the development of electronic communications systems does not produce 'an abstract and inhuman space, strung out on the wire'; rather it produces more sociation, much of it face to face. As we have seen, the construction and operation of CCTV surveillance systems has given rise to a whole new range of human linkages. This has brought together the police, private security managers, department store and shopping centre managers and store detectives. These developments are increasing the integration of police and private security CCTV systems and facilitating information-sharing and liaison between those responsible for managing such systems. As the above examples demonstrate, one of the main reasons for the development of this informal network is that it allows the security personnel to deal with the problem of classification, i.e. the problem of putting names to faces, putting faces to names, and sharing information on 'known' names and faces. In the city centre, for example, police and private security personnel hold bi-monthly City Centre Security Group meetings which provides those involved in the operation of the 'shopnet' with an opportunity to share information on 'known' persons. According to the operations manager of City Centre Mall:

> We discuss particular shoplifters, you know. If you're getting one guy coming round or you may not have seen one guy for a long time and somebody might have had a tip-off through overhearing or actually observing shoplifters and a pattern may be starting to arise, or you may be getting a certain individual behaving in a certain pattern, yes, so we just try and let each other know. So again it's the, er ... collecting information to try and use to combat the problem basically.

Another common practice at the City Centre Security Group meetings is the exchange of photographic information between the security personnel to help with the problem of putting names to faces and faces to names:

> We used to go along with our video and say 'this is so and so, we've got a name for him'.
> (The security manager, department store)

> Well, it's worked in conjunction with the police and a lot of them we know from our own experience. I've actually detained them for shoptheft, the others are well known, what we call 'professional shoplifters' that are passed onto us by the police.
> (The security manager, City Centre Mall)

...the police are quite influential in that, you know, they'll give you information, erm ... and often photographic information to guide you as to the people that you don't particularly want in your business.

(The manager, department store)

Another way of putting names to faces is through informal visits to CCTV control rooms. At Housing Estate Mall, for example, the police are regular visitors to the control room where sometimes they will just sit and chat, usually about the local 'druggies':

We used to sit up here with 'snatch squads', didn't we, to catch the 'druggies'. We'd sit up here watching them and have officers at the exit doors waiting for them.

(Ex-beat officer)

During these informal visits to CCTV control rooms the visitor will often sit and watch the monitors and try to put a name to a face. At Housing Estate Mall most of the security personnel live on the local housing estate and some of the guards went to school with many of the people who visit the shopping centre. This means that the security team have an extensive local knowledge of the people who visit the shopping centre. In the incident below Shaun (the beat officer) sits and watches the monitors with Kevin (the Security Manager) and taps into this local knowledge:

Shaun: 'So what do you know then?'
Kevin: 'Not much.'
Kevin sees a man on the monitors walking through the centre with no shirt on and a large tattoo on his chest.
Kevin: 'That's Steve Brown.'
Shaun: 'Who's Steve Brown?'
Kevin: 'Pete Brown's brother.'
Shaun: 'Oh yes, I know Pete Brown.'

On other occasions security officers or the police will pay informal visits to the control room because they might have a *name* but not a *face*. As Mark Railton, the former security manager, told me: 'You see, if the police get warrants with names on they haven't got the faintest idea who they are.' In this case what happens is the beat officer brings a list of bench warrants to the control room and asks the security personnel if they will contact him if any of the 'wanted' persons enter the shopping centre. During one shift Shaun (the beat officer) arrived in the control room after receiving a tip-off from the guards that a 'wanted' person would be arriving in the shopping centre between one o'clock and two o'clock to collect his methadone prescription from one of the chemists within the centre. Before he arrived in the control room Shaun paid a visit to the chemist and asked the manager of the shop to telephone the control room when the suspect arrived to collect his methadone prescription. After sitting in the control room for about half an hour Shaun received the telephone call from the chemist informing him that the suspect had arrived. The CCTV operative on duty used a camera to zoom in on the suspect through the chemist door. Shaun had a quick look at the suspect on the monitor and left the control room to arrest him.

Another way the security personnel overcome the problem of classification is by constructing 'rogues galleries' of 'shoplifters' and 'troublemakers'. Eleven of the 30 CCTV control rooms which make up the surveillance web contained hard-copy printout machines which allowed them to produce stills from the CCTV footage. The ability to store images in electronic spaces (i.e. video tape), which can then be 'lifted out' and used at some future time and place, is one of the main benefits of CCTV systems. As the operations manager of City Centre Mall explained:

CCTV … gives you the benefit of being an instant record of an event taking place and there again you can use it, you can play it back and extract further information from it … and crime prevention is now on the television. You see it being used where, 'do you recognise this individual?' And that is the total benefit of CCTV equipment. Of being able to take a picture and store that picture, and from a recording you can actually get a better picture and hopefully catch a criminal.

The fact that not all of the control rooms have hard-copy printout machines means that the construction of a 'rogues gallery' depends to some extent on the development of 'face-to-face' meetings between security personnel working in different CCTV control rooms. In City Centre Mall, for example, the security officers employed by one of the stores within the shopping centre do not have the facility to produce photographs on a hard-copy printout machine. To get around this problem they would often monitor the activities of suspected shoplifters from their own CCTV control room and then bring the video recording of the suspects to the shopping centre's CCTV control room and ask the operatives to produce them a photograph.

The security personnel employed by Housing Estate Mall also relied on security officers working in other stores to help them compile their 'rogues galleries'. On my first visit to the control room at Housing Estate Mall, Kevin (the security manager) showed me a 'Banned Persons File' which contains photographs of suspects taken with the hard-copy printout machine and the date the picture was taken. He also showed me a 'Mug Shot File' which contains updated pictures of 'known persons' and 'people to watch out for', and pictures of 'troublemakers' whose identity is not yet known. As he flicked through the 'Mug Shot File' Kevin drew my attention to the quality of some of the photographs which were recorded on disc by the security officers at the local Superstore. Kevin tells me that the two security officers at Superstore used to work as guards at the shopping centre and that they help each other quite a lot with putting names to faces.

This favour was often reciprocated by the security personnel at Housing Estate Mall who helped the security officers at Superstore and other stores to put a name to a face. Also some of the security officers employed by the major department stores in the city centre have worked with Kevin in the past:

> ... the big department stores. I know them all. We meet quite a lot ... when we ban them they're not allowed in here for 12 months. They're still gonna do the shoplifting bit. They hit the resorts a bit in the summer, but mainly it's the town centre. And Geoff at X and Barry at Y was talking about it, and they said: 'We'll try and get some photos of people that's been hitting us hard. We've got the video evidence but we don't know the names. Can you put a name to it Kev?' Things like this.

Informal contacts with the police are also important in the construction of 'rogues galleries'. The police are regular visitors to the CCTV control room at Housing Estate Mall and, as we have already seen, are well known to the security personnel. This provides the police with a pool of information but it also means that the security personnel can ask the police for favours, including helping them to compile their 'rogues gallery'. As Dave explains:

> We caught somebody in X store the other day and when Bill arrived I said: 'Bill, we want a picture of that suspect, is there any chance of bringing him through the centre?' Cos most of them [the police] leave out the back door. So Bill brought this kid out through the centre and said: 'look at that camera'.

Summary

This chapter has argued that the starting point for any attempt to under-stand the impact of visual surveillance systems must be to take as its object of analysis not a separate and discrete CCTV system, but a surveillance web. As we have seen, the surveillance web is invisible, or at least very difficult to discern. A combination of public and private CCTV systems linked with pager systems, panic alarms, radio links and mobile and fixed telephone networks is facilitating the development of sur-veillance webs which weave unseen through the fabric of contemporary cities. The web also entraps its victims. A combination of the surveillance camera and the video replay button means that images can be 'captured' and 'stored' in electronic spaces (on a video tape or computer file) ready to be 'lifted out' of the immediate nexus of social control and authoritative interventions made at some future, as yet unspecified, time and place.

However, we have also seen how the human mediation of technology places limits on panoptic systems, because those responsible for operating them do not take on the essential properties of instantaneity and speed which characterises the 'new' technology. Moreover, the complex interplay between *intimacy* and technology facilitates *and* places limits on the disciplinary potential of panoptic systems. For instance, the integration of discrete surveillance systems depends to some extent on the network of 'human linkages' (i.e. friends, relatives and interpersonal links) that connect the security personnel working in the city's surveillance web. We also saw, however, that whether or not the security personnel communicate with others widely separated in time and space depends to some extent on *where* the other security personnel are located and, more importantly, *who* is at the other end of the electronic link.

In Part 3 we will explore some of these issues in more detail by going inside some of the CCTV control rooms in Northern City. We are going to 'watch the watchers' as they monitor consumers, workers and tenants. These case studies will allow us to explore the context specificity of visual surveillance technology. They will also allow us to explore the two-way relationship between society and technology by posing a number of questions. For instance, how does the introduction of new surveillance technology fit in with existing social relations and cultural traditions? What happens when low-paid, low-status security officers find them-selves monitoring their own locales and workplaces?

Part 3
Three Case Studies of Visual Surveillance Systems

Chapter 4

The panopticon mall

This chapter draws upon detailed observational research conducted in the CCTV control rooms of two shopping malls in Northern City. We have referred to these two sites as City Centre Mall and Housing Estate Mall. City Centre Mall is a 285,000 square foot retail leisure complex, with well over 100 retail units and a 1,000 space multi-storey car park. Built at a cost of £65 million, the shopping mall opened in 1991 and during a six-month period in 1997 made a pre-tax profit of £128.9 million. Housing Estate Mall, on the other hand, has been trading for over 25 years and is situated in the middle of one of the most deprived housing estates in Northern City. This site consists of around 60 retail units, including one super-market and a thriving indoor market. In an attempt to compare and contrast the two surveillance systems on these very different sites, the chapter is divided into three main parts. The first section deals with an account of how suspicion is socially constructed on the two sites. The second section looks in more detail at the nature of suspicion in the two shopping malls and at how this influences the exclusionary potential of shopping mall surveillance systems. The chapter concludes by discussing some of the social and ethical implications raised by the use of shopping mall CCTV systems for exclusionary purposes.

The social construction of suspicion in two shopping malls

The question of who or what gets targeted in a shopping mall has to be understood in relation to the technological sophistication, organisational goals and operational functions of the security systems on different sites.

City Centre Mall has 26 'fixed' cameras and eight fully functional cameras (i.e. cameras with a pan/tilt/zoom facility). This meant that the CCTV operatives had to use a combination of fixed and fully functional cameras when attempting to 'track' suspects throughout the shopping centre. Moreover, only one of the external cameras was fully functional which made it difficult to track suspects once they had left the shopping centre.

The security team at City Centre Mall consists of an operations manager (who is employed by the shopping mall proprietors), a security manager, three supervisors, three stand-in supervisors and 15 patrol guards. This team is responsible not only for any crime or order-related problems that may arise in the mall, but also for a wide range of general operational duties including health and safety issues and the control of access to the 'backstage' of the shopping mall. As the operations manager of City Centre Mall explained:

> I think my main responsibility is contract staff, security, cleaning, contractors that come into the centre, health and safety, assisting the centre manager in the daily running of the centre, and CCTV plays a major part in it because I mean we're sitting and talking now in this office [the operations manager's office] and if you turn around there's a VDU there with coverage of the shopping centre. So without leaving this office we can look at a problem that's going on somewhere inside or outside the centre and communicate our decisions and instructions to our security staff, the same as the security staff can bring situations to our attention by pointing a camera in an area that they want us to look at. I mean some of the things that go on in the centre, and even just safeguarding the security of the centre, with the daily routine we have accidents so again it can be used in that way to investigate what's gone on, how did it happen? Why did it happen? It's a major tool actually.

City Centre Mall is a multi-storey shopping centre comprising five different floors and has a multi-storey car park that holds 1,000 vehicles. The control room is situated at the entrance to the loading bay and the CCTV operators are responsible for a wide range of general operational duties including the responsibility for controlling access to the shopping centre. All contract workers, for example, must report to the control room and sign work permits before the operators allow them access to the site by activating the access control barrier which is adjacent to the control room. The CCTV operators also spend much of the shift dealing with the constant stream of visitors who communicate with the guards through a sliding window. During a typical shift visitors to the control room window include: members of the public, contract workers, business reps, off-duty security staff, patrol guards and cleaners, maintenance workers and electricians employed by the shopping centre. Other more occasional visitors include store detectives employed by stores within the shopping centre, the police, private security branch managers (from head office) and members of the shopping centre management.

With this constant stream of visitors to the control room the CCTV operatives at City Centre Mall cannot dedicate the whole of their time and effort to monitoring the images displayed on the TV screens by the CCTV cameras. The following incident gives some idea of the nature of the CCTV operator's job at City Centre Mall and of how this places limits on the idea of permanent and omnipresent surveillance:

Incident no. 1
At 12.18 a store detective from one of the stores within the centre contacts the control room on the shopping centre radio link (SCRL) to let the operatives know that five known 'lifters' have just left their store and have now entered Sportsworld. Darren acknowledges the call and fixes a camera on the exit to Sportsworld but the image is obscured by a large plant. Darren contacts a patrol guard on the SCRL for an update on the suspect's current location but then leaves the control desk to talk on the intercom system to someone that he has seen on one of the small 12-inch black-and-white TV monitors attempting to gain access to the management car park. Over the intercom Darren takes the driver's details and presses a button to raise the barrier for the management car park. Meanwhile, Alan, the other CCTV operator on duty, has turned up the volume on Radio One to sing along to Echo and the Bunnymen's latest record: 'Nothing ever lasts forever, nothing ever lasts forever -er ... ' Darren returns to the control desk and spots the five suspects who are all dressed in tracksuits, trainers and baseball caps. As Darren tries to track the suspects on camera he receives a call on the SCRL from the operations manager (OM) who wants to know if Bill, the duty engineer, has sorted out the fire alarms yet. Darren contacts Bill on the SCRL and asks him about the fire panels and Bill says that he is on his way up to the control room now. Darren is still trying to follow the suspects but gives up when two off-duty guards (Gavin and Tom) arrive at the control room window to pick up their snooker cues. Darren joins Alan and the two off-duty guards in a discussion about another one of the operatives who everyone agrees has terrible wind. Darren says, 'Oh he's disgusting. He's not on

tomorrow is he?' At this point the duty engineer and his partner arrive and join in the conversation about the flatulent CCTV operator. The patrol guards can be heard on the SCRL passing the five suspects on to one another.

In incident number 1 described above Darren lost track of the five known 'shoplifters'. This is hardly surprising considering that in the five-minute period from the moment the incident began he had to communicate with the driver of a vehicle in the management car park on the intercom system, and with a store detective, two patrol guards, the operations manager and the duty engineer on the shopping centre radio link (SCRL). He was also involved in face-to-face interaction with two off-duty guards, two engineers and Ian, his partner in the control room. All of this while trying to observe five suspects remotely on camera.

As we have seen, the security team at City Centre Mall have to concern themselves with a wide range of general managerial and operational tasks to ensure the smooth running of the mall. In contrast, the six full-time security officers at Housing Estate Mall spend the vast majority of their time using the surveillance infrastructure to monitor the behaviour of those who visit the shopping mall. Also, while Housing Estate Mall has only 13 CCTV cameras (compared with 34 at City Centre Mall), they all have a pan/tilt/zoom facility and are situated to monitor the car parks and surrounding area as well as the main shopping areas within the centre. This allows the CCTV operators to track suspects both inside the mall and the surrounding area.

Another important difference between City Centre Mall and Housing Estate Mall is that the latter is a single-storey complex. This has a number of consequences for how the security system works in practice. Firstly, the ground floor location of Housing Estate Mall means that any outside contractors or delivery vans wishing to visit one of the centre's forty retail units can drive straight to the back entrance of the shop in question without requiring authorisation from the security personnel. Secondly, because Housing Estate Mall is a single-storey complex the security officers do not have to concern themselves with the breakdown of lifts and escalators, incidents which received a high priority from the security guards at City Centre Mall.

The differences between the technological sophistication and organisational goals of the two systems are reflected in Table 4.1. Thus at Housing Estate Mall only 1 in 25 (4 per cent) 'targeted surveillances' (i.e. when a CCTV operator monitored someone/something for 30 seconds or longer) related to property management (i.e. fire alarms, outside contractors working on site, etc.). At City Centre Mall, on the other hand,

Table 4.1 Reason for surveillance in City Centre Mall and Housing Estate Mall

Reason for surveillance	City Centre Mall %	Housing Estate Mall %	Both malls %
Crime/order	77	96	84
Property management	23	4	16
N = 239	100	100	100

almost a quarter (23 per cent) of targeted surveillances were related to this type of incident.

Who was targeted?

The social characteristics of those suspects who were targeted were broadly similar in both shopping centres. As Table 4.2 reveals the vast majority of people surveilled were young: almost nine out of ten (88 per cent) were under thirty with those in their teens (44 per cent) and twenties (44 per cent) having an equal chance of being targeted. Males (71 per cent of targeted surveillances) were targeted more often than females (29 per cent), and exactly one half (50 per cent) of all targeted surveillances were of people dressed in subcultural attire (i.e. tracksuits and baseball caps). The figures for the race of people under targeted surveillance are not discussed in this study because Northern City is basically a 'white' city. Thus out of a total of 168 targeted surveillances, 164 (98 per cent) involved white people, four (2 per cent) involved black people and there were no targeted surveillances of Asian people.

Generally speaking the CCTV operators on both sites targeted young males who were often in groups (45 per cent of targeted surveillances were of groups) and nearly always dressed in tracksuits and baseball caps. The targeting of this population is a reflection of the private security guard's attitudes towards working-class youth in general who were described as 'scrotes', 'scumbags', 'shit', 'druggies', 'G heads' (i.e. 'glue sniffers') and 'scag heads' (see also, Norris and Armstrong, 1998: 22).

Why were people surveilled?

As we saw earlier, a significant number of the targeted surveillances involved incidents related to property management, i.e. fire alarms, lift alarms, contractors working on site, and so on. However, our main concern in this section is to explore how the CCTV systems operated as instruments of social control. So for the purposes of analysis the 'reason

Table 4.2   Age, sex and appearance of primary person under targeted surveillance

	City Centre Mall %	Housing Estate Mall %	Both malls %
Age			
Teens	48	41	44
Twenties	39	47	44
Thirties +	13	12	12
N = 168	100	100	100
Sex			
Male	76	67	71
Female	24	33	29
N = 168	100	100	100
Appearance			
Smart/uniformed	8	2	5
Scruffy	18	23	20
Subculture	45	54	50
Casual	30	22	25
N = 168	101	101	100

Percentage total may not equal 100 due to rounding up.

for surveillance' has been coded under the following headings: property crime, unruly/disorderly and drugs. Following Norris and Armstrong (1999), individuals or groups were assigned to these categories if the operator had explicit grounds for their suspicion. This was regardless of whether or not the person under suspicion was actually involved in any criminal behaviour. Thus the targeting of known 'drug dealers' would be treated as drugs-related even though in all probability the person had entered the shopping centre to buy a loaf of bread rather than 'score for a ten pound bag' (of heroin) as the operators suspected. Similarly, if the operator tracked a known 'shoplifter' this would be treated as shoptheft even though the individual may have been shopping rather than shoplifting.

We can see from Table 4.3 that property crime-related suspicion accounted for six out of ten (61 per cent) of all targeted surveillances, while unruly/disorderly-related suspicion accounted for only three out of ten (30 per cent) and drugs-related suspicion for one in ten of all targeted surveillances (10 per cent). Within property crime-related suspicion by far the largest single category of suspicion, as one might

Table 4.3   Reason for surveillance at both shopping malls

Reason for surveillance	City Centre Mall %	Housing Estate Mall %	Both malls %
Property Crime	50	76	61
Unruly/Disorderly	46	7	30
Drugs	4	17	10
N = 200	100	100	101

Percentage total may not equal 100 due to rounding up.

expect in a shopping centre, was theft from store (86 per cent). The other categories included theft from person (11 per cent), vandalism (2 per cent) and car crime (1 per cent).

However, as Table 4.3 shows, there were significant differences between the two sites. At City Centre Mall, for example, half (50 per cent) of all targeted surveillances were concerned with property crime-related suspicion, while at Housing Estate Mall as many as three-quarters (76 per cent) of targeted surveillances were related to this category. Also, at City Centre Mall, drugs-related suspicion accounted for only one in 25 (4 per cent) of the targeted surveillances compared to almost one-fifth (17 per cent) of the targeted surveillances at Housing Estate Mall. As we shall see later in this chapter, these results are related to differences in the nature of the two sites. For example, the vast majority of targeted surveillances at Housing Estate Mall were focused on known 'shoplifters' and 'drug users', hence the high number of targeted surveillances based on property crime and drugs-related suspicion when compared to City Centre Mall. The two sites also differed in terms of the number of targeted surveillances based on 'order'-related suspicion. This category accounted for only six (7 per cent) of the targeted surveillances at Housing Estate Mall compared to almost half (46 per cent) of those at City Centre Mall. These figures reflect the concern among the security personnel at City Centre Mall with 'nuisance' behaviour and in particular with groups of teenagers 'messing about' and 'making the place look untidy'.

Type of suspicion

We have described the type of incident that the targeted surveillances were directed towards. It is now necessary to examine what in particular prompted the targeting of an individual or group. As Norris and Armstrong (1999) have shown in their observational study of public CCTV systems, suspicion is not unidimensional; rather it is based on a range of assumptions and knowledge held by the CCTV operators. In the present study, over half (55 per cent) of the targeted surveillances were based on 'transmitted' suspicion. In other words, the most frequent reason that a person is targeted is because someone outside of the system (e.g. a patrol guard, store detective, shopworker, CCTV operative from another system or a police officer) has drawn the CCTV operator's attention to a person or incident. The remaining 45 per cent of targeted surveillances were initiated by the CCTV operators themselves.

Table 4.4 presents the figures for all suspicions, i.e. both transmitted and operator-initiated suspicions. As the table shows, well over half (56 per cent) of all targeted surveillances are related to personalised knowledge. One-quarter (27 per cent) are based on a person's behaviour, one tenth (10 per cent) on the individual's personal characteristics, one in 17 (6 per cent) on the location someone was in, and only two cases (1 per cent) were protectional. Once again, however, there were important differences between the two sites. Thus while the majority (41 per cent) of targeted surveillances at City Centre Mall were related to behavioural suspicion, the same category accounted for only 14 (15 per cent) of the targeted surveillances at Housing Estate Mall. And while personalised suspicion accounted for around a quarter (28 per cent) of the targeted surveillances at City Centre Mall, eight out of ten (80 per cent) of the targeted surveillances at Housing Estate Mall were based on personalised knowledge. How can we account for these differences?

The type of suspicion at both shopping malls is shaped by their geographical location which results in them having very different clientele. For instance, Housing Estate Mall is situated in the middle of Banton Estate. Banton Estate is one of the most deprived housing estates

Table 4.4   Type of suspicion involved in targeted surveillances at both shopping malls

Type of suspicion	City Centre Mall %	Housing Estate Mall %	Both malls %
Categorical	16	5	10
Personalised	28	80	56
Behavioural	41	15	27
Protectional	3	0	1
Locational	13	0	6
N = 173	101	100	100

Percentage total may not equal 100 due to rounding up.

in the country and is around six miles away from the city centre. Data compiled on people's lifestyles in Banton by a market research company in 1998 found that three out of five residents are classified as 'striving' (at the bottom of the social league table), which is nearly three times the national average. Almost a third of residents live in areas typical to council tenants with health problems and a quarter of the population live in areas with rates of high unemployment. In the light of this demographic profile it is not surprising that a large number of the estate's inhabitants do not have their own transport which makes travelling to the city centre or out-of-town superstores very difficult.

The residents of Banton Estate are therefore relatively isolated from the rest of Northern City and Housing Estate Mall provides most of the local amenities that people living in the area require on a daily basis. For instance, Housing Estate Mall houses the only supermarkets within walking distance for many of those who live on the estate and contains the only bank and building society in the area. The grounds on which the mall is situated also includes a busy public house, post office, public library, health centre, surgery, probation centre, job centre, fast food takeaways, a taxi rank and the estate's main bus terminal. This combination of factors means that the shopping mall has a very stable clientele consisting of local people who visit the centre day in and day out. As the security manager of Housing Estate Mall explained:

> Well, this was the meeting place for it all. This isn't just a shopping centre, it's not like City Centre Mall where you catch a bus, you go into town, you do what ever you want to do and you get a bus and go home. Ours come here, cause trouble, go across the road, have their dinner and come back again. I mean they only live across the car park. We're in the middle of a residential estate. You don't travel to it and you don't travel from it like City Centre Mall. Our problems are 24-hour-a-day problems. The same people that are pinching newspapers and bread at five o'clock in the morning are the same people that's shoplifting during the day or trying to burgle during the night. It is a meeting place, and not just for miscreants. I mean we have what we call the 'wheel chair brigade'. We've got the Post Office for social security, disability pensions, whatever. We've got Social Services, we've got careers, we've got two probation offices, job centres, library. The Post Office is the main one, we've got the Health Centre. So we've got everything that brings them to this location and unfortunately ... we have about 100,000 to 120,000 people a week coming through and a very, very small proportion of them are the 'undesirables'.

As well as having a stable population of visitors to the shopping mall, most of the security officers who work at Housing Estate Mall are local people with an extensive localised knowledge of the estate and its inhabitants. This means that on many occasions they are able to im-mediately recognise the faces appearing on their CCTV monitors. We can begin to understand, therefore, why personalised knowledge plays such an important role in the operation of the CCTV system at Housing Estate Mall. In stark contrast, City Centre Mall is situated at the heart of the city centre and has a clientele which is much more fluid, comprising mainly of 'weekend shoppers'. Thus at Housing Estate Mall the personalised knowledge of the security personnel meant that in eight out of ten targeted surveillances the CCTV operators knew the person they were observing. At City Centre Mall, on the other hand, the CCTV operators had to rely on other (visual) cues (i.e. a person's appearance, behaviour or location) to inform them of a person's criminal intent. This is confirmed by Table 4.5 which shows the figures for operator suspicion at both sites.

The figures in Table 4.5 show that over three-quarters (77 per cent) of the targeted surveillances initiated by the CCTV operators at Housing Estate Mall were based on personalised knowledge. At City Centre Mall, on the other hand, the CCTV operator knew the suspect under targeted surveillance in less than one-fifth (16 per cent) of observations. On this site the majority (37 per cent) of targeted surveillances initiated by the CCTV operator related to a person's behaviour, a quarter (24 per cent) to the person's location, and one-fifth (21 per cent) to the person's appearance. However, it should be pointed out that the targeting of 'known' persons at City Centre Mall more than doubles (from 16 per cent to 38 per cent) when we look at 'transmitted' suspicions only (i.e. those

Table 4.5   Operator-initiated suspicions at both shopping malls

Type of suspicion	City Centre Mall %	Housing Estate Mall %	Both malls %
Categorical	21	8	14
Personalised	16	77	47
Behavioural	37	15	26
Protectional	3	0	1
Locational	24	0	12
N = 77	101	100	100

Percentage total may not equal 100 due to rounding up.

that come from outside the system on the various radio links) rather than operator suspicions. We would expect these findings considering that most of the transmitted suspicions at City Centre Mall are received on the city centre radio link (CCRL). This radio link was set up with the specific aim of allowing the private security personnel working in the city centre to exchange information on known 'shoplifters' and 'troublemakers'.

Familiar names and familiar faces: personalised suspicion in a shopping mall

At Housing Estate Mall, the personalised knowledge of the security personnel stems from the fact that the majority of the guards are local people who live on Banton housing estate. The main CCTV operator, for example, is a woman called Dawn who has lived on the estate for ten years. Dawn has previously worked as a special constable in the operations room of the police station which is fifty yards from the shopping centre. The security manager is a man in his late twenties called Kevin. Kevin, who has also lived on the estate for a number of years, went to the local school which is two minutes walk from the shopping centre. Kevin says that his local knowledge is useful because it means that he knows the identities of most of the 'troublecausers' who visit the centre. During one incident, for example, he knew the name of the person under surveillance because he played in the same darts team as the suspect's dad. The incident below gives some indication of the extent of Kevin's localised knowledge:

Incident no. 2
At 16.53 Kevin is sat at the control desk and is using the internal cameras to look around the shopping centre. Kevin sees two 'known' people and follows them on three internal cameras. Both of the suspects are dressed in tracksuit tops and one has a white baseball cap on. Kevin follows the suspects and zooms in close on Hobsy when he stops and stands next to the public phone booth which is inside the shopping centre. Hobsy's friend uses the phone and Kevin produces a hard-copy printout of Hobsy as the suspect takes a bite out of his pasty. Kevin turns to me and says, 'I used to go to school with Hobsy. I went to a good school me.' Steve intervenes: 'He went to school with all the scumbags.' Kevin turns around and faces the TV screens. As he does he spots a known 'druggy' called Shipley. Kevin takes a hard-copy printout of the suspect for his new

'Mug Shots Book'. Kevin tells me that Shipley's brother is in prison and that Shipley himself was off drugs but is now back on them.

The localised knowledge of the security personnel at Housing Estate Mall is passed on to any new guards when they arrive. In the following incidents, for example, Barry, who is just beginning his third week at the centre, attempts to tap into his colleagues' localised knowledge in order to learn the names and faces of the regulars:

Incident no. 3
At 14.32 Barry contacts the control room on the SCRL and says to Steve: 'Steve, you've got four kids coming down the West in baseball caps and one of them is pushing a pram. Can you tell me if they're known please?' Steve spots the group on camera and, on the SCRL, says, 'they're known faces but none of them's banned or anything like that'.

Incident no. 4
At 14.55 Barry contacts the control room on the SCRL and says to Steve: 'Steve can you put a camera on the cash point outside Halifax'. Steve puts an internal camera on the cash point and sees a male in his teens dressed in a blue and white tracksuit. Barry says, 'is that Owen or not?' 'Or not', Steve replies.

Incident no. 5
At 12.48 a patrol guard contacts the control room to inform Dawn that Mark Jones is walking down the North. Dawn acknowledges the call but makes no attempt to find the suspect on camera. Barry contacts the patrol guard on radio and says: 'Who's Mark Jones?' The patrol guard replies, 'Shirley Jones's bloke'.

Even those members of the security team with localised knowledge of the shopping centre's regular visitors cannot be expected to know the names of everyone who visits the centre. However, there are other ways of putting names to faces as the following incident demonstrates:

Incident no. 6
At 16.10 Kevin (who is on the mall) contacts the control room on the SCRL to tell Steve that 'Rachel's boyfriend has just gone into the chemist'. Kevin then says, 'Barry, can you watch this kid in the purple top who's just coming up to you'. Barry says, 'who is it, Kevin, do you know?' Kevin says, 'I can't remember his name'.

Steve is in the control room and has picked the suspect up on camera. The suspect is in his twenties and is wearing a tracksuit top, jeans and trainers. On the SCRL, 'Steve says, he's just coming up to you now Barry'. Steve turns to me and says, 'what sometimes happens if we don't know the names and they've gone into the chemist's for methadone, we'll go and ask the pharmacists and if we ask nicely they'll give us their names and addresses which is quite useful really. We get a lot of names like that'. Steve sees the suspect walk into view of one of the internal cameras and looks in the 'Mug Shots Book' to see if there is a picture of the suspect in it.

The localised knowledge of the security officers is also illustrated by the use of local nicknames for the surveilled. As the following extracts from the fieldnotes illustrate, some of these names are based on the appearance of the suspect under targeted surveillance:

Incident no. 7
At 11.44 a patrol guard contacts another guard on the SCRL: 'Bravo Two, you've got "Bandy Legs" in with her boyfriend'. Bravo Two replies, 'I've got the male but there's no "Bandy Legs"'. Dawn hears this conversation and looks for Bandy Legs but can't find her.

Incident no. 8
At 16.18 Kevin is watching the monitors when he sees a ten-year-old boy walking through the centre. Kevin picks up the microphone for the SCRL and says: 'Steve look behind you, you've got little Ginge [the boy has red hair] in the centre'. Kevin tells me that little Ginge is a shoplifter and that 'we just can't do owt with him, so we just keep him out of the centre'. Kevin follows the suspect through the centre on two internal cameras and switches to an external camera and watches little Ginge walk into the amusements arcade which is just outside the shopping centre.

Incident no. 9
At 11.51 two suspects emerge from the shopping centre. Kevin says, 'there's John Harrison and FA Cup'. 'FA Cup' is a male in his twenties with big ears. Kevin says, 'if we don't have names for them we make up nicknames'. Kevin follows John Harrison and 'FA Cup' across the car park and sees them walk into the estate.

While some nicknames are based on the appearance of the suspect others are related to a suspect's past (sometimes criminal) behaviour:

Incident no. 10

At 13.24 Andy is sitting at the control desk when he hears two of the patrol guards talking to one another on the SCRL. The two patrol guards are watching 'Pampers' who is in one of the chemists within the shopping centre. One patrol guard contacts another on the SCRL: 'she's down the nappy isle now'. Andy, who is sat at the control desk, says to himself, 'where are they? X chemist, Y chemist?' On the SCRL Andy says 'where are they, Paul?' 'X chemist', Paul replies.

Incident no. 11

At 14.45 a patrol guard contacts the control room on the SCRL and says to Kevin: 'Kevin watch "Purse Snatcher" will you, he's just heading towards the West'. Kevin picks up 'Purse Snatcher' and follows him out of the shopping centre. The patrol guard calls back and says, 'forget it, he's gone out'. Kevin says, 'yes, he's just gone into the betting shop'. Kevin leaves the camera on Corals. After a couple of minutes 'Purse Snatcher' comes out of the betting shop and runs across the car park. Kevin follows the suspect as he back tracks and runs right around the shopping centre. A patrol guard contacts the control room on the SCRL to tell Kevin that 'Smith, Bandy Legs and Wilson are coming down the Middle'. On the SCRL Kevin says, 'yes, keep an eye on 'em, Andy. I'm just watching "Purse Snatcher" '.

In the two examples above the guards are watching 'Pampers', a suspect who has stolen Pampers nappies in the past, and 'Purse Snatcher', a male in his mid-twenties who once snatched a woman's purse from her handbag while she was shopping at Housing Estate Mall.

Watching the 'druggies'

As some of the examples above have already indicated, many of the targeted surveillances at Housing Estate Mall were focused on what the security officers described as known 'druggies' and 'dealers'. When I asked the former security manager of Housing Estate Mall why the management had decided to install a CCTV system he said:

Drugs. Heroin, pure and simple. Shoptheft is done to feed the habits. Banton is the biggest council estate in Europe and it has a major, major heroin problem. And our biggest problem is we have the very large health centre next door which incorporates DART, the

Drugs and Alcohol Rehabilitation Treatment Team. They give out the prescriptions for methadone, the heroin substitute, and they come to one of our three chemists to have it dispensed. So we've got this congregation of drug addicts whether we like it or not. Unfortunately for every registered drug addict you may have ten or twelve unregistered. But everybody, whether they are a registered drug addict or not, if they want to meet another drug addict to find out whether he's got some gear, know that he has got to come in here during that day. Methadone is dispensed daily.

The CCTV system was installed with the help of the local police in 1992. During the first year of operation local police officers and the security team concentrated their efforts on tackling the shopping centre's 'drugs problem'. During one visit to the control room the former beat officer described how the security officers and the police used to sit in the control room and watch the 'druggies' with 'snatch squads' waiting at the exits to arrest those who were caught dealing. This was reiterated by another police officer who, during a visit to the control room, told me that:

This place used to be a no-go area. There was drugs, dealing. You could get anything you wanted. Colour TV's, you name it. We used to come up here and watch, didn't we? Remember when we caught Paul Smith and I got him in the toilets and said: 'Do ten squat jumps and let me see what's up your arse'. We had one guy tried to break into the control room and steal the radios. We chased him off the roof and he jumped off and broke both ankles, but we made him walk from the pub into the police van.

These stories were supported by Kevin who described how:

'… we used to get the CID down here a lot. What they'd do is they'd sit up here and watch the "druggies" on the phone'. Kevin zooms in on one of the public phone booths in the shopping centre and says, 'what they'd do is zoom in and read the telephone numbers that the "dealers" were dialling. They'd also sit and watch the taxis a lot'. I ask him why they watched the taxis and Kevin replies, 'well a lot of stuff [stolen goods] goes through the taxis and I don't know if you've noticed but the "druggies" are always using taxis and yet they've got no money. Sometimes they'll do a runner and they'll have taxis waiting for them'.

Kevin explained how the 'drugs problem' at Housing Estate Mall was 'sorted out' soon after the CCTV system was installed. However, the CCTV operators who monitor the images displayed by the CCTV cameras still focus their attention on 'known' drug users and dealers who frequent the shopping centre. The targeting of this population is based on the CCTV operator's belief that drug users are visiting the centre for one of two purposes: (a) to 'feed the habit' or (b) to 'make a deal'. As the former security manager, explained:

> We know that they're at it daily, I mean it's not just on a whim, these people live by shoptheft. When you talk to a 'druggy' he says, 'I need £600 a week for me habit', and they sell products at say 20% of the value, that's two and a half thousand quid a week he's got to steal every week. You know they'll get a bottle of something from X chemist for £3.75 and sell it at a £1. So if he needs to get £600 in his hand ...

The security officers also suspect that the 'druggies' may be visiting the shopping centre to make a drug deal. For example, in the following incident:

Incident no. 12
Dawn zooms in on the west car park and sees that Sharon Brown and three males have returned. 'They're waiting for a drop', Dawn says. Then, on the SCRL, Dawn says, 'Sharon Brown and that small group are at the back of the car park again'. Dawn turns to me and says, 'they're all on methadone which is supposed to get them off heroin but it doesn't. And it peeves me cos I don't see why we should pay for their drugs'.

Even the design of the system was influenced by the management's desire to 'weed out the drug dealers'. Thus, according to the former security manager, one of the reasons for making sure that all of the 13 cameras installed at Housing Estate Mall were fully functional (i.e. pan/tilt/zoom) was

> ... so there's nowhere they can hide. 'Druggies' always congregate in little corners or out of sight places. The design of the centre, when it was built, unfortunately they've got the public toilets right next to the telephone, the two main things that drug dealers need: toilets to go inject and telephones for all the calls. That was very evident from when the police did their monitoring from here. They live around

the telephones. But what I also did was have ICB lines fitted to all phones, in-coming calls barred. Because they'd make a phone call and wait for someone to ring them back. We didn't tell them that but after a month they got fed up of waiting for people to ring them back.

The security guards' localised knowledge of the 'druggies' who visit Housing Estate Mall is very useful for the police. As Kevin explained:

> ... the system is used as an information service by the police because they know the problems we've got, they've been here for twenty years. I mean this is not a new centre, this is twenty-three years old now. The police give us the name of a drug dealer and say: 'Can you find out what car he's driving Kev?' 'Yes, there's the car and there's its number plate', when they come in and collect it. [Kevin shows me a hard-copy printout of a car].

As we have already seen, many of the people living on the estate who are addicted to heroin visit the health centre, which is a few yards from the shopping centre, to collect their methadone prescriptions. These prescriptions are then collected from one of the shopping centre's three chemists. Many of those receiving treatment collect their prescriptions on a particular day and at a particular time. This means that the security officers, who know the identity of most of these people, soon become familiar with the weekly routine of many of the local drug users. As the following incident shows, this is very useful for the local beat officer:

Incident no. 13
At 13.35 Darren (the local beat officer) arrives in the control room. Darren has had a tip-off from the guards who have informed him that a 'wanted' person will be arriving at the shopping centre on Thursday between one o'clock and two o'clock in the afternoon to collect his methadone prescription from one of the chemists within the centre. Before he arrived in the control room Darren has paid a visit to the chemist and asked the store manager to telephone the control room when the suspect arrives to collect his methadone prescription. Darren tells us that the suspect has stolen some prescriptions from his doctor when he met him for an appointment and that he has already tried to get sixty tryazapan with the prescriptions. Kevin tells us that he knows the suspect and that he plays darts with his dad. Darren makes us all a coffee and we sit and wait for the wanted person to arrive for his methadone. After about

ten minutes Darren stands up and says, 'I'm gonna go for a walk on the mall'. Stuart says, 'well, when he [the wanted person] comes in and the chemist rings up here I'll tell them to stall him and I'll put a message over the intercom: "could Darren contact the office", or something like that'. Darren says, 'okay', and leaves the control room ...

At 14.33 Kevin receives a telephone call from the manager of the chemist who informs Kevin that the wanted person has entered the chemist shop and is waiting for his methadone prescription. Stuart puts a camera on the entrance to the chemist and, on the intercom microphone, says, 'Your attention please. Would Darren in the shopping centre please contact the office'. Kevin leaves the control room and goes to the chemist to accompany Darren. Stuart zooms in on the chemist and sees Darren leave with the two suspects. Stuart follows the suspects on camera as they are led away by Darren (the local beat officer) and Kevin. At 14.47 two police cars drive away with the wanted person and his friend.

Personalised suspicion and intensity of surveillance

Known people were not only targeted on a regular basis; they also received intensive and intrusive monitoring when under targeted surveillance. For example, targeted surveillances based on personalised knowledge were more likely to result in the production of a hard-copy printout of the suspect, and the duration of the surveillance was also longer when the suspect under surveillance was known to the CCTV operators. More than nine out of ten (93 per cent) of the hard-copy printouts produced on both sites were taken during targeted surveillances based on personalised knowledge. The production of photographs was a regular occurrence at Housing Estate Mall where most of the security officers produced pictures of known persons and their associates. The production of printouts was made easier because of the security guards intimacy with some of the regulars. Take the following incident, for example:

Incident no. 14
At 13.17 Kevin (the security manager) is on the mall when he calls Dawn on the SCRL and asks her to get a picture of a suspect who is using the shopping centre's public phone. Dawn zooms in on two males in their twenties who are both casually dressed. Dawn then picks up the microphone for the SCRL and says: 'Which one is it, Kevin?' On the SCRL Kevin replies, 'it's the one with white sleeves'. Dawn attempts to line up a good picture of the suspect and presses

the button to produce a hard-copy printout. As she presses the button the suspect turns around and Dawn only gets a picture of the back of the suspect's head. The suspect finishes his telephone call and walks away with his friend. Dawn follows the suspects on camera and sees Kevin talking to the suspect as they walk along the mall. Dawn tries to take another picture but this time Kevin's head gets in the way. A couple of minutes later Kevin returns to the control room and asks Dawn if she got a picture of the suspect. Dawn says, 'I would have done if you hadn't got your big nut in the way'. Kevin says, 'I was trying to slow him down so you could get a good picture'. I ask Kevin why he wanted a picture of this suspect. Kevin says, 'he tried to break into Cheapmart a few months ago. I know him, we go way back. I used to go to school with him'. I ask Kevin what his ex-school mates think of him now and he replies, 'they know I'm just doing my job. They're okay. They know how far to push me as well'. Kevin turns to Dawn and says, 'he tells me he's off the drugs now'. Dawn says, 'yes, and I'm a Spice Girl'. Kevin tells me that he wanted an updated picture of the suspect because 'Barry's only been here a few weeks and we're trying to help him get to know the faces'.

In Incident no. 14 Kevin provides us with another example of the relationship between 'intimacy' and electronic communications systems. Kevin is walking on the mall with an old school friend when he decides to deliberately slow him down so that Dawn, who is in the control room, can produce a good picture of the suspect for the rogues gallery. Thus, Kevin's level of intimacy with the suspect under surveillance allows him to communicate with the suspect on a 'face-to-face' basis in the knowledge that this will allow Dawn (who is monitoring remotely from the control room) to produce a hard-copy printout.

The CCTV operators also observed the associates of 'known' people and, on occasions, took their photograph for future reference:

Incident no. 15
At 17.03 Kevin arrives in the control room and asks Steve to put a camera on the middle seats. Steve puts a camera on the middle seats and just to the left of the seats there are two males having a conversation. The two males are in their twenties and both are casually dressed. Kevin says to Steve, 'get a picture of Wilson'. Steve says, 'I'll get his mate as well cos he comes in a lot'. Wilson, Kevin tells me, is a 'lifter'.

Incident no. 16

At 14.48 Steve picks up three males on camera walking towards the shopping centre's public telephone kiosk. Although two of the three males are wearing baseball caps they are scruffy in appearance rather than subcultural. Steve describes them as 'a bunch of smack heads'. One of the suspects uses the telephone and Steve zooms in real close and produces a hard-copy printout of the suspect. He then tries to line up a picture of the other suspect in a baseball cap but says 'shit' as the suspect turns around and Steve produces a picture of only half of his face. Steve follows the three suspects back through the centre and on the SCRL says: 'Hutton and his two mates are on their way up to East now'. I ask Steve what the suspects had done, and he says: 'the one in the green T shirt used to be banned. But even if they're just knocking about with a known "troublecauser" or "scumbag" the chances are they'll be shoplifters or whatever. And the police will come up here and look at the book and say, "yes, we know him, he's a burglar", and they'll give us a name'. Steve cuts up the hard copy print out with only half the suspect's face and pins the other one onto the notice board in front of the control desk.

In Incident no. 16 Steve suggests that anyone who hangs around with known 'troublecausers' or 'scumbags' are likely to be involved in criminal activity themselves. Thus people who know 'known' people are guilty by association and have their pictures taken for future reference. As Steve says, the police will visit and put a name and often a criminal history to the faces collected by the operators at Housing Estate Mall. On other occasions the local beat officer will take a photograph to the police station and pin it on a notice board to see if anyone can put a name to the face.

As well as having their photographs taken on a regular basis, known persons and their associates were also monitored for long periods of time. For instance, one-fifth (22 per cent) of the targeted surveillances based on a person's appearance (i.e. categorical suspicion) lasted for three or more minutes, while the remainder (78 per cent) lasted for one to two minutes. Similarly, only one-third (32 per cent) of the observations based on behavioural suspicion lasted for three or more minutes. However, one half (50 per cent) of the targeted surveillances based on personalised knowledge lasted for this period. On some days the CCTV operators would watch the same (known) faces all day. During one shift I attended the CCTV operators spent hours making sure a known drug user and banned person did not gain access to the centre:

Incident no. 17
At 09.27 a patrol guard calls Dawn on the radio to inform her that Sharon Brown, a banned person, is on the public phone just outside the shopping centre.

Incident no. 18
At 09.37 a patrol guard calls Dawn on the SCRL to inform her that Paul X is coming across the car park towards the centre. Kevin shouts from his office: 'it's druggy day'. 'They've probably got their giros today', Dawn replies. Dawn puts the North car park external camera onto the working monitor and sees a male in his twenties dressed in a tracksuit and trainers walking towards the shopping centre. Dawn then pans away slightly and as she does she sees Sharon Brown again. Dawn leaves the male suspect and follows Sharon Brown.

Incident no. 19
At 11.41 a patrol guard contacts the control room on the SCRL to tell Dawn that Sharon Brown is standing outside of the betting shop which is just to the left of the North entrance. Dawn puts an external camera on the working monitor and follows Sharon Brown across the car park.

Incident no. 20
At 11.45 a patrol guard contacts the control room on the SCRL to inform Dawn that Sharon Brown is entering the North entrance. Dawn puts an external camera on to the working monitor and sees Sharon Brown talking to four teenage males dressed in tracksuits and trainers.

Incident no. 21
At 12.20 a patrol guard contacts the control room on the SCRL to inform Dawn that Sharon Brown is heading towards the West entrance. Dawn puts an external camera on the working monitor and picks up Sharon Brown.

Incident no. 22
At 12.30 on the SCRL one patrol guard says to the other, 'Wilson's in'. Dawn picks Wilson up on camera. He is about 19 years old, dressed in jeans, trainers, a three-quarter length Adidas coat and a white baseball cap. Dawn says, 'yes seen' and follows the suspects across the car park where they meet up with Sharon Brown.

Incident no. 23
At 13.06 a patrol guard contacts the control room on the SCRL to tell Dawn that 'Sharon Brown and them are walking past the betting shop'. Dawn follows the suspects briefly on an external camera but leaves them to deal with the next incident.

Those subjected to such intensive surveillance were aware of the surveillance camera's constant gaze. During many of the incidents above, for example, Sharon Brown, who was banned from the centre, would adopt a 'social face' which gave the impression that she was about to leave the area:

Incident no. 24 (Incident no. 17 continued)
At 09.27 a patrol guard calls Dawn on the SCRL to inform her that Sharon Brown, a banned person, is on the public phone just outside the shopping centre. Dawn uses the control panel to put an external camera (which is at the top of a high mast in the centre of the main car park) on the working monitor and sees the three teenage girls dressed in tracksuits standing by the main entrance. Two of the girls are peering through the glass doors. Dawn turns to me and says, 'they're looking to see where the guards are. She'll [Sharon Brown] try and get back in, she always does'. Dawn follows Sharon Brown on camera as she walks across the car park towards the estate. Sharon Brown turns and waves to her two friends but after walking a few more yards doubles back and starts to walk back towards the centre.

Sharon Brown's attempt to avoid the gaze is thwarted by Dawn, the CCTV operator, who knows what the suspect is trying to do. As the incident unfolds Dawn switches from the use of external cameras to internal cameras to keep Sharon Brown under observation, this time without the suspect knowing she is being watched:

Incident no. 24 continued
... Sharon Brown is standing with her two friends outside the shopping centre and is trying discretely to point towards the cameras to let her friends know they are being watched. Dawn pans away and switches to another external camera on the loading bay which allows her to watch the suspects from a different angle. Dawn picks up the radio and says: 'Sharon Brown is now heading towards the West Entrance'. Dawn uses one of the external cameras at the back of the market to follow Sharon Brown as she walks right round

the centre, past the health clinic, the probation centre and the library towards the West entrance. Before she reaches the entrance Sharon Brown goes to the post office which is just outside the centre opposite a Chinese takeaway. Dawn uses one of the internal cameras to watch Sharon Brown as she stands in the post office queue. She does this by using one of the shopping mall's internal cameras to zoom in on the suspect through the glass doors. A few minutes later Sharon Brown leaves the centre in a taxi. Dawn picks up the radio and says: 'Sharon Brown has left the centre in a red Ford Fiesta'.

One of the reasons for prolonged observations of 'known' people was that the guards believed that the suspect might be about to 'go for it' (i.e. shoplift). A shoptheft incident constituted 'real work' in the eyes of the guards and close and prolonged attention was usually given to incidents involving known 'shoplifters'. Unlike those shopping in the public space of a city centre, who can easily walk out of the camera's view, the suspects under targeted surveillance in a shopping centre like Housing Estate Mall are constantly within the camera's range. Thus, if the suspect decides to use one of the centre's public phones or sit down on one of the benches with their shopping bags, the CCTV operator can observe the suspect very closely to look for evidence of stolen goods:

Incident no. 25
At 15.23 Kevin is flicking through the internal cameras on the working monitor when he sees four known females walking through the shopping centre. There are two women, both 'scruffy' in appearance, one is in her fifties and has bleached blonde hair, the other is in her thirties and is dressed in stone-washed jeans and jacket. The two older women are walking through the centre with two teenagers dressed in tracksuits and trainers. Kevin picks up the radio link and lets the guards know that the Smith family are in the centre. Paul calls Kevin on the radio to let him know that two of the Smith family have gone into the chemist and that he is watching them from an empty unit in the shopping centre which is directly opposite the chemist. Kevin switches cameras to watch the Smith kids who are leaning against some railings outside of Bargain Basement. Paul calls Kevin on the SCRL and lets him know that the two suspects in the chemist have now left the store. Kevin can't find them on camera, so he calls Stuart on the radio: 'Stu, see if you can find Granny Smith, I've lost her'. Kevin finds one of the Smith's sitting down on a bench outside Bargain Basement. He zooms in real

close and looks inside the suspect's shopping trolley as she moves some groceries to make space for two carrier bags full of shopping. As Kevin tries to look inside the trolley a man stands in front of 'Granny Smith': 'Get out the way', Kevin shouts. A couple of minutes later Paul calls Kevin on the radio to tell him that the Smiths have left the centre by the North exit. Kevin uses two external cameras (one on the car park and one on the loading bay) to follow the four suspects back into the estate.

Appropriate use of space in a shopping mall

As a number of writers have argued, 'the mall can be seen ... as a "single minded" space ... a space for one kind of activity which privileges one kind of user – the consumer' (Reeve, 1998: 75). From this perspective, malls are 'instrumental' spaces in which 'users are treated as a means to the ends of consumption, employing a number of socially controlling strategies in management, design, promotion and policing to achieve this' (ibid.: 75). At City Centre Mall in particular, people who disrupted the commercial image were targeted by the CCTV operatives. These people fell into two categories: first, those who behaved in a way which the operatives believed was not conducive to the commercial image of the shopping mall; second, people with certain social characteristics (i.e. subcultural youth) who were believed to be not shopping and subsequently were monitored by the security personnel.

Behaviour that disrupts the commercial image

Some of the types of behaviour that are not permissible in the shopping mall include a whole range of activities that are commonplace in the public space of the street. These types of behaviour include, for instance, walking a dog or pushing a bicycle:

Incident no. 26
At 11.16 a patrol guard calls the control room on the SCRL to inform the operatives that he has seen a man in the centre with a dog. Dave asks a patrol guard on a different level of the shopping centre to intercept this man and ask him to leave. (The security manager, who is working at his desk in the back of the control room and can hear the radio transmissions, shouts: 'How did he get in in the first place?') Dave finds the suspect on camera walking past a fashion store and informs a patrol guard of the suspect's current location:

'Can you stop this man and inform him that only guide dogs are allowed in the centre'.

Incident no. 27
At 14.17 Stuart is sat at the control desk watching the images from the cameras flick over on the monitors. He sees a man and a woman both in their twenties and dressed casually pushing bikes through the centre. Stuart picks up the microphone for the SCRL and asks a patrol guard to tell the two people to take their bikes out of the centre.

Other forms of behaviour that are not allowed include contract workers working on site during the mall's opening hours. The restriction on working is enforced mainly for health and safety purposes. This means that some work can be carried out during opening hours as long as it is in areas where there is no public access. However, as the following incident shows, even this work is not tolerated if it disrupts the commercial image of the mall:

Incident no. 28
A patrol guard contacts Karen and Jim in the control room to tell them that there is someone drilling on the Harbour Deck. Karen decides to contact the shopping centre manager.
Karen: 'Control to CCM 1 [i.e. City Centre Mall 1, which is the shopping mall manager]. Neil, we've got some drilling on the Harbour Deck and apparently it's making quite a noise'.
CCM 1: 'Is it bad?' (Karen looks at Jim who advises Karen to ask CCM 19 (the patrol guard who reported the incident) to liase with CCM 1.)
Karen: 'CCM 19 can you liaise with CCM 1 about this drilling'.
CCM 19: 'CCM 1'.
CCM 1: 'Yes, go ahead'.
CCM 19: 'Neil, this drilling on the Harbour Deck is quite loud and there's also a lot of sawdust flying about'.
CCM 1: 'Okay, can you ask them to stop please'.

Other activities are tolerated but believed to be highly irregular and are monitored closely by the CCTV operatives:

Incident no. 29
Gavin watches a suspect pick a cigarette butt out of an ashtray. 'He's tabbing, he's tabbing', Gavin says to Alan who is also watching the

suspect on the monitors. Gavin then picks up the shopping centre radio link and says: 'He's tabbing. All CCMs, Paul Smith is tabbing, can you watch him?' Alan takes over on the control pad and follows the suspect down one of the arcades but then loses him. He then picks up the microphone for the SCRL to contact CCM 18.

Alan: 'CCM 18, has Paul Smith left the Centre?'

CCM 18: 'Yes I think he's left by the West Arcade'.

Alan (on the city centre radio link): 'City Centre Mall to … store. Paul Smith has just left our shopping centre and is heading towards you'.

Other types of behaviour that are not permissible in the shopping mall include eating, sitting on the floor and lying down. These types of behaviour usually warranted the deployment of a patrol guard who would ask the suspect to position their body in a way conducive to the commercial image of the mall:

Incident no. 30

At 15.38 a shop worker from one of the units within the shopping centre draws one of the patrol guard's attention to a woman who is sat outside a shop eating soup and bread. The patrol guard contacts the control room to inform Alan in the control room about this incident. Alan tells the patrol guard to speak to the suspect and fixes a camera on the woman who is sitting on the floor eating her bread and soup. The patrol guard is seen approaching the woman who stands up and walks away. Alan says out loud to no one in particular: 'Just treat the place like a "doss house" why don't you'.

Treating the place like a 'doss house' obviously disrupts the commercial image of the mall. Most of the security personnel who spent time in the control room expressed their contempt for people who behaved in this manner:

Incident no. 31

At 12.24 Neil says: 'We've got a few people "camping out" [sitting down] down there'. He zooms in and holds a camera on five males in their teens all dressed in tracksuits and three-quarter length Adidas coats. Neil uses the SCRL to ask a patrol guard to move the suspects along but before the guard arrives we can see the five suspects get up and walk out the doors. The guard walks to where the five males had been sitting and picks up a couple of pieces of litter. Karen says: 'I would have gone outside and brought them back in and told them to pick that rubbish up'.

Incident no. 32
At 13.30 Karen is looking at the monitors when she sees two people sitting down on the shopping centre floor. Karen holds the camera on the two suspects and says to Dave: 'Have you seen those two "camping out"?'

The operative's concern with people 'camping out' may reflect their perceived image of the shopper as someone who browses, who is constantly on the move, walking from shop to shop as they decide on their next purchase. However, on most occasions these types of behaviour were considered wrong not only because of the actual behaviour involved, but because of the social characteristics of the people who were behaving in this way, i.e. youth and, in particular, subcultural youth. In the following incidents, for example, those sitting down or lying down are either teenagers or people in their twenties:

Incident no. 33
At 14.49 Neil uses the control pad to have a look around the shopping centre. Neil sees four teenagers, three males and one female, all dressed in tracksuits sitting down on the main stage where the day's promotional performances had earlier taken place. Neil picks up the microphone for the SCRL and asks a guard to move the suspects on.

Incident no. 34
At 15.42 Dave takes the camera fixed on the dock off the spot monitor and sees three males in their twenties, casually dressed, lying down on the main stage (where the day's performances had previously taken place). Dave contacts a guard on the SCRL and asks him to go and tell the three males to sit up.

Incident no. 35
At 14.50 Neil sees four males, all teenagers dressed in tracksuits, sat on a bench outside a shop. On the SCRL he says: 'Control to CCM 12. There's a group of males sat on the bench outside Menswear. They've been there long enough can you move them please'. The patrol guard arrives in a few seconds and asks the suspects to move.

As the following incident illustrates not everyone who sits on the floor is asked to move or stand up:

Incident no. 36
At 13.32 Jim and Shane are sat at the main control desk in front of the monitors. As the images from the cameras flick over Jim sees two people sitting outside one of the shopping centre entrances. He picks up the microphone for the SCRL: 'Control to CCM 8. Alan we've got some people "camped out" on the West Bridge, could you move them please'. In the control room we can see Alan walk towards the suspects but when he reaches them he walks straight past. Alan then contacts the control room on the SCRL to inform Jim that the two suspects were 'a couple of students working out their finances'.

Subcultural youth

A number of studies reviewed by Sibley (1995) on the 'threat to safe shopping' have provided support for the view that 'the boundaries between the consuming and non-consuming public are strengthening, with non-consumption being constructed as a form of deviance at the same time as spaces of consumption eliminate public spaces in city centres' (ibid.: xii). Most of these studies have shown how the category of 'youth' in particular is singled out as 'troublesome'. As we saw earlier, the vast majority of targeted surveillances on both sites were directed at subcultural youth. Almost nine out of ten (88 per cent) of those targeted were under 30 and exactly one half of all targeted surveillances were of people dressed in subcultural attire (i.e. tracksuits and baseball caps). At City Centre Mall, for example, most of the transmissions that came to the control room via the radio links concerned incidents involving youth dressed in tracksuits and baseball caps:

Incident no. 37
At 13.52 one of the stores within the city centre uses the CCRL to send an 'early warning' to the control room. Gavin takes the message and repeats it to the patrol guards on the SCRL: 'Control to all security guards, we've just had an "early warning" from … [names department store]. We've got eight to ten youths in baseball caps heading towards us. If you see them can you just observe please'.

Incident no. 38
At 14.13 Gary and Paul are in the control room when a patrol guard calls the control room on the SCRL to inform the operatives that a group of males in baseball caps have entered the store in two groups.

Incident no. 39
At 12.57 Carl receives a message on the CCRL from the security officers in the control room of a department store who tell him that they have had three males dressed in tracksuits and baseball caps in their store who have been loud and generally causing a nuisance. Carl uses the control pad to look for the suspects and repeats the description from the department store security officers on the SCRL.

As well as tracksuits and baseball caps, any youth dressed in puff jackets (ski-style) or three-quarter length designer sports coats (usually Adidas or Nike) were ascribed malign intent by the CCTV operators. For some of the CCTV operators the combination of 'youth' and subcultural attire was almost synonymous with 'trouble', as the following extract from the fieldnotes illustrates:

> I ask Gary to explain how new recruits at City Centre Mall centre know who the 'troublecausers' are. He replies: 'It's funny you know 'cause they all dress the same. You'll find that the troublemakers all wear tracksuits'.

The targeting of subcultural youth was not based on the CCTV operators' belief that this social group had an over-propensity for criminal behaviour; rather it was based on the belief that subcultural youth were not shopping. In short, subcultural youth were targeted because they disrupted the commercial image of the mall:

> Alan (a CCTV operator) tells me that 'the main problem in the Centre is kids. They're a frigging nuisance. They just come in in groups and loiter. They make the place look untidy. We just move 'em on and in the end they get fed up'.

> I ask Dave what are the main problems in the shopping centre and he replies: 'On a Saturday the main problem is kids. They just treat the place like a playground. If we have to move them on three times then they're out. 'Cause it's obvious they're not shopping'.

Incident no. 40
At 12.42 Carl is looking at the monitors when he notices four males, all in their teens, dressed in sports gear, 'messing around on a bench' (i.e. pushing each other and laughing). Carl asks a patrol guard on the SCRL to move the four males on but they get up and leave before the guard arrives. Carl follows the four males on four cameras but

then loses them. I ask him about the shopping centre's policy on groups of youths. Carl says, 'we don't allow youths to settle anymore. They're not shopping so ... If you let them settle they'll block the lifts and escalators. They think they can do what they want'.

As the preceding examples illustrate, youth are regarded as particularly problematic when they are in groups. The manager of City Centre Mall believes that:

The main problem is with gangs of youths gathering, loitering, now we don't allow them to group, we don't allow them to loiter. So we move them on and move them out. But you're talking about a small percentage, the majority are nice kids, high-spirited, but weren't we all when we were that age? That's not a problem with me. It's when they start getting threatening and using foul language. I don't tolerate that, they're not welcome. It's private property, it's a family centre and out they go.

As Table 4.6 shows, almost half (45 per cent) of all targeted surveillances at the two sites were focused on people in groups. The social characteristics of those groups who were targeted by the CCTV operators were broadly the same as those of the primary person. Thus more than eight out of ten (85 per cent) of the groups who were targeted were under the age of thirty, half (50 per cent) were dressed in subcultural attire, and six out of ten (62 per cent) were male.

But it was not the presence of a group per se that warrants suspicion. Groups were only a problem when they were made up of youths, as the following incident demonstrates very clearly:

Incident no. 41
At 15.04 the security manager (SM) sits down next to Darrel (CCTV operative) at the control desk and starts to use the control pad to pan a camera across the balcony of the second floor of the shopping centre. The SM stops at one of the benches and without saying anything to Darrel draws a circle with his finger around a large group who are standing around the bench. The SM has not zoomed in on the group so it's difficult to make out the social characteristics of this large gathering. Darrel immediately picks up the microphone for the shopping centre radio link (SCRL) and says: 'Control to CM9. There's a large group gathered around the bench outside Electric's UK. Can you move them on please'. A few seconds later CM9 calls

Table 4.6   *Is the target of suspicion alone or in a group?*

Alone or in a group?	City Centre Mall %	Housing Estate Mall %	Both malls %
Alone	31	30	31
With one other	13	33	24
In a group	56	37	45
N = 170	100	100	100

Darrel back on the SCRL: 'Darrel, that group outside Electric's UK. The people there are mostly adults, children and elderly people'. Darrel replies on the SCRL, 'Okay, sorry. It just looked a bit crowded that's all'.

Mobilising a response: the exclusion of youth

Authoritative interventions by patrol guards (involving deployments and ejections) were largely reserved for incidents involving teenagers. For instance, a quarter (23 per cent) of the targeted surveillances involving those in their twenties and one-third (33 per cent) of the targeted surveillances involving those aged 30 or more resulted in a deployment. However, more than four out of ten (41 per cent) of the targeted surveillances of teenagers resulted in a patrol guard being deployed to the scene to deal with the incident. These figures do not tell the full story either, because the deployments dealing with incidents involving teenagers and those in their twenties involved the suspect being questioned, moved on or ejected. The deployments against those aged thirty or more, on the other hand, involved the patrol guard being deployed to give advice to 'older' shoppers who were either lost or had unwittingly found themselves in an unauthorised area of the shopping centre. The security manager of City Centre Mall explained to me the nature of deployments against youth:

People who are sort of verbally abusive towards the guards normally get a 28-day ban, if they come in before their 28 days are up we do extend that to another 28 days and if they abuse that again and try and mess us about that then extends to three months, then six months. A lot of the young kids who come in here come in regularly, it's like a second home to them, a meeting place up on the top floor of the mall. If we take that privilege away from them it hurts them and so they think, you know, 'I'm not gonna prat about because I'll get banned and I won't be able to meet my mates', you know. Even a 28 day ban you can see the looks on their faces, you know: 'Oh no please don't give me a 28-day ban'. And it's a case of, you know, if you come in here you've got to respect our wishes and do what we want you to do. You know, if we don't want you to stand there you don't stand there. At the end of the day it's private property and you're invited in to come to shop as a shopper and not to loiter around. If you continue to loiter around we'll ask you to leave and if you give us any grief then we'll impose a ban on you. And it hurts them. It's quite funny to watch their faces.

Ejecting youths from the centre constitutes 'real work' in the eyes of the security guards as the following examples illustrate:

Incident no. 42
At 14.20 a patrol guard contacts the control room on the SCRL to inform the guards that he is escorting five males out of the car park exit. A few seconds later the same guard calls back to say that the suspects are heading towards a department store near the West entrance. John puts one of the external cameras on the spot monitor and sees the five teenage boys, all dressed in tracksuits and baseball caps, walking past the back of the shopping centre. John quickly switches the external camera on the spot monitor for an internal camera which is fixed on a side entrance near the management office and sees one of the boys pop his head in the door. John picks up the SCRL and deploys a guard to the entrance but the boy runs straight back out and joins his friends who are walking away from the shopping centre. John picks up the statistics book and says, 'is that all we've thrown out today? Five. It hardly seems worth turning up for work'.

I ask Norman (CCTV operator) if it was busy on Saturday and he replies, 'well it's been worse. My record [for throwing kids out] is about 16 to 18 in one day. Horrendous it was. Wall to wall kids. They just treat it as a game in the end'.

The exclusion of youths from City Centre Mall has been formalised by the management who have recently introduced an exclusion policy which is enforced on Saturdays:

Incident no. 43
Just after 12.00 Jim does the 'Saturday Message' on the SCRL:
'Control to all patrol guards, just a reminder that today is Saturday.
If you see any groups of youths hanging around can you ask them to
move along. If you have to tell them more than twice could you
please ask them to leave the centre'.

The formalised exclusion policy at City Centre Mall is reflected in the
figures on the social characteristics of suspects who were ejected from the
mall. As Table 4.7 shows, no one over the age of 30 who was deployed
against was ejected. However, around two out of ten (18 per cent) of those
in their twenties and more than four out of ten (43 per cent) of those in
their teens who were deployed against were ejected from the shopping
centre. Being part of a group also compounds the influence of age. Thus,
although security guards were deployed to deal with incidents involving
groups of older people (aged 30 plus) on four occasions, none resulted in
an ejection. However, half (50 per cent) of the deployments in relation to
groups of teenagers resulted in at least one person being ejected from the
centre. Thus when a guard was deployed to deal with groups of teenagers
there was a fifty–fifty chance that someone would be ejected.

The other category of youth who received intensive surveillance,
particularly at City Centre Mall, were people that the security guards
suspected were of school age. According to the security officers, school
children are not allowed in the shopping centre on weekdays between
9.00 a.m. and 16.00 p.m., although they are allowed in during their dinner
hour. The shopping centre's Truancy Scheme was set up by Neil Lawson,
the manager of City Centre Mall, in conjunction with senior police

Table 4.7   Was someone ejected during a deployment by age of suspect?

		Age		
		Teens %	Twenties %	Thirties %
Was someone ejected?	Yes	43	18	0
	No	57	82	100
	Total	N = 28	N = 17	N = 7

*The results presented in this table are statistically significant at the p< 0.05 level.
†Percentages may not add up to 100 due to rounding

officers and education welfare officers. As the following incidents demonstrate, the scheme involves close liaison between local schools, education welfare officers and the security personnel at City Centre Mall:

Incident no. 44
At 11.18 a patrol guard contacts the control room on the SCRL with the names of two males from Banton High who claim to be doing an Environmental Studies course. Dave picks up the telephone and calls Banton High School: 'Good morning, this is City Centre Mall security. At this shopping centre we have got a policy of letting you know when we have children in the centre that we suspect should be at school. Now we've got a couple of your lads in, Steve Smith and Paul Jones, who claim to be doing an Environmental Studies course … [Dave laughs out loud] … oh so I take it that's not exactly true then. Okay, thank you, bye'.

Incident no. 45
At 10.12 a patrol guard contacts the control room:
CCM 12: 'CCM 12 to control'.
Carl: 'Send'.
CCM 12: 'Carl I've got X down here from Banton High who claims that she has been to the doctors'.
Carl telephones Banton High School to find out if X should be at school. The school inform Carl that X should be at school. Carl then telephones the Education Welfare Officer to inform them of the situation. Carl turns to me and says: 'The Education Welfare Officer will now check with the girl's parents to see whether or not she should be at school. In the past we just used to throw kids out if they were in here during school time. But sometimes we would get the parents ringing up saying that they knew their kids were off school and "what are you doing throwing our kids out of the shopping centre?" So now we do it through the Education Welfare people. It's just to cover ourselves really'.

Incident no. 46
At 11.55 Nigel receives a message in the control room from a patrol guard on the SCRL:
CCM 9: 'CCM 9 to control'.
Nigel: 'Send'.
CCM 9: 'I've got three kids here from Banton High who say that there was a school trip today which they decided not to go on'.

Nigel: 'Well if they're not on the trip then they should be at school. Escort them out please and tell them that their headmaster is waiting for them'.

Nigel telephones the school to tell them that three of their boys have been in the shopping centre. One of the electricians, who is working on a fire alarm panel in the control room, says: 'Nigel you rotten sod. Didn't you ever do that when you were at school?'

Some of the school children had legitimate reasons for being off school and told the guards so. During one incident the CCTV operator telephoned the suspect's parents to check out the validity of their story:

Incident no. 47

At 13.42 Nigel and Karen are sat at the main desk when a patrol guard contacts the control room on the SCRL with the names and home numbers of three young males who he suspects should be at school: 'CCM 12 to Control. I've got three kids here, one from … school, one from … and one from … school. They're saying that they're in town to buy their Dad a birthday present and they've given me their home numbers if you want to check'. Nigel gets on the telephone to one of the children's parents to find out if they are telling the truth about being in town to buy their Dad's present. Nigel says to the parent on the phone: 'They are not supposed to come into the centre on their own during school time, so next time could you ensure that they are accompanied by an adult when they're in the centre'.

The security personnel at Housing Estate Mall experienced problems of a different kind with school children entering the shopping centre. Banton High School is around two minutes walk from the shopping centre. The security guards told me that during the school term (my period of observation at Housing Estate Mall was during the summer holidays) around two hundred children walk across to the shopping centre each day to buy their dinner from the centre which has three bakers shops, a Chinese takeaway and a fish and chip shop. Although the school children are a bit of a nuisance the shopping centre management tolerates their behaviour. As Dave, one of the security officers explained, there are commercial limits to the exclusion of school children:

We were gonna ban 'em at one time but the shops went mad 'cos they make a lot of money out of them.

Managerial concerns

A hierarchy of response

The decision by CCTV operators to respond to incidents which are brought to their attention is filtered through their 'occupational reading' of the situation. As we saw in Chapter 3, for example, during a typical eight-hour shift (between 9 a.m. and 5 p.m.) at City Centre Mall there are likely to be at least thirty to forty descriptions of known 'lifters' or 'troublemakers' sent on the city centre radio link (CCRL). However, only two or three of these are likely to be 'acted upon' by the operatives. In stark contrast, incidents involving health and safety issues (e.g. lift break-downs, fire alarms, unauthorised contract workers on site, etc.) receive a rapid response from the security officers:

> *Incident no. 48*
> At 14.09 a patrol guard contacts the control room to inform the operatives that someone has fallen and that she (the patrol guard) is applying first aid. Jim is at the window having a fag. He says to Norman 'tell all the patrol guards to stay off the air and make a note of it on a piece of paper and I'll DOB [Daily Occurrence Book] it later. Ask Karen [patrol guard] if the woman needs an ambulance':
> *Norman (on the SCRL)*: 'Control to fourteen'.
> *CCM 14*: 'Send'.
> *Norman*: 'Karen, does this woman need an ambulance?'
> *CCM 14*: 'No, she's slipped and hurt her wrist. I've bandaged it now'.
> *Norman*: 'All patrol guards can come back on the air now'.
> *CCM 12*: 'CCM 12 to control. There's a large spillage down there. That's what the woman's slipped on'.
> *John says out aloud*: 'Oh great, she [Karen] never said that. The manager's gonna pick up on that now, "why didn't the guard see the spillage?" '

After applying first aid to the woman who fell down Karen arrives at the control room window to complete her Medical Incident Report Sheets. On her arrival the security manager says: 'Why didn't you see the spillage. If they go for compensation we've got to have something to throw back at them'.

The accident above receives high priority from the CCTV operators. All the patrol guards are instructed to keep off the air (i.e. not use their radios) by the CCTV operators until the incident has been resolved. The incident appears to be going smoothly until one of the patrol guards on the mall contacts the control room on the shopping centre radio link (SCRL) to inform the CCTV operators that there is a large spillage on the floor where the woman has slipped. This worries John who is concerned that the shopping mall manager may pick up on the patrol guard's remarks about the spillage on the radio link. The high priority given by the CCTV operators to safety and management issues is, therefore, mediated by the surveillance infrastructure which allows the management to monitor the behaviour of the CCTV operators and patrol guards. When dealing with these incidents the security officers are aware that 'when things go wrong security will get the blame':

Incident no. 49
The operations manager contacts the control room on the radio link and says to Alan (CCTV operator): 'There's some contract workers on site. Who are they? No one knows who they are'. Gavin, the other operator in the control room, says out aloud, 'here we go security will get the blame again because they haven't got a work permit'. He then turns to Alan and says, 'you know what a security guard needs to be don't you'. 'What', Alan replies. 'He needs to be a hybrid', Gavin says. 'Part fly and part octopus. A fly because they've got more than one pair of eyes, and an octopus so you've got more than one pair of hands. The main thing though would be to have eyes in the back of your head 'cause you get stabbed in the back so many times'.

People behaving in a way that suggests to the security officers that they are under the influence of alcohol or other drugs also receive a high priority. The incident described below, for example, triggers a quick response from Gavin who quickly finds the suspects on camera and uses six cameras to monitor the behaviour of the suspect:

Incident no. 50
At 15.46 a patrol guard (Karen) calls the control room to inform the operatives that there are two drunken males in the centre heading down the escalator. Gavin finds them on camera almost immediately and watches Karen who is asking the men to leave the centre. Alan presses the record button under the desk with his knee as the suspects walk towards the camera. Gavin uses six cameras to follow the suspects out towards the West Arcade and Alan asks another patrol guard to watch the East doors. A couple of minutes

later Karen calls the control room and asks the operatives to inform Black Street that two drunken males are heading that way and that they're accompanied by two females. Alan picks up the radio for the CCRL and informs a member of their security team that the suspects are heading towards their store. The store detective calls Alan back for a description of the second male. Alan asks one of the patrol guards for a description of the second male and is told that the suspects are now heading in a different direction. Alan picks up the radio for the CCRL and passes this information onto the store detective who thanks Alan and can be heard on the CCRL passing the suspects on to another store.

In the above incident the suspects' actions are recorded on the dedicated tape machine (which records the images in 'real time' rather than in time-lapse mode) and an extra guard is immediately deployed to the scene. The suspects are also passed on to a neighbouring high-street retailer on the city centre radio link (CCRL). The reason for pressing the record button, according to Gavin, is because suspects under the influence of alcohol or drugs are believed to be dangerous and capable of a violent response. This means that it is important that their behaviour is tape recorded to provide evidence of such an attack.

While incidents involving intoxicated people may receive high priority from the security guards because of their potential to cause 'on-the-job' trouble, it does not necessarily follow that other institutions (i.e. the police) will treat such incidents with the same urgency, as the following incident at Housing Estate Mall demonstrates:

Incident no. 51
Kevin arrives in the control room and says, 'There's an "alchy" down there with two black eyes. He's just opened a bottle of sherry and I said to him, "you're not drinking that in here". So he said, "you're just picking on me cos I've got two black eyes". I said, "if you open it I'll give you a three-month ban", and he said, "I don't come in here anyway". Then he shook hands and went to kiss me hand and I said, "fuck off" '. Dawn says, 'Did you put antiseptic gloves on and dip them in a bucket of bleach?' Kevin says, 'in the end he just walked off singing "ooh ah Cantona" '...

At 13.16 a patrol guard contacts the control room on the SCRL to inform Dawn that 'there is someone grabbing people at the market entrance'. Dawn puts a camera on the market entrance. She sees the suspect talking to two patrol guards, Steve and Barry, and immediately presses the real-time button on the wall in front of the control desk which means that the images displayed on all the monitors are now being recorded in real time rather than time-lapse. On the SCRL Steve says, 'It's the kid with two shiners that Kevin had spoken to earlier on'. Steve, Barry and the suspect then walk down the side of the market out of view of the camera. Steve contacts Dawn on the SCRL to let her know that Shiners has passed out. At this point Kevin leaves the control room and heads down towards the market. Dawn puts an external camera at the back of the market on to the working monitor and searches for the suspect. She picks the suspect up on camera and sees him square up to Kevin. There is slight scuffle between Shiners and Kevin. Shiners, who is far too drunk to fight, falls down on the floor outside the market. When Shiners falls on the floor Kevin picks up his microphone and says, 'Dawn get hold of the police will you he's doing my head in'. Dawn rings the police at 13.24 and as she does Shiners starts to square up to Kevin once more. Dawn presses the real-time button again as Shiners stands talking to Kevin, Steve and Barry ...

The three guards walk away from Shiners who is sat in the middle of the loading bay outside the market. After a few minutes has passed Kevin contacts Dawn on the SCRL to ask her what's happening with the police. Dawn says, 'I'm on hold at the minute'. Shiners stands back up and is stood swaying at the back of the market. Dawn gets through to the police and says: 'Hello this is Housing Estate Mall, we've got a D and D causing havoc. The guards are trying to get rid of him but he won't have it'. At 13.28 Dawn contacts Kevin on the SCRL and says, 'The police are on route'. Dawn turns to me and says: 'The police will be hanging on in the hope that he's cleared off before they get here. It's the same with "domestics", they leave it for ten minutes before they set off'...

At 13.37 Steve arrives in the control room to take over from Dawn (who was supposed to finish at 13.00) at the control desk. Steve sits at the control desk and starts to monitor the incident ... Kevin picks up his microphone and on the SCRL says: 'Steve, what's the score on the Babylon?' Steve replies, 'You know what they're like on these'. Steve asks me what time the police were called (13.24) and I say that I'm not sure of the exact time ...

At 13.50 Steve calls the police again. While Steve is talking to the police he uses the control panel to follow Kevin who is attempting to lead the suspect by the arm away from the shopping centre. As Steve is talking on the phone he sees on the monitor that a police car has arrived on the scene (13.52) and says to the person on the phone,

'It's okay they're here now' ... A police van arrives on the scene at 14.02 and three police officers pick the suspect up and put him in the back of the van. Steve pans across the back of the market to look at the small crowd that have gathered to watch the events. The police van drives away with the suspect at 14.04. A couple of minutes later Kevin arrives back in the control room and tells us that the suspect has been charged with D and I (drunk and incapable). Kevin says, 'All he kept saying was "sound as a pound. ALL RIGHT!"' '

In the incident described above the security guards wanted a quick resolution. The suspect was not only drunk, he was grabbing other shoppers as they walked past him and had attempted to assault a guard. Also, three security guards were required to deal with the incident which meant that there were no security officers patrolling the malls for the duration of the incident. The police, however, were in no hurry to deal with the incident and took 36 minutes to arrive on the scene. Once again, therefore, our attention is drawn to how the human mediation of technological systems places limits on the disciplinary potential of CCTV surveillance systems. As we saw earlier (in the methadone incident, for instance), shopping mall CCTV surveillance systems are becoming integrated with police deployment practice which extends the exclusionary potential of these systems. However, as the incident above illustrates, the level of integration with police deployment practice depends upon how different social actors perceive the importance of particular types of incident and how this perception is filtered through a different 'organisational reading' of the situation.

Watching the watchers

As Ericson and Haggerty (1997: 35) have shown, the introduction of surveillance cameras and other electronic communications systems which police officers use to conduct surveillance of others are increasingly used to monitor the behaviour of police officers themselves. For instance, police cars are equipped with video cameras and computer terminals, while police buildings are equipped with access cards, surveillance cameras and computers to monitor police officer activity. These developments are also found in the 'wired mall', where electronic communications systems have made the actions of the security officer highly visible to the management:

Incident no. 52
At 17.03 the security manager sits down in front of the monitors, with John who has returned from his break. As the images from the

cameras flick over on the screens he sees one of the patrol guards standing outside a shop. The SM watches the guard for a minute and then picks up the microphone for the SCRL: 'Control to CCM 9. Is that Velcro on your feet?' The guard moves on and the SM turns to John and says, 'He's been there for half an hour'.

Incident no. 53

At 16.30 the security manager arrives back at the control room with Darren (a supervisor) after hearing an exchange on the shopping centre radio link between Jim, the CCTV operator in the control room, and a patrol guard. Darren says to Jim: 'You need to be a bit quicker on your Shop Alert there Jim'. The security manager joins in: 'Yes, you were a bit hesitant in between contacting the guard and deploying him. It might not have seemed like it but there was a long pause on the radio. You've gotta be short, sharp and shit hot'.

Incident no. 54

At this point the Shop Alert alarm sounds in the control room triggering an urgent response from Carl. The shop unit 'under attack' is highlighted and is flashing on and off on the computer screen. Carl attempts to fix a camera on the unit while Darren quickly deploys two guards to the scene, one to investigate and one to back him/her up. A few seconds later all the activity stops and Carl tells me that 'It was only a test by the operations manager to test the response time of the patrol guards'.

Thus, in the 'high visibility' conditions of the 'wired' mall the security guard never knows whether he or she is being watched (on camera) by the management, listened to (on the radio network) by the management, or tested (on computerised panic alarms) by the management. In the following incident the management use the cameras, the radio link and the Shop Alert system to monitor the performance of the security officers:

Incident no. 55

At 14.39 the Shop Alert alarm goes off and Darren moves quickly across to the computer screen. On the screen the unit under attack is highlighted and a 'personal attack' message is displayed at the bottom of the screen. Darren has to take this information in very quickly and at the same time pick up the shopping centre radio link (SCRL) microphone and deploy the correct guards (i.e. those nearest to the unit under attack) to the shop. On this occasion Darren hesitates slightly and calls the guard on the main deck to go to G29 (shop); quickly changing his mind he asks the patrol guard on the West Arcade to make his way there instead and asks another patrol guard to back him up. The security manager returns to the control room to watch the incident on the TV screens and in the confusion one of the patrol guards can be seen on camera running in the wrong direction. The SM turns away and walks to the back of the control room and says: 'Get Steve [patrol guard] down here, he was running to the wrong level'. A patrol guard calls Darren on the SCRL to inform him that the Shop Alert was only a test by the centre manager who is in the unit showing a prospective tenant around the premises. After the incident has finished Darren goes to the back of the control room and says to the security manager: 'I think I might of made a bit of a mistake there actually. I said control to Main Deck when I meant control to West Arcade'.

As we have already seen, because the actions of security officers are highly visible to the management, incidents which the latter regard as particularly important receive a high priority from the security officers. For instance, in a shopping mall some of the most serious incidents, from the management's perspective, are those involving health and safety issues (e.g. lift breakdowns, fire alarms, unauthorised contract workers on site, etc.) which disrupt consumption and, more importantly, can lead to 'comeback' in the shape of complaints or insurance claims:

Incident no. 56
The operations manager enters the control room to inquire about the morning's fire alarm. Darren is getting it in the neck from the operations manager who asks him a number of questions without letting him reply: 'Why was I not informed immediately about the morning's events? Did the escalators stop? Did the shutters open? Why didn't the centre alarms go off? The shutters opened which means we had soaking wet floors out there and customers slipping everywhere costing us a fortune in insurance'. Darren replies, 'Well, to tell you the truth, Dan [OM], we were a bit bewildered by it all, we've never had the alarms do that before'. The operations manager turns his attention to Alan, the supervisor who was on duty: 'Alan, these problems can be avoided. If we control what's going on these problems can be avoided. All we need is a bit of planning. And its up to you to direct the guards to exactly where you want them'. The operations manager leaves the control room and Darren is fuming: 'That guy is full of shit. He makes us look about *that* fucking big.

Don't you think so Alan?' 'Water off a ducks back mate', Alan replies.

Incident no. 57
The operations manager (OM) arrives in the control room looking agitated and wanting a word with Ian. He says that a few months ago a plaster was taken from one of the first aid boxes by the maintenance manager and that the incident was not documented by the operatives. The OM says that 'an insurance claim has gone in and we don't know anything about it because it's not been documented. If anyone comes in here', the OM says, 'including me, and says they want a plaster, then you document it'.

The uncertainty generated by the possibility of 'comeback' when things go wrong is, of course, heightened by the surveillance infrastructure which makes their actions when dealing with incidents highly visible to the management. However, as the following extract from the fieldnotes shows, security officers are not passive recipients of the managerial gaze:

Incident no. 58
At 09.50 Sam, a patrol guard, arrives in the control room to relieve Tony who has gone for a break. Sam looks at the monitors and says to me, 'that's the good thing about coming in here, you can see where all the blind spots are for when you want to stop and talk'.

The CCTV operators also have some degree of choice in shaping the application of the surveillance infrastructure which allows them to turn the tables on the shopping mall management whose behaviour is also highly visible to the security officers:

Incident no. 59
At dinnertime the operations manager arrives in the control room and says to the security manager: 'Come on. I'm taking you for lunch. We're going to a fish restaurant' … Gavin and Alan, the two CCTV operators on duty, turn the radio up and take it easy while the operations manager and the security manager are off the site. At 12.40 Gavin uses eight cameras to try and find out if the security manager is back from his dinner. About five minutes later Gavin and Alan hear the operations manager on the shopping centre radio link which tells them that the security manager must also be back on site because he went for his dinner with the operations manager. Gavin turns the radio down and the two CCTV operators resume

normal duties before the security manager arrives back in the control room.

Incident no. 60
At 13.45 Karen sees one of the managers on an external camera that is fixed on the management access control barrier. The manager is sitting in his car waiting for the barrier to be raised by one of the CCTV operators in the control room. When people are leaving the management car park the drivers side of the vehicle is at the wrong side of the barrier control point which means that they can't reach the intercom button through their window to let the operatives in the control room know that they want the barrier raising. Karen watches the monitor as the driver gets out of his vehicle and walks around the front of his car towards the intercom button on the side of the barrier control point. Just as the man reaches for the intercom button Karen presses the button in the control room to activate the control barrier and shouts, 'Yes, that's the second one I've got today'. The man sees the barrier go up before he has a chance to press the intercom button and walks back round to the driver's side of his car and drives away.

In Incident no. 59, Gavin and Alan decide to take it easy for a while and then use the electronic communications technology to find out when the management are back on site so that they can resume normal working practice. Meanwhile, in Incident no. 60, Karen uses the CCTV system and the intercom system to have a bit of fun with one of the managers in the management car park. Thus, while the surveillance infrastructure allows the management to 'watch the watchers', the security officers also use this technology to carve out 'spaces of resistance'.

Discussion

One of the most important issues raised in this chapter is the use of CCTV for exclusionary purposes. As we have seen, the main preoccupation of the security personnel was the monitoring and exclusion of groups of youths who disrupted the commercial image. More than four out of ten (43 per cent) of teenagers who were deployed against were ejected from the shopping centres, and the influence of age was shown to be compounded by being part of a group. Thus, when a guard was deployed to deal with a group of teenagers, there was a fifty–fifty chance that someone would be ejected. Many of these exclusions were based on what von Hirsch and Shearing (2000) have described as 'profile-based exclusions'. With this type of exclusion 'the idea is to bar from entry certain persons whose characteristics are deemed indicative of a heightened risk of criminal offending. It is not present unacceptable behaviour that is the concern here, but *potential* for future criminal offending' (2000: 88–9). One of the main problems with this form of exclusion, these writers argue, is that 'they bypass the actor's agency' (2000: 89). As they put it, 'the person is being kept out of public or semi-public space, without regard to any choice on his part to engage in harmful or seriously offensive conduct … the person is excluded before he has any chance to show whether he is willing to behave properly' (ibid.: 89).

The formalised exclusion of youth also draws our attention to competing definitions of risk and safety in relation to CCTV systems. Many of those who support the introduction of CCTV surveillance systems have made special reference to how such systems create a safer environment for women and children (see Coleman and Sim, 1996: 17). The managers of City Centre Mall stated that their CCTV system played an important role in creating a safer environment for women and children. The management on this site have also worked closely with the police on a Safe Child scheme which encourages children who become detached from their parents to go to a member of staff in any of the shops displaying the Safe Child sign in their window. However, as we saw earlier, City Centre Mall has also enforced a formalised exclusion policy which aims to keep school children out of the mall during school hours. This policy (which involves close liaison between the shopping mall manager, the CCTV operators, the police and education welfare officers) raises the question of whether school children are being excluded from what could be seen as a relatively safe environment (a busy shopping mall full of other people and patrol guards) to the 'less safe' spaces of public streets.

The exclusion of 'known' offenders raises a number of slightly different issues. One objection, raised by von Hirsch and Shearing (2000), 'relates to the possible unfairness of the procedure for determining that a criminal violation has occurred' (2000: 90). In the absence of detailed dossiers containing the criminal records of suspects who were monitored, information concerning so-called 'known offenders' was shared informally among the security officers. As we saw at City Centre Mall, on some occasions CCTV operators made the decision to deny access to 'known offenders' simply on the basis of what they had heard from other CCTV operators on the city centre radio link. On other occasions, CCTV operators monitored the associates of 'known' offenders. At Housing

Estate Mall, these associates often had their photographs pasted into banning books and 'rogues galleries'. These images were then shown to other CCTV operators and new members of the security team so that they could get to know the 'regulars'. However, these 'banning books' did not always make a clear distinction between 'known' offenders and their associates. This raises the possibility that completely innocent people may be monitored and excluded.

Finally, the exclusion of 'known' offenders and 'known' drug users at Housing Estate Mall raises issues concerning the nature of citizenship in contemporary society. Housing Estate Mall, as we have seen, is relatively isolated from the rest of Northern City which means that many of the local residents have little alternative but to visit the shopping centre for many basic amenities. For instance, the shopping mall contains the only supermarket within walking distance for many of the estate's residents. The shopping mall proprietors also own the surrounding land which includes many basic public services, including a post office, public library, health centre, surgery and probation centre. One obvious question that springs to mind when reflecting on the shopping centre's exclusionary practices is this – how can the excluded obtain access to those services which are delivered on private property from which they are denied access? For instance, if the known heroin addict is likely to be targeted and (as we saw earlier) arrested when visiting the health centre to collect his or her methadone prescription, will he or she abandon the treatment and seek alternative ways of 'feeding the habit'? These are just some of the questions that are becoming important as increasingly many public services are provided on private property where the management have a right to deny access.

Chapter 5

Watching the workers

This chapter tells a story about the introduction of CCTV systems into the workplaces of Northern City. It draws on interviews with the security managers of 7 department stores, 6 major high-street retailers and 16 of the top 20 manufacturing concerns in the area. Further informal interviews and observations were conducted with CCTV operators during visits to several workplace CCTV control rooms. The chapter begins by documenting the use of CCTV to monitor the 'external threat' posed by customers and burglars and other 'outsiders'. It goes on to show how this same technology is increasingly used to target the 'internal threat' posed by the workforce. Here it is shown how the technology is used not just as a means of preventing theft, but increasingly as a general managerial tool. Finally, the chapter concludes with a discussion of some of the theoretical issues raised in the chapter, before going on to discuss some of the unintended consequences that may arise as workers increasingly find themselves under the surveillance gaze.

Managing the threat to profitability: monitoring the external threat

Although it is difficult to put precise figures on the extent of video surveillance in the workplace, it is possible to gain some indication from various business surveys. The annual survey of the business analysts Marketing Strategies for Industry (MSI) revealed the total CCTV market was £115.6 million in 1996 (*CCTV Today*, 1 January 1998: 20). Despite the massive investment in city-centre CCTV systems, public and civil systems still only accounted for 22 per cent of this market with annual sales of £25 million. The remaining 78 per cent of the market was dominated by the retail, commercial and industrial sectors which accounted for 33 per cent (£38 M), 30 per cent (£35 M), and 17 per cent (£17.3 M) respectively. Moreover, Hearnden's (1996) survey of the use of CCTV by small businesses, which included the manufacturing, retail, commercial and transport sectors, found that just over half (51 per cent) of firms had installed CCTV over the last five years. It would appear therefore that workplace surveillance is more extensive than public surveillance and is also growing more rapidly.

The growth of CCTV surveillance in the private sector is partly due to the increased recognition of the extent and impact of business victimisation. One of the most important elements of this growing awareness has been the findings of the surveys of the British Retail Consortium's Retail Crime Surveys which, between 1992 and 1996, have estimated the annual cost of crime for the retail trade to be between one and a half and two billion pounds (Wells and Dryer, 1997). In this context it is hardly surprising that Beck and Willis (1995: 40–41) argue:

> Crime is rapidly becoming one of the most influential factors in retailing. It is a cause of dramatically increasing insurance costs. It creates losses in revenue through lost stock and equipment. Not only does crime increase overheads, it impacts directly on the 'bottom line' of profitability. Retailers are increasingly advised to see their security departments and their strategies less in terms of 'preventing crime' and more in terms of 'protecting profit'.

In all of the retail stores visited the primary purpose of the CCTV system is to act as a deterrent to shoplifting. The cameras are highly visible and are announced by a variety of signs declaring, in one way or another, that the store is under permanent video surveillance. In several of the stores this message was reinforced by large monitors sighted near the entrance displaying live footage from the system to pointedly remind customers that video surveillance was in operation. In addition, the cameras have a major role in the prevention of cheque and credit card fraud which costs retailers over £20 million a year, and the Association of Payment and Clearing Services which underwrites the transactions of a further £165 million (Beck and Willis, 1995: 38). To achieve this, cameras are located to record till transactions so that when, and if, fraud is detected the tapes can be searched to provide a visual identification. Finally, and not inconsequentially, the effect of such systems is to provide a visible deterrent against robbery from the tills and assault more generally. This is especially salient given that the BRCS estimates that over 120,000 retail workers are either assaulted or threatened with physical violence each year.

Not only are the cameras used as a deterrent to customer theft, fraud and assault but also as a means of training staff to recognise the characteristics of shoplifters and to help identify persistent and prolific offenders. The security manager at one retailer, for example, holds monthly security meetings with members of staff where he shows them tapes of shoplifters in action to alert them to 'the body language'. This approach was echoed by the security manager of another high-street retailer who stated:

> We do show staff videos of prolific shoplifters shoplifting. I've got a tape downstairs that … every shoplifter, they are prolific, they're known around the town, they've got several offences against them. So we've got a compilation of shopthefts that we use which amazes the staff when they watch it. Because they don't realise it goes on the shopfloor.

In some stores this is taken a stage further and the staff are actively encouraged to view tapes and images (i.e. photographs) to get to know the shoplifters who are currently active in their stores. One security manager, for example, explained how his company now operates a Retail Crimes Operation (RCO) whereby photographic information is exchanged between the security personnel throughout the country. A news sheet is sent out once a week to all the company's stores listing offenders who are known to be currently active. The sheet includes mug shots captured from the CCTV footage and textual descriptions of locations, modus operandi, etc. The security manager gives the following example of how this works in practice:

> For instance, just before Christmas we had a shoplifter, she was apprehended here for I think it was theft of about £190. She's from down South but she was staying in a caravan park nearby … Following a Section 18 a search on this caravan that she was staying in found receipts from eighteen [of our] stores all over the country. So what we do we have a photographic facility in the control room were we can take any amount of stills from the video. We send these to head office to the collators. They will monitor to see if these people appear in other stores and then they will distribute photographs or reports … to every store.

Indeed the CCTV control room of this store is covered wall to wall with a rogues gallery which includes the suspect's name (if the security staff have a name), address, postcode and known associates. The security manager explained:

> I did an 'open-day' and everybody is like plastered on the wall. We had an open ... well an 'open month' actually, inviting all the staff to come in and view the photographs 'cause obviously it's beneficial if they do see these faces ... It gives us more pairs of eyes on the shop-floor and they can contact security if they recognise anybody ... We have noticed with them being plastered on the wall, we are getting familiar with the faces whereas in a book they're looked at and then forgotten really. It's surprising how many people do spot them in other stores.

The attempt to make shop staff more vigilant and aware of 'known' persons and 'shoplifters' in their stores is also being practised by other stores. In a local chain of 22 medium-sized convenience stores, the CCTV system involves round the clock recording but no permanent monitoring. Only if an incident occurs are the tapes reviewed and then sent to head office where hard-copy printouts can be made. Photographs of known shoplifters are distributed to all the other stores to be pinned on the staff notice boards, frequently with the message: 'This person is not allowed in our stores'.

Unlike the department store or high-street retailers, the industrial workplace does not want to encourage public access to their sites – thus, rather than having multiple exits and entrances, the sites are completely fenced off and all traffic is channelled into one or two access points. On 9 of the 11 sites, the CCTV control room is situated at the entrance to the site which is usually just beyond an access control barrier operated by the security officers in the control room. At every site visitors must report to the control room and sign a visitors book. The control rooms on nine of the sites are monitored on a continuous basis by private security officials, i.e. 24 hours a day, 365 days a year. In the other two sites one has a CCTV monitor placed in the management office which is monitored by the management periodically, and on the other site a private security guard monitors the images at night time when the factory is closed. A typical factory has around ten cameras including a combination of fully functional and fixed cameras. These cameras are usually positioned to monitor the entrances, exits, perimeter fencing, car parks, bike sheds, contractor loading bays and factory floor.

One of the common themes to emerge from all the interviews at the industrial workplace was the use of CCTV systems to monitor the 'external threat' of intruders coming onto the site and for maintaining perimeter security. Unlike the retail sector this threat is not posed by customers but by burglars, dishonest contractors and unwanted intruders. For instance, at one engineering firm, which has a number of defence-related contracts, the security manager explained that the CCTV system had been used most recently to monitor outside contractors (e.g. builders, roof workers) suspected of theft from the premises, peace camps and vigils outside the site, and people tampering with cars in the staff car park. For most companies, CCTV was an integral part of the perimeter security arrangement, often linked to other alarm systems such as motion or infrared detectors, and could be used to quickly visually scan the scene of any alarm.

Managing the threat to profitability: monitoring the internal threat

In the retail sector the primary justification for the installation and expansion of CCTV systems has been the external threat posed by shop-lifters, fraudsters and violent customers. Once such technology is in place it inevitably means that, by default, workers also come under the cameras' gaze. However, default had turned to design in five of the seven department stores and the CCTV systems were explicitly used to monitor staff for the purposes of preventing staff theft in three locations: at the tills, in the cash office and in the loading bays. As one security manager described:

> There's one [a camera] in the stock room, one in the store counting office where they do all the cashing-up, all the others are on the shopfloor or the stairways. The one in the cash office is to stop staff theft. Because there's thousands of pounds in there all on the table where they count it up. In some stores they've had money go missing so it's like a deterrent.

Although in all five stores the main purpose of having CCTV cameras in the cash office is to act as a deterrent against staff theft, as several security managers explained, it also provided a measure of security for the staff if there was an attempted robbery. The cameras are also used to monitor the cleaning staff and those working on the loading bays:

> We look for people sneaking in, drivers dropping one item and taking one back, staff coming onto the loading bay who shouldn't be

there, because they're not supposed to come on here unless they have specific business there, looking for collusions, things like that … Collusion's between drivers and our guys.

(Security manager, department store)

My predecessor had someone who was lifting things out of the stock room, pinching things, and they video'd them actually taking it out the stock room. And we do company searches so later on they did a search and they had the goods on them. He was dismissed and I think the police were called as well.

(Security manager, high-street retailer)

Sometimes I come in early to watch the cleaning staff, to make sure they're not taking anything off the shelves, and to do a couple of searches.

(Security manager, high-street retailer)

The use of CCTV to monitor shop staff in the retail sector, however, is primarily reserved for those working on the tills. All the department stores have CCTV cameras located on the shopfloor and these are perfectly placed to monitor till procedures. This was demonstrated on several occasions and showed that the operators had the ability to zoom in with such clarity that a customer's signature could clearly be read on the video monitor. In many of the retail stores the tills are now linked to stock control computers in an electronic point of sale (EPOS) system. This enables management to look at the electronically recorded takings from each till and compare it with the actual cash taken. If there are any discrepancies, since each member of staff has to individually log into the system before ringing in a transaction, mistakes can be isolated to an individual or, if more than one person has been using the till, a group of individuals. As one manager explained, at the press of a button he could now get a print out of all the expected and actual takings of each till and could see that

… this till took £72,900 in takings and was £20.00 down, that's not a lot, that's 0.03 per cent of takings. But look at that one that's 0.16 per cent down so that's worth investigating … [we] would start in the Accounting Office where they would go through the readings and see if a cheque has not gone through properly or something like that. Then if they don't find anything they might ask me to go through it, and usually it's human error, you know, they've given change for twenty pound instead of a tenner or something. But then if you get an ongoing problem week in week out then you know something might be up. For example, a few months ago we had a kid upstairs on electric's who had an unusual number of 'price overrides' [where an item is bar-coded through the till but no money is taken, usually on prescriptions] so we decided to watch him on camera. It turns out that members of his family were coming in and he was putting kettles through at thirty quid a time and not charging for them. We caught him on camera and he received an instant dismissal.

Several retail security managers revealed that they also use covert (i.e. hidden) cameras to monitor shop staff working on the tills. The security controller of a chain of convenience stores, for example, explained that his company has a team of mobile store detectives who travel from store to store to carry out various covert operations on behalf of the security controller. The security controller says:

> ... we also have other systems where we'll actually go and get ourselves in a room in a store and monitor. Wire up various covert cameras and monitor from within the store. I mean I've got a video tape with a number of incidents on that we've compiled which basically shows various thefts taking place where staff have stolen money out of the tills, given goods away without taking payment for them etc. So, you know, we do have a number of colour cameras for that particular function as well. I think, you know, it's worthwhile spending a bit extra on colour cameras. But we've got about, at any one time we could have covert camera systems in five or six of our stores if we wish to, 'cause we have that many cameras at our disposal ... The staff don't know about it. It's for detection purposes.

Two other retail security managers revealed that they also use covert cameras to monitor shop staff suspected of internal theft. One stated that he used a covert camera which he moves around the store when the need arises. This covert camera is used to monitor shop staff suspected of theft and also to cover various blind spots that the overt system can't reach. Another security manager reported that he had used a covert camera on the loading bay where a night cleaner was caught on camera stealing chocolates. This member of staff received an instant dismissal.

In the industrial workplace while the systems play a central role in maintaining perimeter security and excluding the undesirable, the presence of cameras on the shopfloor is, unlike in the retail sector, unambiguously targeted at the worker. On other sites, with less sophisticated CCTV systems, the cameras are used by the management mainly as a deterrent. The manager of a food processing factory, for example, described how he installed four internal cameras to reduce 'shrinkage'. The cameras are all fixed and the images are not monitored on a permanent basis in a CCTV control room. There is a monitor in the production director's office and he monitors the images periodically. The manager of the factory believes that the main function of the CCTV system is to deter theft as he explained:

> We had a little bit of stealing going on in the stores area and we've just swung a camera around to take that area in. Again it's prevention more than anything else, we tell them what we're doing and er ... because all right, you want to catch the beggar that's doing it, but primarily you want to stop people from doing it. I find that cameras are more of a deterrent than anything else. I mean if you're catching people stealing that's not the course of the exercise. The course of the exercise is to stop people from doing it in the first place.

He also makes sure that the staff know they are being watched in order to maximise the deterrent effect of the CCTV system:

> Well, they know they're on film. We brought every member of staff upstairs and showed them what we could see and what was being recorded, because every camera point is being recorded on a separate film you see. We make a big fuss about making sure that they know the cameras are there. To some extent we have retrained people, or trained people to sort of put it in their mind that these cameras are there, they're under surveillance.

However, if the cameras do not deter the staff then disciplinary intervention can be used, as the following example shows in a case where a worker was seen on camera in an 'unauthorised area':

> Well, generally, when the tapes run through or if it's spotted live then the person's brought to book with it. They're brought upstairs and asked why they were there, and if they deny it they can't 'cause we've got it on tape. And that compounds it 'cause they've lied you see. And they'll get a warning, it'll go down as a disciplinary ruling.

In the food processing plant it was the management themselves that monitored the images displayed by the CCTV system or who reviewed tapes retrospectively after an incident had occurred. However, on the other ten industrial sites the CCTV systems are monitored by private security officials rather than the management themselves. This means management must rely on the security personnel for any information concerning internal theft and other misdemeanours. A CCTV operative employed by a frozen foods company explained how, if he spotted anything, he would report the incident to the management who would then deal with it:

> ... if somebody's actually spotted on site and we think they're a worker all we've actually got to do is get the managers of each factory [there are three factories on the site] together and they'd be able to tell us who it is. The only one we've had is with the No Smoking Policy that we've got on site. We actually spotted some people round the back there [the SM zooms in to a corner at the back of a building] smoking at night time. I mean the cameras are light sensitive so when you light a match or take a draw of a cigarette it actually lights up like a torch. And we actually caught him on the camera ... we informed the management and the next morning they came and reviewed the tape. There was only one fork lift driver who was round there that particular night and they showed him the tape and sacked him.

Internal theft was a particular problem for one security manager employed by a local manufacturer. The cameras on this site were introduced only eight months ago. Three of the cameras monitor the two main entrance points and the staff car park. The other seven cameras are all situated inside the factory to cover 'vulnerable areas' and were introduced to reduce 'shrinkage', as he explained:

> People have broken into caravans to steal microwaves. We've had people walking through the main gate with heavy bags. A lot of drills have gone missing. We've even had people riding off on bikes with big carpets under their arms ... in terms of preventing people from stealing, the law doesn't always back you up ... you can search vehicles and bags but not the person. We were losing stuff in the curtain store and the cameras put a stop to that. But that lasted about two weeks. Now they wait until the curtains are out of the store room and then they steal them. People are more dubious though, they know certain areas are covered and it has stopped the theft of big stuff like carpets. But in factory life they [the workers] know

everything that's going on before you do ... if the cameras are there [nods towards an imaginary camera] we'll stand here.

On two of the industrial sites the security managers acknowledged the use of covert cameras to monitor workers suspected of theft. On one site the use of covert surveillance was prompted by a spate of office thefts in the general office block. The security manager installed several dummy cameras in easily identifiable places in the corridors of the block, while simultaneously installing eight 'pin-prick lens' cameras in strategic places around the building:

> When we arrive at the security manager's office he opens a wardrobe to reveal the hidden monitor and multiplexer which has the capacity for 16 cameras overall. Steve [his deputy] splits the screen into eight pictures and shows me how the system enables them 'to track staff throughout the entire building, covering all the corridors and all floors'. The security manager says, 'the system cost two and a half thousand pounds, but was well worth it. We didn't catch the rogue thief [who had been stealing staff property] but the stealing has stopped'. Steve and the security manager talk enthusiastically about some of the CCTV equipment in the office. They show me their favourite pinprick cameras, saying things like, 'this one's the best ... it can pick out a fly on the wall'. When we leave the security manager's office he tells me that he has also had trouble in the general office block with the 'vending machine thief'. Apparently someone had been emptying the vending machines of goods. This member of staff was caught on film when the security manager decided to place covert cameras directly above the vending machines. On our way out of his office he nods towards the wood panelling on the ceiling directly above a vending machine which has a tiny hole where the pinhole camera had been placed.

On another site the security manager had recently invested in some highly sophisticated covert monitoring equipment to catch a night worker suspected of stealing goods from the factory:

> The security manager takes me to his personal office where he has a 'digital motion detector' system set up on his desk. This system runs on a computer and is linked to an adjacent building by microwave. He explains how it works by drawing a white-shaped rectangle on the screen the same size as the exit door on the building opposite his

office. The member of staff suspected of stealing from this building would have to leave via this exit. The security manager says that when someone walks out of this door it will trigger an audible alarm on the monitor and the image will be recorded. This works, he says, by picking out light change and colour change. If he misses the alarm it doesn't matter because an 'alarm log' stores all the images which he can view at a later date. He goes on to show me the last six alarm calls from the previous evening which he reviewed earlier that morning.

Improving worker performance

Store managers involved in some sites volunteered information about CCTV being used initially to target staff suspected of dishonesty, but then unexpectedly proving to be more valuable in checking whether staff were meeting company requirements, for example compliance with till procedures or rules relating to refunds and exchanges. The use of CCTV as a more general managerial tool in the retail sector was mentioned by five of the security managers interviewed. One security manager explained how a combination of declining resources and the need to become cost-effective meant that surveillance cameras were increasingly being used to monitor areas which were formerly the responsibility of shopfloor supervisors. In this sense, it could be argued that the security manager, armed with information technology (i.e. surveillance cameras and computerised tills), is being used as a more cost-effective supervisory agent following the 'delayering' of middle management.

In one store the company had produced a document which is distributed to all the security managers and store managers in the country. This protocol document is designed to enable the management to gain maximum benefit from the CCTV system which, it states, 'should be thought of as a valuable management tool, not just as a means of deterring and identifying shoplifters or protecting staff and customers'. The document lists the following uses of CCTV as a management tool:

- When contractors are in the store ensure a camera is concentrated on areas of the store they are working in or the main entrance/exit point in the store.

- On a Supervisor's day off, it may be relevant to record that particular area of the store.

- Recording work groups with consistent poor till out-turns will aid identification of poor procedures and therefore training needs required.

- Recording store opening/closing/deliveries/cashing up procedures may highlight opportunities for improvement.

In two of the department stores the management are trained to use the cameras and it would normally be the management themselves who would monitor the staff to ensure they were complying with company procedure. In one store the security manager would sit in the control room himself and then report to the store manager:

> We do operate a system where I watch the cameras. In the CCTV operative's breaks I'll watch the cameras and we look for various things, customer service, till operations, till procedures, everything you can think of really that you can't stand on the shopfloor and watch. I suppose it's a bit of an 'eye spy' really.

The security managers in three other stores said that the CCTV system was particularly useful for what they described as 'customer service':

> Yes, with customer service it's just that the staff are being polite, friendly and are smiling. It's not really a security point of view but it's something that we do exploit the CCTV system for. It's just from a commercial point of view really. Fitting rooms as well, just check the fitting room queues aren't getting too big. Correct procedures again in fitting rooms where the items are counted as they're going in, they're counted as they're going out, you know. It's not always practised that.
>
> (Security manager, high-street retailer)

> A lot of stores also use it like a 'management aid' 'cause erm ... we do a thing here called *Selling The [...] Experience*, it's all about customer care and everything. It's how you are with your customer. You know, your eye contact and all things like that. And I know in some stores they watch a member of staff, how they are on the counter and with the customer and things.
>
> (Security manager, high-street retailer)

As well as watching the body language of the shop staff to make sure they are 'polite' and 'friendly' with customers, the cameras can also be used to monitor the productivity of the shop worker. For example, the management may decide to watch a member of staff for a period of time to see if they are attending to customers or are standing around and talking to their friends:

> ...this system is also used as a management tool. There's a very big emphasis, obviously because of declining resources and personnel, placing the key personnel within different departments, and the personnel function would use this [CCTV] to see if people are adhering to that. I mean, you know, people standing together and not noticing customers and things like that. They might use it for that sort of thing as well.
>
> (Security manager, department store)

> We have like consultants and they're supposed to approach customers to see if they need help. Management can watch them and make sure they are actually approaching people and saying: 'Do you want any help with the word processors?' They're worth a lot of money if you get a good sale on them.
>
> (Security manager, high-street retailer)

In another store the management would actually monitor how many times a shop worker stopped customers to ask them if they were interested in a particular product, as the security manager explained:

> I mean, they don't do it like all the time, but they can say: 'Oh we'll watch so and so for an hour, see how many people she approaches in an hour, or see if she stands talking to her friend', things like that.

In the industrial workplace security managers described how, in addition to the prevention of shrinkage, the CCTV systems were used to monitor compliance with health and safety regulations, time-keeping, access restriction, unauthorised breaks and so on. One of the key themes in the sociological literature of the industrial workplace has been how workers have managed to limit the intensity of work by developing various control strategies for avoiding supervision (Molstad, 1988). However, the surveillance camera allows the management to penetrate some of these spaces of resistance which have been carved out by the industrial worker. On some sites, for example, the monitoring of time-keeping has been passed on to the security personnel, as the security manager on one site explained:

My job is to supervise the site and men ... I'm responsible for people entering and leaving the site. If we see anyone walking through either of the main gates we take their name, clock number, department and the reason they're going off the site. We then log this information and hand it to wages and the managing director. We sometimes get workers clocking-on but not clocking-off ... we get them nipping over the fence 15 minutes early to the sandwich shop, things like that.

(Security manager, caravan manufacturer)

The CCTV camera not only heightens the visibility of working practices on the industrial site, it also increases the accountability for mistakes made on the job. For instance, one security manager described how the surveillance cameras allow him to:

... monitor the loading bays. Loading and unloading, it's amazing what you can pick up. Exactly who's doing what with fork lifts and the like ... are people damaging goods going on to the lorries? Are they damaging trailers? Are they driving forklifts as they should be? We've picked up bad driving practices but they were dealt with. It was brought to my attention that something had gone on and I was then able to go back to the tape and find it on the tape and challenge the person concerned with it. So I say to them 'what have you been doing?' And they say, 'I never did that'. So I say, 'oh yes you did, look'.

(Security manager, pharmaceuticals factory)

Discussion

In the enclosed and controlled setting of the workplace CCTV can easily become an instrument of disciplinary power exercised through the architecture of the panopticon, allowing management to see everything without ever being seen themselves. As we have seen, this enables a honing in on the minutiae of shopfloor workers' presentation of self. In the name of 'customer service' employees' gestures, facial expressions and body language all become subject to the disciplinary gaze. The power of the gaze not only enables management to intervene on the basis of evidence from the cameras, but also, and more effectively, the employee becomes the 'bearer of their own surveillance'. The anticipatory conformity that this induces in employees who recognise that they are always potentially under surveillance presents management with an extremely powerful managerial tool (see Lyon, 1994: 133).

The use of visual surveillance systems in the workplace also disrupts the tacit assumptions governing the exploitation and distribution of what Mars and Nichod (1981) term the 'hidden rewards' of work. In many industries and retail concerns employee theft is a widespread and commonplace activity which has a long historical pedigree and has become embedded in a range of informal organisational structures and practices (see Ditton, 1977; Mars, 1974). These studies have also shown that, within limits, fiddling, including employee theft, is tolerated, accepted and even encouraged by management and that, rather than seeing it as theft, it is regarded as a legitimate perk. The nature of these workplace fiddles is that they are largely hidden from view. Even so they are not completely invisible, but tolerated. Management, by 'turning a blind eye' or 'looking the other way' can facilitate tacit acceptance and absolve themselves from the disruption that would ensue from moral condemnation. The introduction of CCTV systems, however, means that the 'visibility' of a whole range of working practices is increased and with the video recorder, the potential is available for public replay. In this situation turning a blind eye becomes more problematic. The lexical and moral constructions which label certain practices as 'fiddles' and 'perks' find that such ambiguity is hard to maintain when the evidence of workers helping themselves to the stock is replayed for all to see. Since such subterranean practices cannot be defended publicly as 'just a fiddle' they are more likely to become recast as unequivocal cases of 'theft'.

However, the way CCTV systems operate in the workplace is, like any other system, shaped by the people responsible for operating the cameras. Thus, while CCTV systems may be installed for the purpose of general managerial control, whether or not it is used in this capacity depends to some extent on how the introduction of this technology fits in with existing social practices and informal rule systems in the workplace. For example, on 10 of the 11 industrial sites the management do not observe the workforce themselves. This means that they must rely on the security personnel to inform them of any worker malpractice. But the security personnel are not always willing to do this, as one CCTV operator explained:

'We've had workers lifting stuff over that fence'. He then flicks over to a camera that is monitoring one of the offices and says: 'Stuff has gone missing from the offices here as well'. He tells me that he would never report any of these activities to the management. His reluctance to do so is partly to do with the fact that he identifies with the workers rather than the management, and partly to do with the fact that he is also involved in the workplace 'fiddle', as he explains: 'There's no way I'm gonna grass on anyone. If I do my job it would cause a lot of bad feeling when it got back to the staff ... anyway perks are part of the job. If I go to someone and say "have you got a washer for me tap?", they'll say to me, "here, have a new tap" '.

The CCTV operator went on to tell me about a management purge on unauthorised parking. This was another issue on which he sided with the workers rather than the management:

It's the same as when the management asked us to put parking stickers on the workers' cars because of unauthorised parking on the site. It caused a bad feeling between meself and the lads. If someone comes off the site with a toilet and I stop and search them and they say, 'I've got a gate pass', I say, 'fair enough'. One or two of the workers are funny with security, but the majority are all right. If they treat us all right we treat them the same.

There is, therefore, no simple relationship between the imposition of CCTV surveillance and the eradication of workplace deviance. Surveillance systems are mediated by social actors who bring with them their own values and beliefs and these may be more in tune with the occupational culture of the shopfloor than with the management. Given the low status and pay of security guards and their likely class back-grounds, it is hardly surprising that they may not identify their interests as in line with management. Thus where management delegates sur-veillance to others, there is no guarantee that the systems will be used as intended and through tacit acceptance, the security guards will 'turn a blind eye' or more collusively ensure that the cameras are positioned so as not to capture specific events. The inability of technological systems to penetrate existing social practices was found during one visit to a large pharmaceuticals factory, as the following extract from the fieldnotes illustrates:

When I arrived at the control room various members of the security team were present and some of them chipped in with a number of 'CCTV stories'. One of the CCTV operatives zoomed in on the local public house and said: 'We've had some fun outside there on Saturday nights'. He went on to describe how on one occasion a night-shift worker had unwittingly set off an audible alarm in the control room when he crossed an infrared beam while 'nipping over the wall for a pint and a game of snooker in the local'. This was regarded as a good laugh by the security team. The security guard who told me the story turned to the security manager and said, 'We din't report him though, did we, gaffer'. The security manager smiled and shook his head.

Finally, as Beck and Willis (1995: 193) have pointed out, if CCTV is used as a general managerial tool rather than for its stated purposes of monitoring customer and staff theft, then 'the high level of staff confidence in CCTV could evaporate if they felt they were being misled in this way'. This question of the legitimacy of surveillance is central and is raised even more starkly by the increasing use of covert cameras with all the implications of invasions of privacy, the use of unethical and deceptive practices, and breaches of trust. If such activities become public, they may lead to a backlash, calling into question the right of management to place their workforce under such intensive and omnipresent surveillance. In which case we may not be surprised if CCTV becomes the cause of crime rather than its cure as employees sabotage the surveillance systems. This has already happened at two workplaces. The security manager at one manufacturer, for example, described how some of the CCTV fuse boxes had been 'tripped out in suspicious circumstances'. The other act was less subtle, as a CCTV operative in a food-processing factory explained:

We did try putting internal cameras in one of the tea bars, but it was only there for about 14 hours and somebody nicked it ... there was quite a lot of thefts and damage to the tea machines and sandwich machines. People putting their hands in and moving the stuff across so they could get an extra sandwich and then breaking into the machine itself. So we had a camera on the wall overlooking the vending machines. Obviously they didn't like it being in there so they took it. The cabling is still there if we need to use it again.

Chapter 6

Watching the tenants

Over the last decade much academic attention has focused on the emergence of a new division in society between the 'information rich' and the 'information poor'. Castells, for example, has written about the 'dual city' whereby social polarisation consists of 'the cosmopolitanism of the elite, living on a daily connection to the whole world' standing in contrast 'to the tribalism of local communities, retrenched in their spaces' (1989: 30). However, as McGrail (1998) has shown, in his study of high-rise housing schemes in Scotland, the 'information revolution' has not by-passed these so-called 'places of despair', which increasingly are being surrounded by high-tech equipment, including fibre-optic cables, CCTV surveillance systems and electronic sensing equipment. McGrail argues 'that although the specific forms new technologies take in these areas do differ from wealthier districts (in terms of who owns the technology and how it is utilised), they are nonetheless an essential part of the information revolution' (1998: 1).

This chapter explores the uses of electronic surveillance systems in a high-rise housing scheme in one of the most deprived areas of Northern City. As part of the fieldwork for the present study the researcher interviewed several senior Housing Department officials. The fieldwork also included three eight-hour shifts in the control room of a concierge-operated CCTV control room where observations and informal interviews were carried out with the concierge staff. We begin by sketching the background to the introduction of the concierge system at Hampton Court. Next we describe how a concierge system introduced to monitor the 'external threat' of unauthorised access, is increasingly used to monitor the behaviour of the tenants themselves. Finally, we consider some of the unintended consequences of attempts to re-create 'intimacy' by introducing surveillance systems.

Background

In recent years an increasing number of local authority housing depart-ments have begun to install concierge-operated CCTV systems with video entry phones, lift monitoring and access control equipment. In Glasgow, for example, during the early 1990s some 7,000 homes in both low- and high-rise residential sites were fitted with combined CCTV and voice-linked access control and a further 20,000 homes have access control only (*Security Gazette*, 1993: 35). These trends are reflected in Northern City where, since the mid-1980s, a total of 222 fixed cameras (48 external cameras and 174 internal cameras) have been installed in the city's 16 tower blocks and 26 estate offices. These high-rise blocks are spread throughout the city mainly on the large council estates. The six tower blocks in this case study are situated on Oakwell Estate which is some six miles north of the city centre. Hampton Court and Maylane Court comprise six high-rise blocks, housing a total of 636 flats. The estate was built in the late 1960s and early 1970s and suffers from all the popular social indicators of a 'problem' area: high levels of unemployment, poverty, vandalism and other crimes. In a council bid for Home Office funding for upgraded cameras and a new concierge system at Maylane, the council reported that:

> From 1 July to the end of September 1996, for the two sites there were 44 reports of nuisance or public disorder. It is well known that the car parking areas on each site are particularly vulnerable for car break-ins and this is the only area in the city where milk floats have roller shutters.
>
> (Council CCTV bid, Challenge Competition Round 3)

Environmental and heating installation works were carried out in both areas in the 1980s on an Estate Action scheme. In addition a local employ-ment initiative was established, neighbourhood housing offices were opened, and a great deal of tenant involvement work was undertaken. The improvements at the two multi-storey sites concentrated on im-proving the security and environment of the blocks. CCTV and more secure common areas were introduced together with a better use of entrances, lighting and store areas. Following the recommendations of the Hampton Court Neighbourhood Management Committee (NMC), a

24-hour concierge service began at Hampton in 1992. Installed at a capital cost of £180,000, the service is self-financing in revenue terms with a direct charge of £3.00 per week per tenant.

Hampton Court consists of three high-rise blocks of flats which together comprise of 318 flats. The control room is housed on the ground floor of one of the three blocks of flats and is operated by council officials who monitor the images displayed from 27 cameras (nine cameras in each block) on a continuous basis, i.e. 24 hours a day, 365 days a year. The cameras are located in the communal areas of the flats, lifts, car parks, and front and back entrances. In the control room there are four monitors. Three of these display the images from the nine black-and-white cameras in each of the three blocks, while monitor four displays the images from six external cameras that are fixed on the front and back entrance points to the three blocks of flats. The images displayed on monitors one, two and three are displayed and recorded in time-lapse mode, and the images from monitor four are displayed in real-time but are not tape recorded. In front of the control desk, below monitors one, two and three, there are three multiplexers built into the wall. Each has the capacity to display the images from 16 cameras on a split screen. Most of the time these monitors are set to display the images on a nine-way split screen.

External versus internal dangers: the CCTV system

Many of the problems at Hampton Court, according to the neigh-bourhood housing manager, stem from people attempting to gain 'unauthorised access':

A major problem I suppose is unauthorised visitors. By that I mean non-tenants or people the tenant hasn't actually invited in, getting access to the tower block and creating problems. Principally we're talking about youths there, children or youths, getting into the block. They're not particularly visiting anybody, they'll be running round. It'll be a bit of a game for them, leaving graffiti here etc. And inevitably it creates problems.

To prevent unauthorised access to the flats the council erected eight-foot-high fencing around the blocks. The main entrance, however, remains accessible to tenants and the public who can gain entry to the flats through the electronically operated sliding doors. While all the tenants at Hampton are issued with an electronic 'fob key', which allows them to gain access to the buildings, non-tenants can only gain access to the flats by contacting a tenant or a member of the concierge staff on the electronic door panel. Anyone wishing to visit a tenant, therefore, must tap in the tenant's door number on the 'door station' panel which is fixed to the wall at the entrance to each of the three blocks of flats. The visitor can then communicate with the tenant on a two-way intercom system before the latter presses a button to activate the sliding doors.

When the visitor contacts a tenant in this way a buzzer sounds in the control room and the door number of the tenant being contacted lights up in red on a door station panel on the control desk. At the same time as the buzzer sounds in the control room and the door number lights up on the panel, an external camera, positioned to monitor the entrance point where the visitor is standing, automatically displays an image of the visitor on the 'working monitor'. This allows the concierge staff to monitor those entering the flats and, if necessary, prevent unauthorised access. If the visitor for whatever reason cannot remember the door number of the tenant they wish to contact, then instead of pressing the tenant's flat number they can press the number 600 which allows them to communicate with the concierge staff on the two-way intercom system.

The internal cameras also have two-way intercoms with loudspeakers. This is operated by what the concierge staff describe as a 'zone switcher' which is on the right-hand side of the control desk and consists of three rows of lights (red, yellow and green), one row for each high rise block. Next to each light there is a button which, when pressed, allows the concierge staff to talk (and listen) to tenants in those areas of the building which have internal cameras. During one shift Vance explained how he uses the zone switcher system to deny access to visitors:

> The zone switcher's useful because you can hear the tenants deny access so when the person asks us to let them in we know the tenant doesn't want them in and we can say 'no, you're not coming in'.
>
> (Vance)

While the concierge system at Hampton Court was introduced to monitor the external threat of unauthorised access, the senior concierge officer described how the system is used to monitor the tenants themselves. The senior concierge says 'ten years ago these tenants would have been denied access to accommodation because they're not capable of keeping a place'. In his description of the tenants below, the senior concierge uses a number of cultural stereotypes (alcoholics, drug dealers, schizophrenics and prostitutes) which marginalise the realities of poverty at Hampton Court:

Well, we've got six to seven alcoholics. We've got four or five drug dealers. The police have raided their flat God knows how many times but they've never found a thing. We've got needles all over the landings, we've had 'em defecating on the landing. We've had two deaths. One night a kid had 'O D'd' and his mate dragged him out onto the landing and rang us to get an ambulance. We've got George who's a schizophrenic. He was walking around the block with a knife one night and the blood vessels in his eyes had burst. He looked like he'd had his eyes pulled out of their sockets. Bloody horrible it was. We've got little old ladies who are very sweet. They bring us biscuits and things. We've got two prostitutes. You see, we're in a village if you like, and we're on top of it. We can't walk away from it. It's part of the job.

The use of the CCTV system to monitor the residents is limited in the sense that all the cameras on the site are fixed. This means that the concierge staff do not have the facility to 'track' suspects throughout the blocks of flats. What they can do is use the control pad to display a single image at a time and zoom in on suspects as they pass each camera or are standing in the lift. During one visit to the control room Trevor sees a man leaving the flat with a television and uses the control pad to monitor the suspect:

At 12.37 Trev and Vance see a suspect on monitor one carrying a television out of the back door and into the boot of a taxi that is waiting in the car park. The suspect is a male in his twenties and is dressed casually in jeans and a denim jacket. Trevor puts the camera that monitors the back door onto the working monitor and zooms in on the suspect as he puts the television into the boot of the car and walks back into the block of flats. Trev says, 'well he's got a PAC key', as he watches the suspect use his key to get back into the block of flats. A minute later the suspect emerges from the flats and Trev produces a hard-copy printout of him as he enters the car. Trev then stands up and looks out the control room window to try and get the registration of the taxi. 'It's H something', he says, before adding, 'well at least we've got the time [on the hard-copy printout] if anyone reports a TV missing'.

While tracking tenants as they move around the flats is difficult, the system has created an intelligence base for police operations directed against the tenants. The CCTV system at Hampton Court is useful for a number of organisations, including the police who often arrive to collect tapes after incidents have been reported by the concierge staff. I ask Trev if the police are regular visitors to the control room and he says:

> Yes, they come and they ask us to review tapes. We had one the other day where we were looking for a stolen car off the car park. But you have to stop all the cameras on the monitor to review the tapes. But yes, we have good liaison with Holbrook Police Station, Transport Police, Bradley Police, the Child Protection Unit, the Divisional Intelligence Unit. We don't have much to do with the town centre police.

During one of my visits to the control room a member of the CID arrived and asked Vance if the tape had been saved from the other night, and if he knows anything about 'the Jennings job'. When DC West leaves the control room Vance looks in the Incident Log Book and tells me what happened:

> *Vance*: 'What happened was one of the "drugs flats", 472 in Block One, rang Gary in the concierge at 16.20 and said "there's somebody trying to kick my door down, can you ring the police?" It was probably a dispute over drugs or money. Then at 17.03, 472 called the concierge again and told Gary that they'd set fire to his door. So Gary had to go up with a fire extinguisher and put the fire out. Gary then viewed the tape with the police but couldn't find anything'.
> *MM*: 'Why did DC West want the tape saving?'
> *Vance*: 'What I think has happened is DC West has collected some stills from the tape in Block One [where the fire took place] but he knows that one of the flats in Block Three was involved as well so he wants the tape saving from Block Three. Mr Davis [one of the tenants involved in the dispute] was arrested in Block Three and put up a bit of a fight. He was done for possession of heroin and stolen goods. I think the stolen goods were from the flat of the people who set fire to the door of 472'.

The installation of CCTV systems in Northern City's high-rise flats was very much inspired by the Crime Prevention Through Environmental Design (CPED) movement (Jacobs, 1961; Jeffery, 1971; Newman, 1972). The main conceptual models behind the CPED movement were the notions of the 'urban village' and 'defensible space' where the stress is on recreating the social spaces for mutual recognition, surveillance, good neighbourliness, intimacy and communal responsibility (Cohen, 1985: 215). In this sense it is hoped that the introduction of CCTV systems would allow council staff to monitor the 'external threat' of burglars and other intruders who were making their way into the communal areas of the high-rise flats.

The CCTV system is also connected to the tenant's communal television aerial system on a dedicated channel. This latter feature enables the tenants themselves to visually identify callers before admitting them into their flats. When the door entry system is used and somebody rings a flat the tenant can turn their television onto Channel Nine which displays the same image as the camera monitoring the main entrance to the flats. The main reasoning behind the introduction of a communal television system was to reduce unauthorised access to the flats. However, its introduction has produced some unintended consequences, as the housing officer who installed the system explained:

> What's happened in the odd block is some people sit and watch Channel Nine all the time, find out who's going out and then go and do their flat. So they've actually had it disconnected in a couple of blocks.

These problems with the communal surveillance system should not surprise us because, as the criminological literature has shown, a large proportion of offences within an area are in fact committed by 'insiders', i.e. local residents (Bottoms and Wiles, 1988). In this event, the 'defensibility' of an area against 'outsiders' may be immaterial to its crime rate.

The senior concierge (Stan), meanwhile, explained how he sometimes receives a telephone call from the police who inform him that someone's flat is going to be raided over the next few days. When this happens Stan turns the communal TV aerial system off for a couple of days so that the tenants can't see the police arrive at the flats on the day of the raid. Stan says that if the tenants ask why the communal channel is not working he tells that it's broken and that he is waiting for an electrician to come and fix the system.

The access control system

As we have already seen, the concierge surveillance system at Hampton Court was inspired by the Crime Prevention Through Environmental Design (CPED) movement. This movement promotes 'an elaborate process of negotiation with tenants, local authority departments, police, and local agencies' in an attempt to restore informal processes of social control (Downes and Rock, 1998: 356). According to a council document, the primary purpose of the concierge system at Hampton Court is 'to help secure a safer internal and external environment for those people who live within the high rise flats, the neighbouring area and all visitors to the area'. The main focus of the scheme, the council believes, 'is to uplift the quality of life and the perceived quality of life to a level that will encourage people to view the area as a permanent home for themselves and their families'. The key objectives are listed by the council as follows:

- Reduce the fear of crime and reassure the public.

- Prevent and respond directly to harassment.

- Detect and prevent the high incidences of vehicle crime in the area.

- Provide accurate information to the police to assist in their response to incidents of crime.

- Increase the general public safety on the site.

- Reduce criminal damage and graffiti within the area.

- Provide on-site control room staff accessible to the public at all times to give general security and caretaking support 24 hours a day.

- Contribute towards instilling a sense of worth and belonging to the residents of the area, who perceive to exist in a 'forgotten problem area' of the city.

(Council document)

The attempt to re-create a feeling of community is enshrined in the concierge job description which states that staff should 'provide a general reception service to the residents and others by establishing and fostering links within the blocks including the Neighbourhood Management Committee and the Community Association members'. They are also encouraged to 'take an active interest in the welfare and well being of all residents within the blocks'. One way the concierge staff can do this is through the use of the access control system. All the tenants at Hampton have a 'fob key' which allows them to open both the front and back sliding doors. All uses of this fob key are linked to a computer which stores all the information on each individual tenant's use of the fob key. The system also produces printouts every morning which contain 'health warnings' and 'absconds'. The health warnings allow the concierge staff to check if elderly or sick persons have been using their 'fob key'. If one of the elderly tenants has not used their fob key for a couple of days, one of the concierge staff will either contact the tenant on the two-way intercom system or knock on their flat door to check if they are okay.

Anyone without a 'fob key' wishing to contact a tenant must press the tenant's flat number on the 'door station' panel outside the entrance to the flats and speak to the occupier on the two-way intercom system. Each tenant has an internal phone which is fixed to the wall next to the door in each flat. The tenants can let the visitors in by pressing a button on their Entrycom system which activates the sliding door. The Entrycom system is also used by tenants to talk directly to the concierge staff who have an internal phone in the control room. The paid council official who installed the security systems on the site told me that the Entrycom system:

> adds that personal touch ...actually having the physical presence of the staff on site, it gives people somebody to talk to. They're just on the end of the phone for the door entry system.

As the senior concierge says: 'tenants will often call down here. What time is it? Has the postman been? Can you ring the emergency services? You know, that type of thing'. During the time I spent in the concierge control room tenants would often call the concierge staff for various favours or just to chat:

> At 13.00 one of the tenants in the block of flats where the concierge staff control room is situated [Block Three] contacts the concierge staff in the control room on the internal Entrycom system and asks them to pass a message on to one of their friends who lives in Block One. Trev turns to me and says, 'they do this a lot. One minute they're slagging you off and the next minute they're asking you to do them a favour'. Vance says, 'I don't mind passing messages on, but only once. If they ring me and ask me to do it again I say "well I've already asked them once I'm not doing it again" '.

> At 20.02 Trev receives a telephone call. The caller asks if Clare is still in at flat number 146. Trev calls 146 on the Entrycom system and is told by one of the tenants of 146 that 'Clare has gone to Steve's house'. Trev picks up the telephone and passes the information on to the caller.

Thus, in the wired high-rise flat those residents who cannot afford a telephone can maintain contact with friends and relatives who ring the CCTV control room and communicate with the tenants through concierge staff on the intercom system.

However, the access control system is used not only to check on the well-being of elderly tenants or to allow those without a telephone to maintain contact with the outside world. The absconded messages, which record non-use of the fob key, for example, 'has implications for taking the flats back':

Yes, we record all of the 'non-uses' of the 'fob key' and especially those that are only used once a fortnight 'cause it means they're probably only coming to collect their giros. But the Housing people are not that bothered at the minute 'cause they've got a lot of empty flats and this way they're still getting rent.

(Dave)

The tenants living in the flats are not the only people with a 'fob key'. The social services, housing staff, DSS, doctors and the police are also on the access control system. The Chief Constable doesn't like the police being on it but we do because it means we don't look like we're grassing by letting the police in and taking them to the flats every time they want to speak to somebody. We liaise closely with the police though. We give them a 'tenants list' and they give us any information they can on any dodgy people who we perhaps shouldn't be giving a flat out to. We also liaise with the Yorkshire Electricity Board as well. If people are not using their electricity tokens you know, they'll come down and say, 'these people haven't bought tokens for a while'.

(Stan)

If any tenant is not using their fob key on a regular basis, Dave can report them to the neighbourhood housing manager or one of the neighbourhood housing officers who are based at the local estate office which is about thirty metres away from the concierge control room. Dave says:

Yes, well I report to the neighbourhood housing manager. You know, if somebody's not using the flat, noise problems, nuisance problems, I'll tell the neighbourhood housing office and then it's up to one of them to go and visit the person.

Similarly, while the Entrycom system provides access to the 'outside world' for those tenants without a telephone, it can also be used for purposes of social control. For instance, anyone wishing to visit a tenant in the three blocks of flats must tap in the tenant's door number on the 'door station' panel which is fixed to a wall outside the entrances to the three blocks of flats. As we saw earlier, when the visitor does this a buzzer sounds in the control room and the tenant's door number lights up in red on a door station panel. I asked the concierge staff if it was useful to have the flat number light up in the control room every time a visitor contacts a tenant:

> Yes it is, 'cause we can watch the 'drug flats' and count how many visits there are to those flats. We've got a list there where we jot down the number of visits which we can then show to the police ...the police often have surveillance units here as well. They'll have one sat in here watching the faces and others scattered about around the flats.
>
> (Concierge worker)

> We liaise with the Child Protection Agency. I'll keep a record of how many young kids visit the flats of suspected paedophiles and then tell the NHO what's happening.
>
> (Senior concierge)

> Well, we gather information for the police. They'll say, 'where does so and so live?' or 'we think this flat's dealing, keep an eye on it'. I'll keep a record then of who visits the flat and pass it on to the intelligence field officer. And I'll also say to them, 'what do you know about this guy?' and they'll say, 'well he's a Twocker (taken without owner's consent), he's a junkie', you know.
>
> (Senior concierge)

The Entrycom system also helps the concierge staff overcome the problem of classification. The concierge staff know the names and faces of most of the tenants, and the senior concierge always asks the tenants to come to the control room when they receive their 'fob key' so that he can 'get a good look at their face'. However, if an incident occurs and the concierge staff don't know the name of the tenant involved, they will know his or her flat number which they can give to the Housing staff or to the senior concierge both of whom have a record of all tenants. The problem here is not so much one of putting names to faces, but one of putting names to door numbers. Take the incident below, for example:

Trev and Vance talk about an incident that happened the previous night where one of the tenants, who the concierge staff tell me is a 'dealer', smacked another tenant for throwing his keys down the rubbish chute. The tenant who did the smacking arrived at the control room door earlier in the shift with his hand strapped up and asked the concierge staff if he could have the keys to a friend's flat because his friend had gone away for a few days and had asked him to look after his two children:

Trev: 'He smacked Muffet in the mouth for throwing his keys down the chute'.

Vance: 'He smacked someone else the other day'.

Trev: 'Smacked who?'

Vance: '202'.

Later in the shift, Vance receives a telephone call from the neighbourhood housing manager (NHM) about the incident described above. It sounds like the NHM is trying to find out what happened and who was involved:

Vance: 'I'm not sure what happened. I think there was a gang of kids outside 156 and they dropped some keys down the lift. This morning 190 turned up saying he needed the keys to 156 while 156 is away because he's looking after 156's kids. I'm not sure ... I'm not sure but Dave'll be back any minute he's just popped across the road for a sandwich'. [Dave arrives back in the control room and takes the phone call from the NHM.] 'Yes, he's five foot six, stocky and clean-shaven.

Apparently he flattened somebody last night for dropping his keys down the lift'. About ten minutes later one of the office workers from the neighbourhood housing office arrives in the control room and asks Dave for some information on the tenants of flats 156 and 190.

The Entrycom system helps the concierge staff in other ways. For example, by watching the door numbers that visitors tap in on the door station panel the concierge staff soon become aware of who knows who in the housing block. When I asked Tom what type of things he would regard as suspicious when monitoring the images displayed on the screens he said:

Well, somebody standing at the door and not doing anything. Somebody just pressing lots of flat numbers. Somebody pressing lots of flat numbers that are 'connected' is okay. Like 146, 157 and 201 all know each other, so that's not suspicious.

Other flat numbers become associated with 'trouble'. If any incidents are reported from these 'numbers' the concierge would ring the police immediately, whereas incidents reported by other 'numbers' may be dealt with informally by a visit to the flat, for example. According to Tom:

If anything goes off in some flats you would always ring the police immediately. Flats like 459 and 372 are 'drug flats' and you just don't know what you're going into.

The 'violence of poverty'

Over the last two or three years the 'violence of poverty' (Damer, 1974) on Oakwell Estate has been retold in the local newspaper as the 'violence of drugs culture'. One of the central figures in the media-led 'war on drugs' is Chief Inspector Nicholson who is the Divisional Commander of the area. Chief Inspector Nicholson holds meetings with the Director of Housing and was closely involved in the recent bid for funding from the Home Office for a new concierge system and upgraded CCTV cameras in the high-rise flats. Chief Inspector Nicholson has used the local news-paper to 'declare war on drug dealers' living in the flats and the sur-rounding area. In one week the newspaper dedicated a total of 18 articles to what was described as the 'Enough is Enough' campaign. In one of three front-page spreads ('WE'RE AFTER YOU') Chief Inspector Nicholson had a stark message for 'the dealers in death who are cashing in on the misery of ordinary citizens':

If you are dealing, think. Will the next knock on the door be another burglar wanting to buy his next fix or an undercover police officer? Can you sleep at night knowing that your door will be knocked down in the early hours of the morning? Think. Is it worth five years in prison? We are not pretending, we mean it. It's going to happen.

The following evening's front page – THIS SHOWS WE MEAN BUSINESS – showed a picture of eight officers smashing down the door of a suspected 'drug dealer' whose name had been given to the police by a local resident on one of the telephone hotlines set up by the police. At the end of the week-long media campaign the Chief Inspector stated that the police couldn't keep the crackdown up forever. However, he went on to say that the police had helped the local residents 'get off to a flying start' by providing 'a foothold on the climb back to a safer, less drug-ridden community'.

The council also believes that one of the main reasons for the unpopularity of the flats is the local 'drugs problem'. In its bid for Home Office funding for a new concierge system and an upgraded CCTV system on the site, the council said:

> Due to the age and lifestyle of current tenants there seems to be a significant amount of drug abuse in the flats. This is evidenced by the number of discarded hypodermic needles and other debris of drug abuse. There are also associated problems of certain flats being a focus for large numbers of callers, presumably seeking drugs. There have been three drugs related deaths since the summer of 1995. Only one of these young people was a tenant.
> (Council CCTV bid, Challenge Competition Round 3)

To tackle the 'drugs problem' in the flats the council has recently signed an Information Sharing Agreement with the local police. Under the agreement, senior housing staff and senior operational police staff have already started to meet regularly to discuss appropriate cases and to share information to be better able to take civil tenancy enforcement or criminal action respectively. The principles of the agreement are to:

> Establish meetings twice a year between Divisional Commanders and the Director of Housing to discuss mutually relevant issues; establish model arrangements for liaison and communication between Housing Managers and Police Sector Commanders; set up agreed methods to obtain details of relevant convictions and police knowledge and evidence of incidents involving council tenants in order for legal action to be considered for enforcement of the council's tenancy agreement, both in connection with repossession proceedings and injunctions.
> (Information Sharing Agreement)

The high-profile media campaign and increased police presence at Hampton may indicate that the police and the council are 'doing something' about the problems on the estate. However, it may also add to the stigma of the estate as a 'problem' area infested with a drug problem. As Damer (1974) argues, if this is the case we should not be surprised if the inhabitants of a 'dreadful enclosure' such as Hampton are also in collusion with their negative label. When this happens 'locals retreat into the womb of their houses whence they view the outside world of their neighbours with fear and suspicion' (ibid.: 203; see also Taylor, 1999: 118). This is already happening at Hampton, as one of the concierge staff explained:

> ... some of the residents with 'mental problems' will sometimes sit and watch Channel Nine [the tenants communal television aerial system] all day and scare themselves to death thinking someone's gonna come and get them. We used to have a paranoid schizophrenic who used to sit and watch Channel Nine and the kids in the block would frighten him and tell him people were coming in to get him. One night they frightened him so much that he ran out of his flat and kicked a window in. He was covered in blood and ran to another tenant's flat and kicked their door down. This woman called down here that somebody had broke into her flat covered in blood. She then ran out leaving her child in bed so I had to go up and let the child out.

Despite the police crackdown the high-rise flats continue to be known to the community, the police and other professionals to have a particularly high incidence of crime. The city council has also become increasingly concerned at the high turnover rate in the flats which is approximately 50 per cent, compared with an average annual turnover rate in the city's council properties of around 15 per cent. A recent 10 per cent random survey of the blocks carried out by housing staff stated that:

> the picture of life that is emerging in the flats is one where the majority of the new tenants are under 25; very few (2 per cent) are under 18; most are unemployed, never having worked; they have little commitment to the area/flats; they have little furniture or effects when moving in; new tenancies last on average less than a year.
>
> (Housing Committee report, 1997)

The Housing Committee report proposed a series of measures aimed at reversing the decline of the blocks in both the short and medium term. These included (a) a minimum age of 18 for all applicants onto the housing register; (b) the removal of choice of area for all new tenants and homeless families; (c) more tenancy regulations in the first year of a tenancy; (d) active promotion of the flats by the council; (e) disposing of all or part of the blocks to another landlord such as a housing association;

(f) 'mothballing', i.e. closing off flats until demand picks up or; (g) demolition. In 1997 the council made a bid to the Home Office for a new concierge system at Maylane and upgraded internal and external colour CCTV cameras for both Maylane and Hampton. This bid failed, however, partly due to the fact that the council failed to secure any private funds towards the system. In July 1999 the city council announced that the three-high rise blocks of flats at Hampton Court are to be demolished.

Discussion: the 'context specificity' of visual surveillance systems

As we have seen in the three case studies above, the same technology is applied differently by different people in different contexts. Recognition of the 'context specificity' of surveillance systems forces us to rethink some of the theoretical assumptions in the existing literature on 'new surveillance' technologies. For instance, in an attempt to come to grips with the 'new surveillance' many writers have seized upon Foucault's idea of the panopticon to explore the disciplinary potential of electronic surveillance systems. The panopticon, it is argued, induces conformity on the basis of a potential response, and allows the possibility of a rapid intervention at any moment if something suspicious is detected. However, the extent to which CCTV surveillance systems mirror these panopticon principles in their operation and effects depends upon how this technology is used by different social actors in different institutional settings. We can illustrate this point by briefly contrasting open-street public CCTV systems with the shopping mall, workplace and housing systems reviewed above.

As Norris and Armstrong (1999) have shown in their observational study of public CCTV systems, the panopticon effects of CCTV systems are limited in three main ways. First, the activities of those monitored by open-street CCTV systems in public spaces are not restricted to an enclosed environment which makes continuous monitoring virtually impossible. In contrast, shopping malls, workplaces and high-rise housing schemes are all relatively enclosed and controlled spaces which means that it is more difficult (though not impossible) for people to move out of sight of the camera's gaze. In the retail sector, for example, till operators spend the entire working day under the gaze of a surveillance camera, as well as having every transaction electronically recorded by electronic point of sale (EPOS) technology. Similarly, for the tenants of Hampton Court, moving out of sight of the cameras would mean moving into alternative accommodation, an option that is not open to most of the residents. The same applies to many of those who shop at Housing Estate

Mall who have little choice but to use the facilities (health centre, probation centre, library, etc.) on this site which are all covered by the external CCTV cameras.

Secondly, Norris and Armstrong (1999) found that the ability to mobilise a rapid response to monitored non-compliance in public space was constrained by two factors: that CCTV operators could not themselves intervene to deal with incidents, and that they were not in a position to demand intervention by the police (1998: 87). Thus out of a total of 600 hours of observation these writers witnessed just 45 deployments to deal with monitored non-compliance. In the case studies reviewed here the situation was very different. For instance, in the retail sector some CCTV systems were monitored by the management themselves who could respond immediately (or retrospectively by reviewing the tapes) to monitored non-compliance. Meanwhile, in the shopping mall CCTV operators had direct radio links with patrol guards whose remit was to respond rapidly to incidents that were brought to their attention. These differences between public and private CCTV systems are reflected in the level of deployments initiated by CCTV operators. For instance, Norris and Armstrong found that one in 20 (5 per cent) of the 'targeted surveillances' at their three CCTV control rooms resulted in a deployment, compared with one in three (34 per cent) of those at the two shopping malls in this study.

A third difference between public CCTV systems and private or semi-public CCTV systems concerns the problem of classification. As Poster (1990) has pointed out, the disciplinary power of the panopticon is only complete when one-way total surveillance is combined with a detailed 'dossier that reflects the history of his deviation from the norm' (1990: 91). As Norris and Armstrong point out, the street population monitored by open-street CCTV surveillance systems are unknown to the observer, which means that those watching the screens are unable to systematically identify and classify people in public space. This was reflected in their findings which revealed that only 1 in 33 (3 per cent) of the targeted surveillances in public space were based on the personalised knowledge of the security officers. However, as we saw at Housing Estate Mall, dossiers on the behaviour of the surveilled were stored in the memories of security officers who went to the same schools, drank in the same pubs and played for the same football teams as those they were monitoring. This detailed localised knowledge meant that at Housing Estate Mall the security personnel knew the identity of the person they were monitoring on the TV screens in 8 out of 10 (80 per cent) targeted surveillances.

Part 4
Back to Theory

Chapter 7

Back to theory

The history of communications is not a history of machines but a history of the way the new media help to reconfigure systems of power and networks of social relations. Communications technologies are certainly produced within particular centres of power and deployed with particular purposes in mind but, once in play, they often have unintended and contradictory consequences. They are, therefore, most usefully viewed not as technologies of control or freedom, but as the site of continual struggles over interpretation and use. At the heart of these struggles lies the shifting boundary between the public and private spheres .

(Murdock, 1993; in Graham and Marvin, 1996: 382)

The 'electronic panopticon'

One of the most significant impacts of the 'information revolution' has been the remarkable capacity of new surveillance technologies to transcend both spatial and temporal barriers. Today surveillance is no longer confined to controlled and arranged spaces and no longer requires the physical co-presence of the observer. As this book has shown, the 'distanciated' relations produced by the developing CCTV surveillance networks are creating new forms of human interaction and leading to new forms of social control. However, while recognising that techno-logical developments have played an important role in changing the nature of surveillance systems, one of the main aims of this book was to avoid the 'technological determinism' found in much of the writing on electronic communications technologies. As David Lyon has argued, the problem with technological determinism is that 'it underestimates both the role of social factors in shaping the technology in the first place, and also the variety of social contexts that mediate its use' (1994: 9). Following Lyon, this book has focused on the 'social dimension' of surveillance technologies to show how 'technological determinism' fails in several ways.

The human mediation of technology

As Gary Marx (1992: 225) has argued, in 'the hype accompanying current technological efforts to control crime and deviance', 'new surveillance' technologies have been presented as 'silver bullets' which can provide utopian solutions to complex social problems surrounding crime and disorder. But as Graham (1998) has argued, 'the reality of technological innovation is a great deal less deterministic and a great deal more "messy", difficult, [and] contingent' than the idea of a techno-fix would seem to imply (1998: 29). One of the main concerns of this book, therefore, has to been to show how the human mediation of technological systems places limits on the disciplinary potential of panoptic systems.

The human mediation of technology occurs in a number of ways. For instance, the way 'new surveillance' technologies are applied in practice depends upon how they fit in with the existing organisational, occupational and individual concerns of those responsible for monitoring the systems. We saw earlier, for example, how the integration of private security surveillance systems with police deployment practice depends upon how such systems fit in with the 'occupational culture' of the police. At Housing Estate Mall the mobilisation of a response to monitored non-compliance was filtered through different 'organisational readings' of particular types of incident. Thus, while incidents involving intoxicated people received a high priority from the private security officers, it did not automatically follow that the police treated such incidents with the same kind of urgency. This was illustrated on a number of occasions when the police failed to respond quickly to incidents which had been brought to their attention, such as 'domestics' or 'drunk and disorderlys'.

Similarly, at City Centre Mall, the decisions made by CCTV operators concerning whether or not to respond to incidents that were brought to their attention was filtered through their 'organisational reading' of the situation. From the management's perspective, some of the most serious incidents were those involving health and safety issues, including accidents, lift breakdowns, fire alarms and the presence of unauthorised contract workers on the site during opening hours. These incidents were considered as particularly important because they disrupted consumption and, more importantly, could lead to 'comeback' in the shape of complaints or insurance claims. The speed of response from the security officers was therefore mediated by their organisational reading of which incidents could involve 'comeback'. The uncertainty faced by the security officers when dealing with these incidents was compounded by the surveillance infrastructure (cameras, radio links and the computerised 'Shop Alert' system) which allowed the management to monitor their performance.

In the 'high visibility' conditions of the 'wired mall', therefore, CCTV operators became more tense, alert and time-conscious. However, as Nigel Thrift (1996: 1471) has pointed out, electronic communications media do not necessarily 'communicate their essential properties of instantaneity and speed to their users'. We saw on many occasions, for example, that monitors were not watched, messages sent by radio link were ignored, and pager systems were turned off. The ability to mobilise a rapid response to monitored non-compliance was also limited by the fact that some security officers had insufficient knowledge of the technology to respond quickly to the messages they received. Newburn and Hayman (2001) have reported similar findings in their study of the introduction of CCTV into the custody suite of a busy police station. These writers found that a number of custody officers lacked the technological know-how required to use the CCTV system effectively, and that the nature of their job often precluded continuous monitoring of the images displayed on the TV monitors (2001: 69).

The mutation of surveillance systems

One of the main problems with much of the (administrative) criminological literature on CCTV is that it tends to take as given the way such systems are applied in practice. The majority of effectiveness studies, for example, attempt to evaluate how effective CCTV systems are as a crime prevention tool. But as we have seen in this study, while the stated aims of the vast majority of CCTV systems were related to crime control, once in play they were used for entirely different purposes. In the commercial-retail sector the CCTV system was used also to check whether staff were meeting company requirements – for example compliance with till procedures or rules relating to refunds and exchanges. On some sites the cameras were used to monitor the body language of the shop staff to make sure they were being 'polite' and 'friendly' with customers. Other security managers explained how the cameras could be used to monitor the productivity of the shop worker. This was done by watching members of staff for a period of time to see if they were attending to customers or standing around and talking to their colleagues.

The use of CCTV systems for undeclared purposes is nothing new. As early as 1973 the Central Integrated Traffic Control system installed by the Greater London Council was used to monitor political demonstrators in Grosvenor Square rather than for its intended aim of monitoring traffic flow (Fay, 1998: 325). More recent examples include the use of Edinburgh's traffic control CCTV system for purposes of crowd control, and the use of Shipley's town centre CCTV system to monitor road protestors (ibid.: 326). As Fay points out, there is also increasing evidence that such systems are being used to monitor forms of behaviour which constitute only a minor offence or no crime at all. The CCTV system in King's Lynn, for example, is used to monitor littering and under-age smoking. Meanwhile, in the Bulwell area of Nottingham, the police and welfare agencies are planning to use a CCTV to target the problem of truancy (Fay, 1998: 327).

The above examples would seem to confirm the view held by many critical writers that CCTV surveillance is bound up with wider relations of power and discipline. From this perspective, visual surveillance systems allow powerful individuals and organisations to monitor the activities of marginalised groups in a form of 'top-down' scrutiny (Haggerty and Ericson, 2000). Coleman and Sim (2000), for example, argue that the surveillance 'continuum with its gaze turned almost continuously downwards can be contrasted with the lack of upward surveillance of the powerful whose often socially detrimental and harmful activities remain effectively beyond scrutiny and regulation' (2000: 637). However, as a number of writers have argued, electronic surveillance systems have transformed 'hierarchies of surveillance' by allowing the wider society to scrutinise the activities of the powerful (Mathiesen, 1997; Haggerty and Ericson, 2000). An example of 'bottom-up' surveillance is provided by the introduction of CCTV systems into custody suites and police cells which potentially means that the activities of custody officers could come under just as much scrutiny as the inmates (Newburn and Hayman, 2001). The monitoring of the powerful has also been facilitated by the proliferation of video cameras that allow the general public to tape instances of police brutality (Haggerty and Ericson, 2000: 618). Meanwhile, a number of CCTV systems operating in public space have recorded examples of police brutality (*Guardian*, 24 August 1999; *Hull Daily Mail*, 20 February 1998; *Guardian*, 7 August 1999; *Guardian*, 22 February 2000). In one court case, the prosecution produced a video recording taken from the Bournemouth CCTV system which showed a police constable bouncing a suspect's head off the back windscreen of his patrol car (*Guardian*, 22 February 2000).

CCTV systems can therefore be viewed as both 'top-down' and

'bottom-up' forms of observation. However, whether this dichotomy fully captures the complexity of the surveillance process is another question. We have seen in this book, for example, that 'hierarchies of observation' are not simply reversed by 'new surveillance' technologies; rather they are constantly in flux. Take the operation of shopping mall CCTV surveillance systems. At City Centre Mall, several managers explained how CCTV was installed to deal with the 'external threat' posed by 'shoplifters' and 'troublecausers'. However, once the system was up and running the management began to realise its potential as a general managerial tool which could be used to deal with non-disciplinary issues (e.g. lift breakdowns, accidents and other health and safety issues). The introduction of cameras and radio links in City Centre Mall also made the actions of the security officers highly visible to the management, and it wasn't long before the latter began to use the communications technology to monitor the performance of the security staff. The use of the system mutated further when the security officers used the surveillance infrastructure to monitor the behaviour of the management. For instance, by listening to the communication between the managers on the shopping centre radio link (SCRL), the security officers knew exactly where the managers were at any given moment. This allowed the security staff to 'take it easy' when they knew the management were not around, and to resume 'normal' working practices before the management arrived on the scene. As this example shows, the operation of surveillance systems is a dynamic 'process' in which 'hierarchies of observation' are constantly negotiated and never settled.

Intimacy and sociation

As Nigel Thrift (1996: 1473) has argued, much of the recent literature on information technology gives the impression that the introduction of electronic media has created a more abstract and inhuman world where the 'life world' is increasingly taken over by the 'system' (Habermas, 1984). However, as Thrift points out, the development of electronic communications systems does not produce 'an abstract and inhuman space, strung out on the wire', rather it produces more sociation, much of it face to face. Thrift's argument is very pertinent for those who are attempting to assess the impact of electronic surveillance systems. For instance, the way electronic communications systems are applied in practice is greatly influenced by what Thrift might describe as 'patterns of sociation'. In his study of the role played by ICT in the context of intelligence-led policing, Peter Gill reported that cooperation between different units 'is more likely if previous contacts have produced trust between those involved'

(Gill, 2000: 257). Meanwhile, in their observational study of three CCTV control rooms, Norris and Armstrong (1999: 171) found that the number of deployments initiated by CCTV operatives varied enormously between the three sites. They go on to report that this variation in levels of deployment was highly dependent on the facilitation of a shared set of values and informal understandings between CCTV operators and the police.

Similar findings have been reported in this book. We saw, for example, that while telecommunications systems may facilitate instantaneous communication between people widely separated in time and space, security officers are more likely to communicate and share information with people they know personally. For example, the construction and operation of Northern City's CCTV network was made possible by the existing networks of interpersonal links, friends and even relatives that exist within the city. Conversely, while close interpersonal relations between the security personnel facilitated the integration of separate surveillance systems, the absence of such relationships placed a barrier to communication between those responsible for operating CCTV systems. For instance, the security personnel at Housing Estate Mall preferred to deal with the local police station. This was because they had spoken to most of these police officers in the past during informal visits to the CCTV control room. In contrast, when the security officers rang the police and were transferred to the new Police Communications Headquarters (which is about ten miles away from the shopping centre), they were dealing with a 'faceless bureaucrat'. The police officers at the new head-quarters were unfamiliar with the informal processes of information-sharing that had been built up at the local level between security officers and the police. Recall, for example, when Steve telephoned the police to inform them that there was a 'wanted person' in the mall only to find that the person at the other end of the line 'didn't know who we are or where Housing Estate Mall is'. Steve preferred to deal with the local police station because, as he said, 'we can ring them direct and they'll come straight out'.

A further illustration of the complex interplay between 'new technology' and 'sociation' is provided by the use of electronic communications systems to order face-to-face interaction (Thrift, 1996: 1485). At City Centre Mall, for example, the shopping centre radio link (SCRL) was used by the CCTV operators to arrange tea breaks with friends who were on patrol duty. The security officers on this site also used the surveillance infrastructure to monitor the whereabouts of management. By listening to radio messages between the managers and using the CCTV system the security officers knew when members of the management team had left the building. In this instance, time-space transcending technologies were used to facilitate 'easing' behaviour while managers were not around.

A similar story of technology being used to order face-to-face interaction was found at Hampton Court. Many of the tenants who lived in this extremely deprived high-rise housing scheme did not have a telephone. However, their flats did contain an intercom system which allowed them to communicate directly with CCTV operators in the control room. As we saw in Chapter 6, this technology allowed acquaintances of the tenants to contact the CCTV control room and ask the concierge staff to send messages to the tenants via the intercom system. In this respect, the surveillance infrastructure introduced by the council to monitor the tenants was used by those without a telephone to maintain contact with friends and relatives in the outside world. On the same site, security officers had access to electronically stored information on the tenant's use of 'fob keys'. This information was used to provide a (face-to-face) check on the well-being of elderly tenants who had not used their 'fob keys' for a number of days (see also McGrail, 1998).

While the examples above draw our attention to the 'social dimension' of 'new surveillance' technologies, it could be argued that the digitalisation of surveillance systems has made this approach redundant. As Stephen Graham (1998: 15) points out, 'technological developments towards the digitisation of CCTV, and its linkage with databases, seem likely to lead to much higher degrees of automation and a much greater reliance of linked surveillant-simulation techniques'. These developments raise a number of questions concerning the role of 'sociation' in the surveillance process. For instance, what part does the human mediation of technology play when automated speed cameras can scan the number plates of speeding cars and send digital records to police computer operators who then send a fine to the owner's address in the mail? Do automated systems spell the end of the human mediation of surveillance technologies? Or does the 'social shaping' of technology simply move to an earlier stage in the surveillance process?

To answer these questions let us take a brief look at two automated systems: 'intelligent scene monitoring' and 'face recognition' technology. Intelligent scene monitoring uses computer-based pattern recognition software to automatically monitor and interpret complex scenes and trigger an alarm when 'unusual' events occur. For example, 'a stationary vehicle can trigger an alarm as can a person heading in the "wrong" direction' (Norris and Armstrong, 1998: 264). Meanwhile, the ability to store visual information on computerised databases means that cameras can be linked with sophisticated computer software which can convert images into numerical data and automatically match facial features against a pictorial database of known offenders (Norris, 1996: 7). For instance, Software and Systems International (SSI), claims to have developed 'a fully automated facial recognition system based on neural network software ... which can scan the faces of the crowd in "real" time and compare the faces with images of known "troublemakers" held on a digital database' (Norris and Armstrong, 1999: 217).

At first sight, it would appear that there is very little room for subjectivity and discretion in the operation of these fully automated systems. Having said this, when intelligent image-processing systems identify 'unusual events' and trigger an alarm, surely it still requires a knowledgeable social actor to decide whether or not any action should be taken to investigate the 'event'? Similar questions arise in the context of facial recognition systems. For instance, who decides which 'faces' are to be stored on the digital database? How long should these images be stored on computer files? And so on. Computers also need to be told (by software designers) how to recognise faces. But what criteria do software designers use when deciding how to differentiate between faces? Are computers programmed to recognise that certain facial expressions or gestures may be indicative of deviance? In other words, is it possible that subjective evaluations can be inscribed into an algorithmic formula? In relation to automated systems, therefore, it could be argued that the 'social shaping' of technology does not disappear, but simply moves back to an earlier stage in the surveillance process. Further detailed empirical research of the design of automated surveillance systems is required before we can begin to fully understand the complex interplay between 'simulation' and 'sociation'.

Governance and risk

In recent years, a number of writers have drawn upon the 'governmentality' literature to show how 'neoliberal' strategies of crime control are increasingly addressed not only by agencies of the central state, but also by the organisations, institutions and individuals of civil society (Garland, 1996: 451; O'Malley, 1992). David Garland describes this as a 'responsibilization strategy' which involves state authorities seeking:

> to enlist other agencies and individuals to form a chain of co-ordinated action that reaches into criminogenic situations, prompting crime-control conduct on the part of 'responsibilized' actors ... Central to this strategy is the attempt to ensure that all the

agencies and individuals who are in a position to contribute to these crime-reducing ends come to see it as being in their interests to do so. 'Government' is thus extended and enhanced by the creation of 'governors' and 'guardians' in the space between the individual and the state.

(Garland, 1997: 188)

The success of 'reponsibilization' strategies depends upon the extent to which the actions and objectives of individuals and organisations can be aligned with those of the state. In some respects, the development of open-street CCTV surveillance networks fits neatly with these develop-ments. Thus, from the perspective of the police, CCTV systems provide a means of devolving the responsibility for, and shifting the costs of, crime prevention, while at the same time allowing them to retain a coordinating role which enables them to develop new structures of information exchange. Town centre managers, on the other hand, are being en-couraged to accept that setting up (and paying for) open-street CCTV surveillance systems is essential if they are to stem the 'retail migration' to out-of-town superstores (Beck and Willis, 1995: 113).

However, as this study has shown, the extent to which the actions of individuals and organisations can be aligned with those of state authorities is limited. In the city centre, for example, the attempt to construct a publicly funded open-street CCTV system was thwarted by opposition from the city council whose members did not believe that the city council was *responsible* for protecting private property in the city centre. As one of them put it, 'we should not be spending public money to protect the insurance policies of businesses'. While many councillors were opposed to a publicly funded city-centre CCTV scheme, there was unanimous backing for surveillance schemes to protect council-owned property (e.g. bus station, car parks, art gallery, marina, cleansing depot, etc.) which, as several councillors explained, 'are our responsibility'.

The council also made a successful bid for a £50,000 grant from the Home Office which represented approximately 50 per cent of the capital costs of developing a CCTV system on the Northern City industrial estate. The remaining funding was to be provided by members of the industrial association with contributions based upon each occupier's 1995 rateable value. However, despite the concerted effort by the council and the police to persuade the industrialists to contribute towards the funding of the system, many refused to back the scheme and the cheque was eventually returned to the Home Office. As one council official explained: 'We kept banging our heads against a brick wall. We had to really grab these people by the throat and say: "JOIN THE SCHEME"

... But every time I went to these places they just weren't interested. Basically I got abuse: "Why aren't you paying for it? Why isn't the council paying for it? We pay enough in rent. We get nothing from the council" '. The industrialists on this site refused to back the scheme for a number of reasons. Some were sceptical of the attempt by the police to 'offload' what was perceived as a 'problem area' onto a private security company. Others had their own CCTV systems and consequently did not want to incur the further expense of contributing to the revenue costs of the proposed system. A number of industrialists were worried about 'free-riders', who were to gain free coverage without contributing towards the system. Other industrialists dropped out because they suspected that leading members of the Northern City Industrial Association (NCIA) were out to make a profit from the new security system. Finally, some local managers of national concerns supported the scheme but had to pull out because their head office refused to back the scheme.

Private justice

As we saw in Chapters 2 and 3, government–intitiated 'responsibilization strategies' are leading to the development of surveillance networks which blur the boundaries between 'public' and 'private' policing. These developments are giving rise to what Johnston (1992) has described as new forms of 'hybrid policing'. First, the development of Northern City's CCTV network has led to an increase in 'joint operations' (Johnston, 1992), including, for example, the covert surveillance of council premises occupied by suspected drug dealers. This operation involved close liaison between the police, the city council and private investigation companies. Secondly, there has been an increase in 'new organisational forms', including the creation of a City Centre Security Group (CCSG) whose members include senior police officers, educational welfare officers, department store managers, security managers, and CCTV operators. Thirdly, there has been an increase in the 'exchange of in-formation' between the public police and private security officers (Johnston, 1992). While much of this process is carried out informally (i.e. during control room visits), it has also been formalised by the formation of security group meetings and the signing of information sharing agreements. In this respect, the deregulation and privatisation of crime control supplements rather than replaces state resources. As Barbara Hudson (2001) points out, privatised schemes provide 'extra eyes and ears for the police, extra "pieces of evidence for prosecutors", and new "clients" for the social control network' (2001: 156). Thus, what we are witnessing, 'is a "rolling out" rather than a "rolling back" of the state' (ibid.: 156).

These developments raise a number of important issues including the possibility of a shift in the nature of policing from 'due process' to 'private justice'. As we saw in our discussion of shopping mall systems, the 'private justice' administered by security officers differs in important respects from punishments administered by the state. As von Hirsch and Shearing (2000) point out, after the completion of a state-sanctioned punishment, 'the person has the right to return to the public space in question' (2000: 83). However, many of those who were monitored and excluded from semi-public spaces in this study received permanent 'banning orders'. Thus, unlike punishment administered by the state 'the response is not "over" when a proportionate sanction has been carried out' (ibid.: 91). Moreover, the right to return to the semi-public space of the shopping mall is often based on the whim of a private security officer rather than due process. At City Centre Mall, for example, those who tried to re-enter the mall before they had completed their 28-day exclusion order could have their ban extended to three months and, if they tried to re-enter again, their ban could be increased to six months. Meanwhile, at Housing Estate Mall the decision to pass on the names of 'wanted persons' to the local beat officer was often based on the nature of the private security officer's previous relationship with the suspect. Thus whether or not a local suspect came into contact with the criminal justice system was dependent upon their degree of familiarity with local private security officers.

Post-Fordism, folklore and class solidarities

The exclusionary vision

As a number of writers have argued, the demise of Fordism and the Keynesian welfare state has witnessed a shift in strategies of crime control from welfare and reintegration towards the more punitive goals of incapacitation, the militarisation of public space and exclusionary practices (Davis, 1990, 1992). In Chapter 1, we explored the possibility that the construction of surveillance networks could be seen as part of this broader shift towards exclusionary strategies of social control. As Norris and Armstrong (1999) have argued, CCTV surveillance systems are exclusionary and 'net-widening' to the extent that they can be used to mobilise a response in a number of ways. For example, CCTV systems extend the 'disciplinary gaze' to wide areas of public and semi-public space which allows those in authority to mobilise a response to previously unnoticed acts and to expel potential deviants from specific locations. In public space 'the expulsion function has traditionally been performed by the police: the officer informs the person that he had best leave, if he does not wish to be arrested' (von Hirsch and Shearing, 2000: 93). However, today exclusionary practices are increasingly taken over by private security officers who monitor and patrol the semi-public spaces of shopping malls, industrial parks, recreational domains and residential communities. As we saw at City Centre Mall, the exclusionary potential of shopping mall surveillance systems is enormous. The main pre-occupation of the security personnel at City Centre Mall was with behaviour that disrupted the commercial image, and in particular with the behaviour of groups of youths who were not shopping. More than four out of ten (43 per cent) of teenagers who were involved in incidents that led to the deployment of a security officer were ejected from the shopping centre, and the influence of age was shown to be compounded by being part of a group. Thus, when a guard was deployed to deal with a group of teenagers, there was a fifty–fifty chance that someone would be ejected.

The exclusion of individuals from the public space of the city centre is more difficult, although the increasing use of by-laws to ban drinking and other activities in public spaces (see Reeve, 1998) increases the exclusionary potential of public CCTV systems. Moreover, as we have already seen in this study, CCTV systems are not separate and discrete systems but are part of a 'surveillance web'. A combination of informal liaison between security personnel and the police, and the use of time-space transcending technologies (e.g. mobile radio links, pager systems, computerised panic alarms and telephones) are increasing the integration of CCTV systems by allowing security personnel to communicate with others across greater distances. As public and private systems become more integrated one important question raised in this study is whether the interests of the private sector could play a leading role in decisions about who does and does not belong in the new territories of con-sumption (see also Coleman and Sim, 2000: 627). Thus, the exclusionary potential of shopping mall CCTV systems may not be confined to the enclosed and controlled space of the mall. The integration of such systems with other public CCTV systems may increase the exclusionary potential, currently widely practised in the semi-public space of the mall, to wider public spaces.

Visual surveillance systems are also exclusionary in the sense that they produce images which can be 'lifted out' and used to provide evidence against deviant populations to justify exclusion (Norris and Armstrong, 1999). As we have seen in this study, with the aid of hard-copy printout machines security officers are able to produce photographs of known suspects which can then be stored in 'rogues galleries' for future reference. Moreover, once these photographs are taken they can be 'passed around' a multiplicity of social actors who are involved in the operation of the surveillance web and used to identify and exclude potential deviants. For instance, the security manager responsible for the operation of Northern City's hospital CCTV network has recently compiled a 'rogues gallery' of known 'drug addicts' and is working closely with the police in an attempt to exclude these people from the city's four hospitals. Meanwhile, the security controller employed by a chain of 22 stores, comprising 198 CCTV cameras, has distributed photographs of suspected shoplifters to all the stores in the city with the message: 'This person is not allowed in our stores'. And in the city centre, senior police officers and members of the Chamber of Trade have recently distributed photographs of a 'dirty dozen' known 'troublemakers' and 'shoplifters' to the security personnel working in the shopping centres, department stores, high-street retailers and smaller shops in the city centre.

This raises the important issue of how long these images remain in rogues galleries and banning books. As the security manager at Housing Estate Mall told me, some of the pictures in his rogues gallery were 'taken years ago' and he also takes new pictures of suspects every year in case they have changed their appearance. One question we might ask is whether the 'data image' takes on a life of its own and outlives the deviant identity of the 'real self' who, as David Matza (1964) long ago pointed out, will usually 'drift' out of crime in his or her early twenties. However, while the 'data image' may take on a life of its own, the security guards are perfectly aware that the 'real self' changes over time. This was illustrated by a number of their comments about the surveyed which included: 'We can let X back in [to the shopping mall] now 'cause I had a word with him the other day and he seems to have grown up a bit'.

The focus on exclusion becomes even more pertinent when it is realised that the growth of CCTV surveillance systems is bound up with broader and more permanent economic and political changes which may be leading us towards a society which relies on exclusionary, rather than inclusionary, strategies of social control. The emergence of city-centre CCTV systems, for example, must be placed in the context of the rise of the 'entrepreneurial city', which has brought increased inter-urban competition for positions as centres of consumption (Harvey, 1994). In this context, CCTV has played an important role in selling the image of city centres as risk-free environments that will attract inward investment, consumers and tourists. However, the transformation of city spaces into privatised places of consumption has also meant that 'the boundaries between the consuming and non-consuming public are strengthening' (Sibley, 1995: xii). It is against this background that several writers have warned that 'panoptical' methods of control such as CCTV may increasingly be used to monitor and/or exclude the so-called 'underclass', those 'flawed consumers' who 'cannot be integrated through the consumer market' (Bauman, 1992: 51).

This so-called 'underclass' is increasingly regarded by the wider society not as a group to be integrated but 'as a risk to be policed' (Nelken, 1994: 4). These developments are bound up with the emergence of the 'risk society' and the move towards crime control strategies which seek to regulate groups as part of a strategy of managing danger (Feeley and Simon, 1994: 173). The move towards a 'risk society' reflects developments already well under way in America where, as Mike Davis (1990, 1992) has shown, the privatisation of security has seen a marked expansion in housing and specialist estates which are 'gated' and 'guarded' to keep out the 'dangerous classes'. In his account of 'Fortress LA', Davis (1990: 224) shows how the search for absolute security in Los Angeles has led to the creation of a 'fortress city', 'brutally divided between "fortified cells" of affluent society and "places of terror" where the police battle the criminalized poor'. However, before going any further down this path towards a dystopian vision, this book will conclude by saying something about the relationship between 'exclusion' and 'sociation'.

Folklore and class solidarities

As the central state attempts to devolve the responsibility for crime control onto local state and non-state agencies, it creates a greater role in policing for the private security industry. One interesting issue to emerge from the present study is the question of how low paid, low status, mainly working-class security officers respond when they find themselves monitoring their own locales and workplace situations. As we saw earlier, the shopping mall provides a new meeting place for young people, but also a new site for conflict between youth and private security officers who attempt to defend the moral character of the new consumer spaces. At City Centre Mall, for example, subcultural youth are targeted because they disrupt the commercial image of the mall. On this site, the attitudes expressed by the guards towards working-class youth are very similar to those expressed by the police (Reiner, 1994). Thus, the CCTV operators at City Centre Mall described working-class youth as 'scrotes', 'scumbags', 'shit', 'G heads' (i.e. 'glue sniffers'), 'druggies' and 'scag heads'.

However, at Housing Estate Mall, the relationship between the security officers and working-class youth is a little more ambiguous. Most of the security officers on this site are local people with extensive knowledge of the estate and its inhabitants. The security manager, for example, has lived on the housing estate for most of his life and, like most of the other guards, he went to the local school which is two minutes walk from the shopping mall. The security manager says that his local knowledge is useful because it means that he knows the identities of most of the 'troublecausers' who visit the centre. During one incident, for example, he knew the name of the person under surveillance because he played in the same darts team as the suspect's dad! Other members of the security team also have extensive knowledge of the local area and its inhabitants, such as Dave who plays in a local Sunday League football team with some of the shopping centre's regular visitors.

The degree of familiarity between the security officers and the local suspect population is reflected in the security officer's use of local nicknames to describe the 'surveilled'. For instance, 'The Teenage Temptress', 'Purse-Snatcher', 'FA Cup', and 'Little Ginge' are just some of the characters monitored on the TV screens at this site. The security officers do use a number of derogatory terms to describe the local 'druggies', but the use of terms like 'Little Ginge', demonstrates a measure of familiarity, and even sympathy, with the local individuals under surveillance. It should come as no surprise, therefore, to find that some of these low-level security officers are not always willing to cooperate with the police. For instance, the local beat officer has given the security personnel a list of 'wanted' persons and asked them to give him a ring (either at the local station or on his mobile phone) if they see any of these suspects on camera. However, whether or not this information reaches the beat officer depends upon the degree of familiarity between the security officers and the local 'surveilled' population. This was illustrated on a number of occasions when 'wanted' persons were identified on camera but the security officers decided not to contact the local beat officer. Recall, for example, the security officer who said, 'I wouldn't grass [i.e. pass the name of a wanted suspect on to the local beat officer] on Tommo 'cause he's all right, he's never given me any bother. Anyway, he's off the smack now'. In this respect, local class solidarities placed a limit on attempts to incorporate commercial security into policing networks.

Local class solidarities also placed limits on the disciplinary and exclusionary potential of panopticon systems in the workplace. On most of the industrial sites visited the management did not observe the workforce themselves; rather they had to rely on the security personnel to inform them of any worker malpractice. However, most of the security officers in the industrial workplace had similar class backgrounds to the workers. In this setting the security officers identified their interests as more in line with the occupational culture of the workforce than with management. The influence of class on the operation of workplace surveillance systems was illustrated on a number of occasions in the industrial workplace. On some sites, for example, the security officers vigorously pursued the misdemeanours of the middle-class office worker while turning a blind eye to the deviant activities of the industrial worker. For instance, at one local manufacturing plant the security officers were perfectly happy to ignore the activities of 'the lads' which involved 'lifting stuff over the fence' and 'nipping for a pint' during the night shift. However, the same security team were willing to spend over two thousand pounds on covert surveillance equipment designed to catch the 'Vending Machine Thief', a white-collar worker suspected of stealing from a vending machine in the general office block. Thus, while CCTV systems may be installed for the purpose of the general managerial control of the workforce, whether or not it is used in this capacity depends to some extent on how the introduction of this technology fits in with existing social practices and informal rule systems in the workplace.

And so we reach the end of this story about a Northern City and its relationship with CCTV. As stated at the beginning of this book, the study had two main aims: first, to locate and analyse the emergence of CCTV in relation to the central concerns of theorists of modernity; and secondly, to provide a micro-sociological account of the construction and operation of a CCTV network in one city. We are now in a position to state what implications this case study has for theories of surveillance and social control. The central message is very simple. The relationship between surveillance and society is a two-way process. The introduction of surveillance systems always has a 'social impact'. But equally, the way 'new surveillance' technologies, 'new modes of governance' and 'exclusionary practices' are applied in practice depends upon how they fit in with the existing social relations, political practices and cultural traditions in different locales and institutional settings.

Bibliography

Ackroyd, S. et al. (1992) *New Technology and Practical Police Work*. Buckingham: Open University Press.

Allan, S. (1998) 'News from NowHere: Televisual News Discourse and the Construction of Hegemony', in A. Bell and P. Garrett (eds), *Approaches to Media Discourse*. Oxford: Blackwell.

American Civil Liberties Union (2000), 'Court Rejects Michigan's Attempt to End ACLU Challenge to Urine Testing of Welfare Recipients', 18 April, http://www.aclu.org/news/2000/n041800a.html

Amin, A. (ed.) (1994) *Post-Fordism: A Reader*. Oxford: Blackwell.

Bannister, J., Fyfe, N.R. and Kearns, A. (1998), 'Closed Circuit Television and the City', in C. Norris, J. Moran and G. Armstrong (eds), *Surveillance, Closed Circuit Television and Social Control*. Aldershot: Ashgate.

Barry, A. Osborne, T. and Rose, N. (1996) *Foucault and Political Reason: Liberalism, Neo-Liberalism and Rationalities of Government*. London: UCL Press.

Bauman, Z. (1992) *Intimations of Postmodernity*. London: Routledge.

Bauman, Z. (1993) *Postmodern Ethics*. Oxford: Blackwell.

Bauman, Z. (1997) *Postmodernity and Its Discontents*. Cambridge: Polity Press.

Beck, A. and Willis, A. (1995) *Crime and Security: Managing the Risk to Safe Shopping*. Leicester: Perpetuity Press.

Beck, U. (1992) *Risk Society: Towards a New Modernity*. London: Sage.

Beck, U. (1994) 'The Reinvention of Politics: Towards a Theory of Reflexive Modernization', in U. Beck, A. Giddens, and S. Lash, *Reflexive Modernization: Politics, Tradition and Aesthetics in the Modern Social Order*. Cambridge: Polity Press.

Becker, H. (1963) *Outsiders: Studies in the Sociology of Deviance*. New York: Free Press.

Bell, A. (1991) *The Language of News Media*. Oxford: Blackwell.

Bianchini, F. and Schwengel, H. (1991) 'Re-imaging the City', in J. Corner and S. Harvey, (eds), *Enterprise and Heritage: Crosscurrents in National Culture.* London: Routledge.

Bijker, W. E., Hughes, T. P. and Pinch, T. J. (1987) *The Social Construction of Technological Systems: New Directions in the Sociology and History of Technology.* London: MIT Press.

Boddy, T. (1992) 'Underground and Overhead: Building the Analogous City', in M. Sorkin (ed.), *Variations on a Theme Park.* New York: Hill & Wang.

Bottoms, A. E. and Wiles, P. (1988) 'Crime and Housing Policy: A Framework for Crime Prevention Analysis', in T. Hope and M. Shaw (eds), *Communities and Crime Reduction.* London: HMSO.

Bulos, M. (1995) 'CCTV Surveillance: Safety or Control', paper given at the *Annual Conference of the British Sociological Association*, Leicester, 10–13 April.

Carriere, K. D. and Erikson, R. V. (1989) *Crime Stoppers: A Study in the Organization of Community Policing.* Toronto: University of Toronto.

Castells, M. (1989) *The Informational City: Information Technology, Economic Restructuring and the Urban-Regional Process.* Oxford: Blackwell.

Chatterton, M. R. (1979) 'The Supervision of Patrol Work Under the Fixed Point System', in S. Holdaway (ed.), *The British Police.* London: Edward Arnold.

Chibnall, S. (1981) 'The Production of Knowledge by Crime Reporters', in S. Cohen and J. Young (eds), *The Manufacture of News.* London: Constable.

Christie, N. (1993) *Crime Control as Industry.* London: Routledge.

Christopherson, S. (1994) 'The Fortress City: Privatized Spaces, Consumer Citizenship', in A. Amin (ed.), *Post-Fordism: A Reader.* Oxford: Blackwell.

Clarke, R. (1980) 'Situational Crime Prevention: Theory and Practice', *British Journal of Criminology*, Vol. 20, No. 2, pp. 136–47.

Cochrane, A. (1993) *Whatever Happened to Local Government?* Buckingham: Oxford University Press.

Cohen, S. (1985) *Visions of Social Control.* Cambridge: Polity Press.

Cohen, S. (1994) 'Social Control and the Politics of Reconstruction', in D. Nelken (ed.), *The Futures of Criminology.* London: Sage.

Coleman, R. and Sim, J. (1996) *From the Dockyards to the Disney Store: Surveillance, Risk and Security in Liverpool City Centre*, paper presented at the Law and Society Association Conference, University of Strathclyde, July.

Coleman, R. and Sim, J. (2000) ' "You'll Never Walk Alone": CCTV Surveillance, Order and Neo-Liberal Rule in Liverpool City Centre', *British Journal of Criminology*, Vol. 51, No. 4, pp. 623–39.

Crime Prevention News (1993) 'Pictures by Phone Now', 21 July.

Damer, S. (1974) 'Wine Alley: The Sociology of a Dreadful Enclosure', *Sociological Review*, Vol. 22, No. 2, pp. 221–48.

Dandeker, C. (1990) *Surveillance, Power and Modernity: Bureaucracy and Discipline From 1700 to the Present Day.* Cambridge: Polity Press.

Davies, S. (1996) *Big Brother: Britain's Web of Surveillance and the New Technological Order.* London: Pan Books.

Davis, M. (1990) *City of Quartz*. London: Vintage.

Davis, M. (1992) 'Beyond Blade Runner: Urban Control', *Open Magazine Pamphlet Series*, No. 23, December, pp. 1–20.

Delbridge, R., Turnball, P. and Wilkinson, W. (1992) 'Pushing Back the Frontiers: Management Control and Work Intensification under JIT/TQM Factory Regimes', *New Technology, Work and Employment*, Vol. 7, No. 2, pp. 97–106.

Deutsche, R. (1991) 'Uneven Development: Public Art in New York City', in D. Ghirardo (ed.), *Out of Site: A Social Criticism of Architecture*. Seattle, WA: Bay Press.

Ditton, J. (1977) *Part-Time Crime: an Ethnography of Pilfering and Fiddling*. London: Macmillan.

Donzelot, J. (1991) 'The Mobilization of Society', in G. Burchell, C. Gordon and P. Miller (eds), *The Foucault Effect: Studies in Governmentality*. Hemel Hempstead: Harvester Wheatsheaf.

Downes, D. and Rock, P. (1998) *Understanding Deviance*. Oxford: Oxford University Press.

Ericson, R. (1994) 'The Division of Expert Knowledge in Policing and Security', *British Journal of Sociology*, Vol. 45, No. 2, pp. 149–75.

Ericson, R. and Carriere, K. (1994) 'The Fragmentation of Criminology', in D. Nelken (ed.), *The Futures of Criminology*. London: Sage.

Ericson, R. V. and Haggerty, D. (1997) *Policing the Risk Society*. Oxford: Clarendon Press.

Fairclough, N. (1992) *Discourse and Social Change*. Cambridge: Polity Press.

Fay, S. (1998) 'Tough on Crime, Tough on Civil Liberties: Some Negative Aspects of Britain's Wholesale Adoption of CCTV Surveillance During the 1990's', *International Review of Law, Computers and Technology*, Vol. 12, No. 2, pp. 315–46.

Feeley, M. and Simon, J. (1994) 'Actuarial Justice: The Emerging New Criminal Law', in D. Nelken (ed.), *The Futures of Criminology*. London: Sage.

Fielding, N. (1993) 'Ethnography', in N. Gilbert (ed.), *Researching Social Life*. London: Sage.

Forensic Science Service (2000) 'DNA Profiles on National Database Top One Million', 13 November.

Foucault, M. (1977) *Discipline and Punish: The Birth of the Prison*. London: Allen Lane.

Foucault, M. (1984) *The Foucault Reader*, ed. P. Rainbow. Harmondsworth: Penguin Books.

Fowler, R. (1991) *Language in the News: Discourse and Ideology in the Press*. London: Routledge.

Furedi, F. (1997) *Culture of Fear: Risk-Taking and the Morality of Low Expectation*. London: Cassell.

Fyfe, N. R. (1995) 'Law and Order Policy and the Spaces of Citizenship in Contemporary Britain', *Political Geography*, Vol. 14, No. 2, pp. 177–89.

Fyfe, N. R. and Bannister, J. (1994) *The Eyes on the Street: Closed Circuit Television Surveillance in Public Spaces*, Presented at the Association of American Geographers Conference, Chicago, March, pp. 1–13.

Gandy, Oscar, H. Jr (1993) *The Panopticon Sort: A Political Economy of Personal Information*. Oxford: Westview Press.

Garland, D. (1996) 'The Limits of the Sovereign State: Strategies of Crime Control in Contemporary Society', *British Journal of Criminology*, Vol. 36, No. 4, pp. 445–71.

Garland, D. (1997) ' "Governmentality" and the Problem of Crime', *Theoretical Criminology*, Vol. 1, No. 2, pp. 173–214.

Garrahan, P. and Stewart, P. (1989) *Working for Nissan*, paper presented at the Conference of Socialist Economics, Sheffield Polytechnic, July.

Giddens, A. (1985) *The Nation State and Violence: Volume Two of a Contemporary Critique of Historical Materialism*. Cambridge: Polity Press.

Giddens, A. (1990) *The Consequences of Modernity*. Cambridge: Polity Press.

Gill, P. (2000) *Rounding Up the Usual Suspects? Developments in Contemporary Law Enforcement Intelligence*. Aldershot: Ashgate.

Gilliom, J. (1994) *Surveillance, Privacy and the Law: Employee Drug Testing and the Politics of Social Control*. Ann Arbor, MI: University of Michigan Press.

Glaser, B. and Strauss, A. (1967) *The Discovery of Grounded Theory*. Chicago, IL: Aldine.

Graham, S. (1998) 'Spaces of Surveillant Simulation: New Technologies, Digital Representations, and Material Geographies', *Environment and Planning D: Society and Space*, Vol. 6, pp. 483–504.

Graham, S. and Marvin, S. (1996) *Telecommunications and the City: Electronic Spaces, Urban Places*. London: Routledge.

Graham, S., Brooks, J. and Heery, D. (1996) 'Towns on Television: CCTV in British Towns and Cities', *Local Government Studies*, Vol. 22, No. 3, pp. 3–27.

Grint, K. and Woolgar, S. (1997) *The Machine at Work: Technology, Work and Organization*. Cambridge: Polity Press.

Guardian (1994) 'Major Says Some Opt to be Homeless', 25 April, p. 3.

Guardian (1995) 'Anger Over Straw Blast on Beggars', 6 September, p. 1.

Guardian (1999) 'PC Found Guilty of Assaults and Perverting Justice', 24 August.

Guardian (1999) 'Race Action', 3 April.

Guardian (1999) 'Security Video Showed Police Beating Man', 7 August.

Guardian (2000) 'CCTV Filmed Assault by Constable', 22 February.

Guardian (2000) '3m Face DNA Tests in Blair Crime Initiative', 1 September, p. 1.

Habermas, J. (1984) *The Theory of Communicative Action*, Vol. 1, *Reason and the Rationalization of Society*. Boston: Beacon Press.

Haggerty, K. D. and Ericson, R. V. (2000) 'The Surveillant Assemblage', *British Journal of Sociology*, Vol. 51, No. 4, pp. 605–22.

Hall, S. and Held, D. (1989) 'Citizens and Citizenship', in S. Hall and M. Jaques (eds), *New Times*. London: Lawrence & Wishart.

Hall, S. and Jaques, M. (eds) (1989) *New Times*. London: Lawrence and Wishart.

Hall, S., Critcher, C., Jefferson, T, Clarke, J. and Roberts, B. (1981) 'The Social Production of News: Mugging and the Media', in S. Cohen and J. Young (eds), *The Manufacture of News*. London: Constable.

Hammersley, M. and Atkinson, P. (1983) *Ethnography: Principles in Practice*. London: Routledge.

Harvey, D. (1989) *The Condition of Postmodernity: An Enquiry into the Origins of Cultural Change*. Oxford: Blackwell.

Harvey, D. (1993) 'From Space to Place and Back Again: Reflections on the Condition of Postmodernity', in J. Bird et al. (eds), *Mapping the Futures*. London: Routledge.

Harvey, D. (1994) 'Flexible Accumulation Through Urbanization: Reflections on Postmodernism in the American City', in A. Amin (ed.), *Post-Fordism: A Reader*. Oxford: Blackwell.

Hearnden, K. (1996) 'Small Businesses' Approach to Managing CCTV to Combat Crime', *International Journal of Risk, Security and Crime Prevention*, Vol. 1, No. 1, pp. 19–31.

Hoeffel, J. C. (1990) 'The Dark Side of DNA Profiling: Unreliable Scientific Evidence Meets the Criminal Defendant', *Stanford Law Review*, Vol. 42, No. 2, pp. 465–538.

Holtorf, K. (1998) *Ur-ine Trouble*. Scottsdale, Arizona: Vandalay Press.

Home Office (1979) *The Private Security Industry: A Discussion Paper*. London: HMSO.

Home Office (1988) *Practical Ways to Crack Crime*. London: Home Office.

Home Office (1989) *Safer Cities, Progress Report 1988–89*. London: HMSO.

Home Office (1992) *Safer Cities and Community Safety Strategies*. Crime Prevention Unit. Series Paper No. 38, London: Home Office.

Home Office (1996) *Closed Circuit Television Challenge Competition 1996/7 Successful Bids*. London: Home Office.

Home Office (1999) *Proposals for Revising Legislative Measures on Fingerprints, Footprints and DNA Samples*. London: Home Office.

Hornsby-Smith, M. (1993) 'Gaining Access', in N. Gilbert (ed.), *Researching Social Life*. London: Sage.

Hubbard, P. (1996) 'Urban Design and City Regeneration: Social Representations of Entrepreneurial Landscapes', *Urban Studies*, Vol. 33, No. 8, pp. 1441–61.

Hudson, B. (2001) 'Punishment, Rights and Difference: Defending Justice in the Risk Society', in K. Stenson and R. R. Sullivan (eds), *Crime, Risk and Justice: The Politics of Crime Control in Liberal Democracies*. Cullompton: Willan Publishing.

Hull Daily Mail (1996) 'People on Patrol', 15 March.

Hull Daily Mail (1996) 'Stop The Burglar', 29 June.

Hull Daily Mail (1997) 'Bridlington Traders', 28 April.

Hull Daily Mail (1997) 'Mail Readers Praised for Drugs Calls', 18 February.

Hull Daily Mail (1997) 'Wanted: Do You Know These People?' 17 January.

Hull Daily Mail (1998) 'PC is Caught on Camera', 20 February.

Independent on Sunday (1998) 'Random Testing Puts Drug Users' Jobs on the Line', 22 November.

Jacobs, J. (1961) *The Life and Death of Great American Cities*. New York: Penguin.

Jeffery, C. R. (1971) *Crime Prevention Through Environmental Design*. London: Sage.

Johnston, L. (1992) *The Rebirth of Private Policing*. London: Routledge.

Kling, R. (1996) 'Information Technologies and the Shifting Balance Between Privacy and Social Control', in R. Kling (ed.), *Computerization and Controversy: Value Conflicts and Social Choices*. San Diego, CA: Academic Press.

Lash, S. (1994) 'Reflexivity and its Doubles: Structure, Aesthetics, Community', in U. Beck, A. Giddens and S. Lash. (eds), *Reflexive Modernization*. Cambridge: Polity Press.

Lash, S. and Urry, J. (1994) *Economies of Signs and Space*. London: Sage.

Latour, B. (1987) *Science in Action: How to Follow Scientists and Engineers Through Society*. Milton Keynes: Open University Press.

Lyon, D. (1993) 'An Electronic Panopticon: A Sociological Critique of Surveillance Theory', *Sociological Review*, Vol. 41, No. 4, pp. 653–78.

Lyon, D. (1994) *The Electronic Eye: The Rise of the Surveillance Society*. Cambridge: Polity Press.

Lyon, D. (2001) *Surveillance Society: Monitoring Everyday Life*. Buckingham: Open University Press.

McGrail, B. (1998) *Communication Technology, Local Knowledges, and Urban Networks*, paper presented at Telecommunications and the City, University of Georgia, March.

Manning, P. K. (1992) 'Information Technologies and the Police', in P. Gill (2000) *Rounding Up the Usual Suspects? Developments in Contemporary Law Enforcement Intelligence*. Aldershot: Ashgate.

Mars, G. (1974) 'Dock Pilferage', in P. Rock and M. McIntosh (eds), *Deviance and Social Control*. London: Tavistock.

Mars, G. and Nicod, M. (1981) 'Hidden Rewards at Work: The Implications From a Study of British Hotels', in S. Henry (ed.), *Can I Have it in Cash?* London: Astragal Books.

Marx, G. T. (1988) *Undercover: Police Surveillance in America*. Berkeley, California: University of California Press.

Marx, G. (1995) 'The Engineering of Social Control: The Search for the Silver Bullet', in J. Hagan and R. Peterson (eds), *Crime and Inequality*. Stanford, California: Stanford University Press.

Mathiesen, T. (1997) 'The Viewer Society: Michel Foucault's "Panopticon" Revisited', *Theoretical Criminology*, Vol. 1, No. 2, pp. 215–34.

Matza, D. (1964) *Delinquency and Drift*. New York: Wiley.

Meyrowitz, J. (1985) *No Sense of Place: The Impact of Electronic Media on Social Behaviour*. Oxford: Oxford University Press.

Mitchell, W. J. (1992) *The Reconfigured Eye: Visual Truth in the Post-Photographic Era*. London: MIT Press.

Molstad, C. (1988) 'Control Strategies Used by Industrial Brewery Workers: Work

Avoidance, Impression Management and Solidarity', *Human Organization*, Vol. 47, No. 4, pp. 354–60.

Mulgan, G. (1989) 'A Tale of New Cities', *Marxism Today*, March, pp. 18–25.

Murdock, G. (1993) 'Communications and the Constitution of Modernity', *Media, Culture and Society*, Vol. 15, pp. 521–39.

Murray, R. (1989) 'Fordism and Post-Fordism', in S. Hall and M. Jaques (eds), *New Times*. London: Lawrence & Wishart.

Nelken, D. (1994) *The Futures of Criminology*. London: Sage.

Nelkin, D. and Andrews, L. (1999) 'DNA Identification and Surveillance Creep', *Sociology of Health and Illness*, Vol. 21, No. 5, pp. 689–706.

Newburn, T. and Hayman, S. (2001) *Policing, Surveillance and Social Control: CCTV and Police Monitoring of Suspects*. Cullompton: Willan Publishing.

Newman, O. (1972) *Defensible Space: Crime Prevention Through Urban Design*. London: Architectural Press.

Newton, D. E. (1999) *Drug Testing: An Issue for School, Sports, and Work*. Aldershot: Enslow.

Norris, C. (1995) 'Algorithmic Surveillance', *Criminal Justice Matters*, No. 20, summer, pp. 7–8.

Norris, C. and Armstrong, G. (1998) 'Categories of Control: The Social Construction of Suspicion and Intervention in CCTV Systems', draft manuscript of material being prepared for *The Maximum Surveillance Society: The Rise of Closed Circuit Television*. Oxford: Berg.

Norris, C. and Armstrong, G. (1999) *The Maximum Surveillance Society: The Rise of Closed Circuit Television*. Oxford: Berg.

Norris, C., Moran, J. and Armstrong, G. (1998) 'Algorithmic Surveillance: The Future of Automated Visual Surveillance', in C. Norris, J. Moran and G. Armstrong (eds), *Surveillance, Closed Circuit Television and Social Control*. Aldershot: Ashgate.

Observer (1999) 'Beware: That Bagel Could Get You Fired', 12 December.

O'Malley, P. (1992) 'Risk, Power and Crime Prevention', *Economy and Society*, Vol. 21, No. 3, pp. 252–75.

Patten, J. (1988) 'Foreword' in T. Hope and M. Shaw (eds), *Communities and Crime Reduction*. London: HMSO.

Phillips, S. and Cochrane, R. (1988) *Crime and Nuisance in the Shopping Centre: A Case Study in Crime Prevention*, Crime Prevention Unit Series Paper No. 16. London: Home Office.

Piore, M. and Sabel, C. (1984) *The Second Industrial Divide*. New York: Basic Books.

Poole, R. (1991) *Safer Shopping: The Identification of Opportunities for Crime and Disorder in Covered Shopping Centres*. Birmingham: West Midlands Constabulary.

Poster, M. (1990) *The Mode of Information: Poststructuralism and Social Context*. Cambridge: Polity Press.

Pratt, J. (1999) 'Governmentality, Neo-Liberalism and Dangerousness', in

R. Smandych (ed.), *Governable Places: Readings on Governmentality and Crime Control*. Dartmouth: Ashgate.

Ramsay, M. (1989) *Downtown Drinkers: The Perceptions and Fears of the Public in a City Centre*, Crime Prevention Unit Series Paper No. 19. London: Home Office.

Reeve, A. (1996) 'The Private Realm of the Managed Town Centre', unpublished manuscript, Joint Centre for Urban Design, Oxford Brooks University (a revised version also published in *Urban Design International*, Vol. 1, No. 1, pp. 61–80).

Reeve, A. (1998) 'The Panopticisation of Shopping: CCTV and Leisure Consumption', in C. Norris, J. Moran and G. Armstrong (eds), *Surveillance, Closed Circuit Television and Social Control*. Aldershot: Ashgate.

Reiner, R. (1994) 'Policing and the Police', in M. Maguire, R. Morgan and R. Reiner (eds), *The Oxford Handbook of Criminology*. Oxford: Clarendon Press.

Reiner, R., Livingstone, S. and Allen, J. (2001) 'Casino Culture, Media, and Crime in a Winner-Loser Society', in K. Stenson and R. R. Sullivan (eds), *Crime, Risk and Justice: The Politics of Crime Control in Liberal Democracies*. Cullompton: Willan Publishing.

Robins, K. (1995) 'Collective Emotion and Urban Culture', in P. Healey et al. *Managing Cities: The New Urban Context*. New York: John Wiley & Sons.

Robins, K. and Webster, F. (1988) 'Cybernetic Capitalism: Information, Technology, Everyday Life', in V. Mosco and J. Wasko (eds), *The Political Economy of Information*. Madison, Wisconsin: University of Wisconsin Press.

Rose, N. (1993) 'Government, Authority and Expertise in Advanced Liberalism', *Economy and Society*, Vol. 22, No. 3, pp. 283–99.

Rose, N. (1996) 'Governing Advanced Liberal Democracies', in A. Barry, T. Osborne and N. Rose, (1996) *Foucault and Political Reason: Liberalism, Neo-liberalism and Rationalities of Government*. London: UCL Press.

Schlesinger, P. and Tumber, H. (1994) *Reporting Crime: The Media Politics of Criminal Justice*. Oxford: Clarendon Press.

Schonberger, R. J. (1982) *Japanese Manufacturing Techniques: Nine Hidden Lessons in Simplicity*. New York: Free Press.

Security Gazette (1993) 'Crackdown! on Tower Block Crime', January, pp. 34–5.

Sennett, R. (1990) *The Conscience of the Eye: The Design and Social Life of Cities*. New York: Alfred A. Knopf.

Sewell, G. and Wilkinson, B. (1992) 'Someone to Watch Over Me: Surveillance, Discipline and the Just-in-Time Labour Process', *Sociology*, Vol. 26, No. 2, pp. 271–89.

Seyd, P. (1990) 'Radical Sheffield: From Socialism to Entrepreneurialism', *Political Studies*, XXXVIII, pp. 335–44.

Shearing, C. and Stenning, P. (1983) 'Private Security: Implications for Social Control', *Social Problems*, Vol. 30, No. 5, pp. 493–506.

Sibley, D. (1995) *Geographies of Exclusion: Society and Difference in the West*. London: Routledge.

Signal Magazine (1995) 'Intelligent Scene Monitoring Drives Security Surveillance', July, pp. 29–31.

Simpson, L. C. (1995) *Technology, Time and the Conversations of Modernity*. London: Routledge.

Skinns, D. (1998) 'Crime Reduction, Diffusion and Displacement: Evaluating the Effectiveness of CCTV', in C. Norris, J. Moran and G. Armstrong (eds), *Surveillance, Closed Circuit Television and Social Control*. Aldershot: Ashgate.

Smandych, R. (1999) 'Introduction: the Place of Governance Studies in Law and Criminology' in Smandych, R. (ed.) *Governable Places: Readings on Governmentality and Crime Control*. Dartmouth: Ashgate.

Smart, B. (1985) *Michel Foucault*. London: Tavistock.

Sparks, R. (2001) 'Bringing It All Back Home', in K. Stenson and R. R. Sullivan (eds), *Crime, Risk and Justice: The Politics of Crime Control in Liberal Democracies*. Cullompton: Willan Publishing.

Spitzer, S. (1987) 'Security and Control in Capitalist Societies: The Fetishism of Security and the Secret Thereof', in J. Lowman, R. Menzies and T. Plays (eds), *Transcarceration: Essays in the Sociology of Social Control*. Aldershot: Gower.

Squire, J. (1994) 'Private Lives, Secluded Spaces: Privacy as Political Possibility', *Environment and Planning: Society and Space*, Vol. 12, pp. 387–401.

Stenson, K. (2001) 'The New Politics of Crime Control', in K. Stenson and R. R. Sullivan, *Crime, Risk and Justice: The Politics of Crime Control in Liberal Democracies*. Cullompton: Willan Publishing.

Stenson, K. and Edwards, A. (2001) 'Rethinking Crime Control in Advanced Liberal Government: The "Third Way" and Return to the Local', in K. Stenson and R. R. Sullivan, *Crime, Risk and Justice: The Politics of Crime Control in Liberal Democracies*. Cullompton: Willan Publishing.

Stenson, K. and Watt, P. (1995) *Young People, Public Space and Sovereignty*, paper presented at the British Sociological Association Annual Conference, April.

Sunday Times (2000) 'Police use DNA to Beat Racists', 2 April.

Tagg, J. (1988) *The Burden of Representation*. London: Macmillan.

Taylor, I. (1994) 'The Political Economy of Crime', in M. Maguire, R. Morgan and R. Reiner (eds), *The Oxford Handbook of Criminology*. Oxford: Clarendon Press.

Taylor, I. (1999) *Crime in Context: A Critical Criminology of Market Societies*. Oxford: Polity.

Taylor, I. et al. (1996) *A Tale of Two Cities: Global Change, Local Feeling, and Everyday Life in the North of England*. London: Routledge.

Thrift, N. (1996) 'New Urban Eras and Old Technological Fears: Reconfiguring the Goodwill of Electronic Things', *Urban Studies*, Vol. 33, No. 8, pp. 1463–93.

Tilley, N. (1998) 'Evaluating the Effectiveness of CCTV Schemes', in C. Norris, J. Moran and G. Armstrong (eds), *Surveillance, Closed Circuit Television and Social Control*. Aldershot: Ashgate.

van Dijk, T. A. (1996) 'Discourse, Power and Access', in C. R. Caldas-Coulthard, and M. Coulthard (eds), *Texts and Practices: Readings in Critical Discourse Analysis*. London: Routledge.

van Dijk, T.A. (1998) *Opinion and Ideologies in the Press*, in A. Bell and P. Garrett (eds), *Approaches to Media Discourse*. Oxford: Blackwell.

Van Maanen, J. (1978) 'On Watching the Watchers', in P. Manning and J. Van Maanen (eds) *Policing: A View From the Street*. Santa Monica, CA: Goodyear Publishing Company.

von Hirsch, A. and Shearing, C. (2000) 'Exclusion from Public Space', in *Ethical and Social Perspectives on Situational Crime Prevention*. Oxford: Hart.

Webster, F. (1995) *Theories of the Information Society*. London: Routledge.

Webster, F. and Robins, K. (1993) 'I'll Be Watching You: Comment on Sewell and Wilkinson', *Sociology*, Vol. 27, No. 2, pp. 243–52.

Wells, C. and Dryer, A. (1997) *Retail Crime Costs Survey 1995/6*. London: British Retail Consortium.

Werrett, D. (1999) *The National DNA Database*, paper presented at the First International Conference on Forensic Human Identification in the Millennium, http://www.forensic.gov.uk/forensic/conference/papers_list.html.

Winner, L. (1992) 'Electronic Office: Playpen or Prison', in R. Kling (ed.), *Computerization and Controversy: Value Conflicts and Social Choices*. London: Academic Press.

Young, J. (1994) 'Incessant Chatter: Recent Paradigms in Criminology', in M. Maguire, R. Morgan and R. Reiner (eds), *The Oxford Handbook of Criminology*. Oxford: Clarendon Press.

Young, J. (1999) *The Exclusive Society*. London: Sage.

Index

access control systems, 172–8
accidents, response to, 138–9
action plan, City Centre Task Force, 50
active citizen news frame, 62–5
age, targeted suspects, 108t
alcohol, people under influence, 139–42
appearance
    period of surveillance, 122
    targeted suspects, 108t
associates, of known offenders, 121–2
authoritative interventions, 133
awareness, of surveillance, 124–5

Banton Estate, 74, 110–11
behaviour, that disrupts commercial image, 126–30
Bentham, Jeremy, 4, 5
bicycles, in shopping malls, 126
BID TO BOOST SECURITY, 58
BIG PUSH FOR CITY CAMERA WATCH BID, 63
body language, monitoring, 151, 187
bottom-up observation, 188–9
British Retail Consortium's Retail Crime Surveys, 150
British Telecom, image transmission, 6

bus station, CCTV system, 36, 37, 55, 76
business areas, segregated from retail and residential, 19

CALL FOR MORE CITY SECURITY CAMERAS, 57
CAMERA BID TO TACKLE CRIME, 58
CAMERA CASH WORRIES, 58
CAMERAS CLICK WITH CHIEF, 56–7
camping out, in malls, 128–9
car park, CCTV system, 36, 37, 55, 76
CCAG *see* City Centre Action Group
CCRL, 72, 86–8, 89–91
CCRL II, 91
CCSG *see* City Centre Security Group
CCTV
    distanciated relations, 6–7
    facilitation of surveillance networks, 8–9
    increasing fear and insecurity, 20
    instruction manual, 21
    literature, xiv
    monitoring of staff, 10–11
    moral regulation, city centres, 14
    Northern City *see* Northern City

segregation, residential, retail and business areas, 19
self, criminology of the, 62
sex, targeted suspects, 107, 108t
Sheffield, economic realism, 12
shift data, case study, 28
Shop Alert system, 72–4, 84–5
shoplifters
    learning to recognise, 151
    prolonged monitoring, 125
    rogues galleries, 97–8
shopnet system, 70–6, 86–8
shoppers, concerns, 14
shopping, review, Northern City, 49–50
shopping centre radio link, 72
shopping malls see City Centre Mall; Housing Estate Mall; overstreet malls; panopticon mall
SHOPS ON SHOPLIFTING ALERT, 67
shrinkage, reducing, 156
silver bullet news frame, 56–9
site visits, case study, 24
sitting down, in shopping malls, 128–9
skyway systems, 19
small business, use of CCTV, 150
social characteristics, targeted suspects, 107
social construction
    of reality, news media, 54
    of suspicion, 103–13
Social Construction of Technology, xiii–xiv
social control
    Entrycom system, 176–7
    master shift in discourse of, 17
social divisions, reinforcement of, xii
social practices, limitations, technological systems, 164–5
social relations, shaping surveillance, xii
sociation
    and intimacy, 189–92
    surveillance and, 7–9

society, and surveillance, xi–xvii
space
    appropriate use of, shopping malls, 126–37
    management of, urban design, 19
    see also electronic spaces; public spaces
SPY CAMERAS CRACK CRIME, 57
staff monitoring
    covert cameras, 155, 158–9, 200
    in industrial workplace, 156
    retail sector, 153–4, 155
    supermarket checkouts, 10–11
statistics, crime control, 56–7
store detectives, mobile, 155
stranger society, 19
Straw, Jack, 13
subcultural youth, 130–3, 198
subject populations, targeted surveillance, 14–15, 103–4
success stories (CCTV), publicised, 58–9
supermarket checkout operators, CCTV surveillance, 10–11
surveillance
    case study, 22–30
    post-Fordism, 9–16
    risk society, 16–22
    and society, xi–xvii
    time-space distanciation and the panopticon, 3–9
surveillance systems
    context specificity, 181–2
    mutation of, 187–9
surveillance web, Northern City
    council network, 76–9
    other systems, 80–4
    shopnet system, 70–6
    system integration, 84–98
suspects
    identification and exclusion, 16
    reasons for surveilling, 107–9
    social characteristics, 107
suspicion
    personalised, 113–26
    social construction of, 103–13